THE COMPLETE IDIOT'S GUIDE® TO

Personal Finance with Quicken®

by Ed Paulson

A Division of Macmillan Computer Publishing
201 W. 103rd Street, Indianapolis, IN 46290

The Complete Idiot's Guide to Personal Finance with Quicken®

Copyright © 1999 by Que Alpha

International Standard Book Number: 0-7897-1751-4

Library of Congress Catalog Card Number: 98-85917

Printed in the United States of America

00 99 98   4   3   2   1

Trademarks

Executive Editor
Jim Minatel

Acquisitions Editor
Jill Byus

Development Editor
Rick Kughen

Managing Editor
Thomas F. Hayes

Project Editor
Tom Stevens

Copy Editor
Shanon Martin

Indexer
Lisa Stumpf

Technical Editors
Jim Grey
Jeremy Dunlavey
Graham Schweer

Proofreader
Jeanne Clark

Layout Technician
Brad Lenser

Illustrator
Judd Winick

Contents at a Glance

Introduction

Congratulations on taking an important step toward getting your personal finances under control. Starting today you are on your way to a comfortable and possibly early retirement.

As with any trip, you want to know what to expect from the destination and how to get there. Taking a few minutes to read this introduction increases your familiarity with this book and turns it into the most valuable resource it can be.

What Can You Expect from This Book?

No book can really cover all the complexities of personal financial management. For starters, the book would be a few thousand pages long and probably so technical that nobody with a social life would want to read it. I have read a few of these books and assure you that they are not only a good physical workout (because you have to carry around this few thousand-page book) but they also cure insomnia (for obvious reasons.)

My goal in writing this book was to present you with the critical items that you really must address when creating a financial plan for you and your family; however, nobody knows your life and you better than you do. No recommendation that any-one makes can replace the responsibility you have for your own financial well being. For this reason, I not only make recommendations to you regarding the topic under discussion, but I also present you with the principles behind the recommendations, because no standard set of recommendations is right for everyone.

How much, for example, should you spend for medical insurance and what level of coverage should you sign up for? These are questions that only you can answer, armed with the combination of guidance in this book, other reference sources, and your insurance agent. Assimilating the information and formulating a course of action is your responsibility. My intent is to arm you with knowledge and the questions to ask. Understanding the questions to ask and the underlying philosophy behind medical insurance, or any other financial decision, makes you a more intelligent buyer.

You need to treat your personal finances like a business. Face it. You trade your time for money, which is then used to provide the quality of life you want for yourself and your family. A company must track its finances to make sure that it remains financially viable. Why should *your* finances require any less attention? Remember that it is your time and money. Managing both properly provides you with a higher quality of life and enables you to reach those personal lifestyle goals that you imagine when dozing off at your desk. And, by the way, the more you know about your finances, the easier it is for you to present yourself as a credible borrower when applying for a loan. More personal freedom, peace of mind, and easier loan qualification make the time spent tracking your personal finances an excellent investment.

I not only want you to read this book and understand the material presented, I also want you to take action that is specific and right for your circumstances. These actions should be molded not only by what you read here, but heavily dependent upon your own decision process. Some of my recommendations will feel right to you and others might feel off the mark. That's okay. Do something, because almost any planning is better than no planning at all.

Where Does Quicken Fit In?

One step that you can take is to purchase Quicken and begin using it for your accounting and financial planning software package. I used the Quicken Deluxe version in writing this book, so some features might vary from your version if you are not on the Deluxe version. But the basics of what makes Quicken a great accounting package for the home financial planner remain consistent between versions, so push forward through the exercises outlined in this book, using your version of Quicken. You won't regret it. Also, if a feature is mentioned in the book that doesn't appear in your version, check the Help screens to make sure that the features isn't hiding in an unexpected place.

This book was designed to be 20 percent about Quicken. Entering the data into Quicken is really the easy part. Understanding what to do with the data after it is entered is the hard part, which is why 80 percent of the book is about financial management.

Remember that financial management is your goal. Quicken is the tool you use to accomplish that goal. Get to know Quicken from Part 2 and spend time with the other chapters to really use Quicken as the incredible tool that it is.

How This Book Is Organized

This book has several parts, with each part building on those preceding.

Part 1, "Can We Talk?" deals with some basic concepts that help you to understand the importance of financial planning in your life. It also presents a few fundamental financial management concepts that you use not only in the rest of the book, but in your daily life.

Part 2, "Getting It into the Computer," is an introduction to Quicken. It covers the installation, initial setup, transaction entry, setup for taxes, and other information important to the operation of Quicken. This is a must-do part.

Part 3, "Give Yourself Some Credit," is about credit. How to get it. How to use it. When to not use it. How to preserve your credit rating. Part 3 is also about real estate and its specific financial benefits. Your home is probably the largest single investment you make in your lifetime. Read Part 3 to manage it to your best advantage.

Part 4, "Getting Better Mileage with Smarter Choices," deals with insurance and investment. Insurance is critical to well-defined financial plans and investments are an integral part of today's business environment.

Part 5, "The Future Starts Today," looks to future events such as your children's college education and your retirement. The emphasis is on how you plan to pay for both and how much money you need after you get there. The final chapter of the book is about estate planning and its importance to you and your heirs financial well-being.

What Do All These Clever Pictures Mean?

As you work your way through the chapters, you find certain items that provide additional information regarding the topic being investigated. Each has a rhyme and reason behind it.

QuickTip items provide you with a little extra interesting information or a shortcut for performing a certain action.

QuickCaution items warn you about those sleeping circumstances that might bite you later if you do not plan. You really should read each of these just to be on the safe side.

Voice of Experience items are about something that happened either to me or someone I know. These are the real world brought to you in print.

Talkin' Money items present the definition to a term that is important to your understanding of the topic. Most of these terms are also in the glossary, but reading them on the page helps to maintain the educational flow.

Summary

My hat is off to you for taking the time to read this book, understand its concepts, familiarize yourself with Quicken, and eventually provide for a secure retirement. Many people talk a good story about getting their finances together. You are really doing it. Thank you for your interest in this book and for taking me along as your tour guide. Enjoy the ride.

Part 1
Can We Talk?

This part leads you through the process of accurately determining your current financial situation and where you want to end up. The right financial direction for you depends on your stage in life and personal family situation. Work your way through Part 1 to determine where you are and where you are headed.

It's Never Too Early to Start Planning

In This Chapter

- Learn the most important thing to do when first starting out
- Do the right things if you get married
- Cover yourself if you are an unmarried couple or partner
- Understand why you should start planning to save for your family
- Learn the financial steps needed to secure your marriage

Start-Out Saving Early

until I was in my late 30s. That is not old, but I also had lost almost 20 years worth of investment that could have been a down payment on a house or something else important.

My parents always encouraged me to save and even set me up with my own savings account when I was around 10 years old. It never had more than a few hundred dollars in it, but it did break the mental barrier of having me take responsibility for my own money.

If you are a parent, I suggest that you start your kids out with a savings plan at the earliest age possible. Have them put as little as $5 per month into the account, but have them do it on a regular basis. You might even encourage them to look for ways that they can earn that $5 and then make sure that it gets deposited.

This might sound a little trite, but my intent is not to have them retire early, but to develop the discipline needed to save a portion of their income in the form of a savings deposit.

It makes a good story when they are older, and they appreciate the fact that they have some money put aside.

Voice of Experience

My parents' training paid off when I was in the Army. I bought a savings bond with each paycheck I received while on active duty. When I got out, I needed a few hundred dollars to buy something that was important to me. My roommate reminded me of the savings bonds, which I contended were there for a rainy day. I looked outside and it was actually raining. So I cashed in the bonds and made my purchase. Buying those bonds surely paid off for me on that occasion.

Plus, you rest easier as a parent knowing that your kids can provide for their own financial health. It is always nice to know that family will help, but it is even nicer to know that the help probably will not be needed.

Going It Alone

If you are single, under 35, and without children, you are in a great position to start creating a financially security future. Your financial obligations are minimal and you have many possible work years ahead of you, which allows you to take higher investment risks. If the risk doesn't work out, you can always start over again because you are not close to retirement. In addition, you have not put your family's financial well being in jeopardy.

So, I suggest that you put as much as 80% of your investment money into the highest-risk investments that you can tolerate. But beware. This is a high-risk gamble, and you need to keep track of things. In fact, the secret to successful gambling is effective money control.

Let your money ride in a higher-risk investment until it has earned you some money, and then shift a portion of your earnings to lower-risk investments. In this way, you protect a portion of your portfolio from a major high-risk crash assuming your lower-risk investments stay stable. By the way, you should strongly consider moving your high-risk investments to a lower-risk, lower-yield investment if your high-risk investments start losing money. The right time to pull out of an investment is an art form and hard to quantify. Stock market investors invest for the long run, and typically don't move stocks on a daily basis, but if your stock takes a nose dive of, say, 80% loss in a few days, you should consider putting your money somewhere else. At times like this, it is handy to have a seasoned investment mentor around for questioning.

The following are a few items that you should take care of as early as possible in your financial life:

> ➤ Get a good credit rating established. This may require that you get a credit card at a department store, and then work your

Voice of Experience

Assume that you play a certain number and color at a roulette table, and it hits. You get a lot of money for that turn of the wheel. If you just let it ride on that number again, you might win again because the odds on the next spin are the same as the prior spin. But if you lose, you lose all the money you just won. A more effective money management approach might be to take half of your winnings and spread it over lower risk bets while letting the other half ride on the same number again. In this way, you are not left empty handed should your number not hit.

If it hits again, let half ride again and play the other half on lower risk bets. Do you see a pattern forming here? I always like to leave an evening of gambling with my winnings in my pocket. My goal is not the adrenaline rush. My goal is to make money, and that should also be your goal.

Don't be afraid to take the risk, but also don't expect the risk to pay off every time. Make sure that you shift your money around so that it is always working for you at the risk level that is right for you.

way up to Visa and MasterCard. Make sure that you buy something with the card and pay it off. In this way, you not only have the card but show a solid payment history. Do this even if it is for a $5 pair of socks.

➤ Keep your car expenses as low as possible. Cars are a major investment drain, and spending your early dollars on an expensive car may impress your friends but won't get you any closer to financial independence. (See Chapter 14, "Cars, Cars, and More Cars," for details regarding car ownership.) On the other hand, if you are a car lover, by all means enjoy your hobby by getting the car you want, but I suggest cutting back in other areas to cover the higher car expenses.

➤ Try to get into some type of real estate ownership position as quickly as possible. This might be a condominium or town home. It might be a fixer upper that takes up so much of your time that you won't want that expensive car. Know that your early real estate ownership payments are a larger portion of your monthly income (probably between 30% and 36%), but that this percentage drops as your income increases. Buy the property and rent out a few rooms to help with the payments. You still get all the appreciation and tax benefits. (See Chapter 12, "There's No Place Like Home," for additional information on home ownership.)

➤ Start putting money into a mutual fund with a higher rate of return. Shoot for depositing 10% of what you earn every month. But even if you put only $100 a month into it, you see it grow over time. For example, $100 put monthly into an account bearing 15% interest over 10 years turns into an account balance of more than $27,000. You put in $12,000 and get out $27,000. Now that is pretty cool. (See Chapter 18, "Taking Risks Doesn't Mean Betting the Farm," for additional information on compounded interest and risk.)

➤ As raises come along, invest the incremental income in a savings vehicle of some type. In other words, get into a habit of maintaining a more consistent cost of living and bank those raises. Otherwise, you are never able to save any significant amount of money because your cost of living continues to rise as you make more money.

➤ Avoid the temptation to charge your credit cards to their limits when you first get them. Keep their balances as low as possible, with a zero balance being a first priority goal.

➤ Make sure that you have medical insurance and enough term life insurance to cover your funeral and other expenses related to your passing away, which is a very small but also very real possibility. (See Chapters 15, 16, and 17 for additional information on the various insurance types.)

➤ Put as much money as possible into your employee benefits investment options such as a 401(k) or stock purchase plan. These things pay off over time, and money put into them and the interest earned on the account are not taxable until you reach age 59 1/2, which makes them particularly attractive.

➤ Have a simple will drawn up that reflects your wishes should you pass away. Once again, this may sound unreasonable if you are young, but accidents happen. Your family will appreciate your letting them know your wishes. (See Chapter 23, "You Can't Take It with You, So Plan Your Estate Now," for additional information.)

Planning for your retirement means starting early. If you take the previously outlined steps, you just started planning for your retirement. All these investment vehicles combine into a substantial nest egg when compounded over 30+ years.

Retirement may seem so remote to you at this point that planning for it is right up there with preparing for a major meteorite to impact the Earth. Just remember that time passes more quickly than you expect, and you may very well wake up one day and be in your late forties. At that point, you will be thankful that you started putting a little away each month.

Going It as a Couple

Congratulations on finding each other. You not only get to enjoy the personal benefits of having a life partner, you also get to enjoy the financial benefits of sharing expenses. For purposes of this section of the book, I assume that your family fits the dual income no kids (DINKs) model and that your incomes are about the same. The overall concepts presented here, however, are the same if your incomes are different.

Every item presented in the prior section related to a single person applies to couples, too. You should start with creating and protecting your credit record, take care of a will, minimize your car expenses, and do the other recommended actions. All the previous investment recommendations apply to you except that you should get ahead more quickly because you have two contributing incomes instead of one. I suggest that you still take risks with your investment portfolio and manage your money as recommended in the earlier section.

QuickTip

If you are single or married with a single income, the following ideas can be helpful to you, especially if you see your current situation changing into one that involves a financial partner.

In addition, you might be in a position to allow one person's income to cover the living expenses and use the other person's income for savings and wealth building. This might allow you to put more than 10% per month into savings or investments.

You might decide to combine incomes and buy a more expensive house, which is probably a good idea as long as you don't make yourselves house poor. You know people who are house poor, don't you? They are your friends who own a house and cannot do anything outside of it because every nickel they own goes into the house. Sure, they own a house, but is it worth the cost to the rest of their lives? You should work diligently to ensure that your total payments required to support your house don't exceed 36% of your gross income. Even at this rate, there isn't much left over, but at least you can afford to go out for burgers every now and then.

The good news is that your combined incomes give you more flexibility and enable you to build wealth more quickly as long as you don't follow the common wisdom of spending more than you make.

QuickCaution

Just because you make more money doesn't mean that you have to spend more money. A higher mortgage payment makes sense because you get to live in a nicer house and get a tax deduction, but buying a more expensive car when you don't have a savings built up seems like the wrong financial approach. I know people who make four times the money they made ten years ago, and they are still as broke as they were ten years ago. Think about it. That makes no sense to me. Extra money does not have to be spent. It can and should be saved or invested.

A few things do change as you become a couple. Think about these recommendations as you plan your financial future:

➤ Your will becomes more important because you now jointly own some items and probably came into your marriage with items you owned before getting married.

➤ Health insurance is probably best handled with one party being the primary insured and the other being the additional party on the policy. I suggest that you make the person with the most stable job and best benefits the primary insured, and make the other person the additional party.

➤ You might plan on having kids. If so, start saving today for their college expenses. The longer you put money into a college fund, the larger the college fund becomes. It is just that simple.

➤ Look for other ways to consolidate expenses such as with automobile insurance and car pooling. If you can get by with one car instead of two, you save thousands of dollars a year that can be put to better use as the down payment on a piece of real estate.

➤ It is a good idea for each of you to have your own clean credit history, just in case something happens to either of you or the marriage dissolves. Sorry. These things do happen, and it is a good idea to cover yourself as long as it doesn't hamper daily living. If one spouse handles all the finances and goes deeply in debt without the other spouse's knowledge, the innocent spouse is usually still responsible for the debts. You don't want to lose your marriage and your credit rating on the same day.

➤ Now for some not so good news if you just got married. You probably find that your income tax bill is higher as a married couple filing jointly than for two unmarried people filing separate returns. Married filing separately usually drive the tax bill higher than the married filing jointly return. So, if you don't feel the need to get married, want to live together, and dislike paying taxes, you might consider not getting married and keeping more money to yourselves. On the other hand, you give up benefits such as spousal coverage on health insurance and other legal benefits provided to married couples.

➤ Decide on a budget target for your monthly living expenses and then stick with it. Think of this as a couple thing because you both are pulling together to keep under budget. Now is that exciting or what? Just kidding, but making a game out of it takes some of the dryness out of the budget process.

➤ The sharing of credit cards, checking accounts, and savings accounts minimizes the expenses associated with these items but might make one or both of you feel like your independence is being curtailed. Talk about it and decide on the right approach for you two as a couple. Just remember that the bills must be paid from some account, and a single checking account is easier to work with than having accounts for each of you.

➤ Finally, I suggest that you two have a heart-to-heart discussion about your long terms goals. When do you want to retire? Where do you want to live and eventually retire? What are your family and professional aspirations? How much will these things cost? Talking about them today, planning for them, and then taking action makes them all much more likely to happen as you plan.

Be aware that unmarried couples, or "domestic partners," do not share some of the default legal privileges of married couples. Some of the areas to watch out for if you are in this situation include the following:

➤ Spouses can transfer money between each other without tax implications, whereas the domestic partner who receives a cash gift may need to treat it as a gift for tax purposes. Pay your domestic partner's medical bills and you could actually be giving them a taxable gift.

➤ If you decide to sell a house that you jointly purchased and owned but one of you does not qualify for the exemption because you sold a primary residence within the past two years, only $250,000 in gain can be excluded, not the $500,000 that would be allowed a married couple under the same circumstances.

expensive and frustrating process for those left behind, especially your children. (See Chapter 23 for information regarding guardianship.)

The preceding is only a partial listing of the things that you should consider when having children. My interest is to alert you to the major areas of consideration, getting you to think about things and to realize that along with the personal impact there is a financial and legal impact associated with having children.

The Least You Need to Know

➤ Developing a credit history is a critical part of financial security.

➤ The younger you start saving for retirement, the more time works in your favor.

➤ Domestic partners do not share the same laws as spouses. Domestic partners should take extra precautions to protect their legal standing with respect to each other.

➤ Your financial needs change as you move from single, to married, and to parent. Cover all the critical items to ensure that your family is protected.

➤ Become a real estate owner as quickly as possible. It is by far the best personal investment you can make.

Chapter 2

Planning Ahead in Your Middle Years

In This Chapter

➤ Determine the right investment portfolio risk combination

➤ Find your optimal retirement pastime

➤ Take a "dependent" deduction for a parent

➤ Be informed when taking an early retirement package offer

➤ Help your family prepare for a sick parent needing long term care

---

It intrigues me how our roles in life change the longer we stick around. We start out as children needing assistance. We then move into being individual adults with our own lives. Most of us meet a special someone, marry, and have children of our own. At some point our parents might age to the point that we become their caretakers. Even more interesting, we eventually age to the point that we may need our children to take care of us. It is a cycle that is independent of geography, ethnic background, or gender. We are born, age, and eventually pass away.

Within that framework there are variations on how things can turn out, many of which are heavily dependent upon your own particular circumstances. Planning for the predictable items such as retirement, Medicare, and Social Security is only the starting point of effective retirement planning.

This chapter presents many of the steps that you should be taking to prepare for your retirement. These are steps that you should take independently of whether you use Quicken for your home accounting package or not. The information is presented in a predominantly non-Quicken format with the Quicken references added. Part 2,"Getting It into the Computer," presents the details of Quicken operation.

Work your way through this chapter and verify your retirement preparation status, and then extend the contents as applicable to your particular life. Taking the time today can make the future better for all parties involved.

Ages 45–62—Preparing to Take It Easy

Hopefully, by the time you are about 55 years old you are in a financially secure position—one that lets you start thinking about retirement. (See Chapter 1, "It's Never Too Early to Start Planning," for information pertaining to folks under 45.) Unfortunately, many people fail to start thinking about retirement until it is just a few years away. By not planning ahead, you jeopardize not only retirement, but your ability to retire and do the things you've always dreamed of doing after finishing your career. This is why I urge you to start planning for your retirement as early as possible.

If you began putting money into a retirement portfolio fund while you were in your 20s, you have already had your money working for you over a number of decades, and you can probably look forward to a retirement free of financial concerns.

Age 45 is really the right time for you to perform a financial check up. If things aren't where they need to be, you still have time to set things right with 17–20 potential working years still ahead of you.

QuickTip

You might plan to still work after retirement. Many retirees I talk with believe that working after retirement keeps them more active and helps them live longer, more productive lives. Know that any money you earn cuts into the amount of money you receive from Social Security, depending on your age, and upon Social Security even being there at all when you retire. Working after retirement also helps people who do not have a standard company pension with its associated benefits.

You can either perform this check up yourself or bring in a professional to do it for you, but you certainly want to do it. The following are a few items that should be on your retirement preparedness checklist:

➤ Will your home mortgage be paid off by the time you retire? Do you need to pay a little extra every month over the next few years to make sure that you retire mortgage free?

➤ Can you afford the property taxes on the home you currently own? In some locations, the property taxes can be more than $1,000 per month, which is a payment on a smaller house. Is it unrealistic to expect to live in your current house after you retire?

➤ How is your health insurance set up to handle the transition from working to Medicare? Medicare kicks in at age 65, and you might retire at an earlier age. Will your insurance cover you during that period and will it transition to being the secondary coverage behind Medicare parts A and B? What will it cost? Will Medicare even be there when you retire? (See Chapter 17, "An Apple a Day Won't Keep the Doctor Away," for additional information about Medicare coverage and health insurance.)

➤ Are your children independent, or are you going to have to support them in some way? What about your grandchildren? Will their parents provide for them, or is that going to fall under your roof? Sorry. This is a reality of life in our modern day, and being honest with yourself now can keep you from living like a pauper later on.

➤ Are your investments predominantly in high-risk areas where a major market downturn could put you in financial crisis? Perhaps you should consider moving your investments into medium or lower risk categories. I suggest that you start mixing your portfolio so that you have around 25% in lower risk vehicles, 45% in medium risk vehicles, and 30% in higher risk vehicles.

➤ Verify that your life insurance coverage is up to the level you want today and expect to need after retirement. (See Chapter 15, "Cover Your Personal Assets," for additional information regarding life insurance.) If retirement coverage will cost you more money, have you factored the increase into your retirement budget?

➤ Are you going to have a parent of your own to take care of while you work toward retirement, and beyond? If so, you should analyze that person's living expenses and income situation, and make the proper financial arrangements required to cover any shortfalls on his or her part.

➤ Start doing some soul searching about your personal interests. Life doesn't stop when you retire. Only your conventional work requirements stop. Creating interests outside of work before you retire helps you with the retirement transition.

The complexities of your life make it impossible to provide a list that is totally complete for you and your particular situation. This list covers the major items that affect all of us. My hope is that you take this list as a starting point and start looking today at your needs when you reach retirement age. Planning today increases your chance of reaching your goals successfully.

Voice of Experience

A great place to start with your retirement preparation research is to talk to people who are already successfully retired. Ask them about the unexpected things that they encountered, how they planned their retirement, and how close their estimates were. You can learn a lot from their experiences, so ask the questions today. There is a wealth of experience around you if you just ask and are willing to listen.

Over 65 and Enjoying Retirement

Well, here you are—all this free time on your hands and money in the bank. It sounds pretty good, doesn't it? It does to me, but I'm not retired yet. What is interesting to me is that my retired friends often complain about having nothing to do. It is ironic that you should work your whole life to retire, and then sit around wondering what to do with yourself.

There is bound to be a period of disorientation as you move from working at a job that created a certain amount of structure in your life, to being in a position where you define your own structure. Accept that as a reality and be thankful if it doesn't happen. It passes as you get into your new schedule.

If you were a person with diverse interests outside of work, you probably find that those interests continue after retirement, but their importance to you may change. Instead of being an escape from work, they now become what you do.

The following are some retirement options that may be of interest to you:

➤ Golf, golf, and more golf. Not only do you get some exercise, but you keep socially active and somewhat competitive depending on your skill level. Notice that this passion might require a move to a warmer climate where you can play year round.

➤ I know another man who retired so that he could sail every day. He and his wife moved to Florida and bought a nice sailboat that was ocean worthy. They spent a lot of time on the boat, and had a great time.

➤ Managing your investment portfolio is a great hobby that not only contributes to your financial well being, but keeps you mentally active. This is particularly true for those retirees who have health challenges. I suggest that you start by taking a portion of your portfolio that you can afford to lose, say 5%–10%, and make a game out of beating the market indexes. As you get better at it, you find your own challenges. Make sure that you don't gamble with your retirement nest egg. You can't afford to lose it all at this point.

➤ Writing is a great avocation for a retired person. You have the time to research events that you plan to include in your books, time to write and rewrite until it is right, and minimal financial pressure to take the first publishing deal offered. For you budding writers, using a computer to do your writing is a great segue into the next bullet item.

➤ More than one retired person I know has gotten hooked on his computer and spent his retired time either using it as an investment analysis tool (such as with Quicken) or using it to cruise the Internet or to send electronic mail. I suggest that you purchase a computer and take classes at a local junior college or other adult education center. The computer can be a great companion for someone who is house bound because it can play chess, bridge, checkers, and other interactive games. It can also aid in functional ways such as online ordering of groceries, stock market analysis and transactions, mutual fund assessment, electronic mail, chat groups where people interact on a real time basis over the Internet, and newsgroups where people of similar interests share information.

➤ Volunteering is a great way to stay active and give back to the community. Libraries, hospitals, and other community service organizations are always looking for volunteers. Pick your area of interest and give a local organization a call.

➤ Have you ever wondered why retired people have such perfect gardens and lawns? They have time to take classes, prune those bushes they always planned to get at, fertilize the lawn when needed, and make sure things get watered properly. You might even find that a former employer pays for gardening education classes as part of a retirement transition package.

➤ Have you always wanted to go back to school? Here is a perfect chance to do just that. Depending on you goals, you might be happy with a junior college or you might want to look into major colleges or universities. There may be a Ph.D. out there with your name on it.

➤ Travel is one area that most people agree on as a primary reason to retire. This area is as diverse as the people who retire. Travel can run from a major trip each year, to owning and traveling in an RV for the winter, to owning a home in another location where you spend your time. There are tours specifically set up for seniors where the pace and itinerary is set up to accommodate older people from both an interest and physical limitation basis. The National Park and Forest Service even offers a Golden Age Passport that gets you discounts in all national parks and forests. Almost every airline, bus, and train company offers discounts to seniors.

QuickCaution

Traveling abroad is great fun, but persons on Medicare need to remember that Medicare does not provide medical coverage outside of the United States. Make sure that you have supplemental insurance that covers you outside of the United States before taking that well-deserved trip abroad. (See Chapter 17 for additional information regarding Medicare.)

➤ You might want to start a new business. In some ways you are better off starting a business as a retired person than at an earlier age. You have a guaranteed income, so the early stages cash drain is reduced. You have more experience than someone in her 30s, which may make you more marketable to someone else. Colonel Sanders was retired when he started Kentucky Fried Chicken. And he looked great in those white suits.

➤ Don't forget the possibility of teaching. After all, you have a lifetime of experience that might help younger people get a head start on their lives. Junior colleges are always looking for adjunct faculty to teach. Call the personnel office at a local college.

Whatever course you take after retirement, simply know that the more financially prepared you are, the broader your retirement options become. You could easily live 25 years after you retire. Planning ensures that those years are not only productive but also personally rewarding.

Enjoying Early Retirement

Oh, oh. Your company has just offered you the option of retiring early. What? Retired? You are only 50! How does this work out? It can work out great, but know what you are getting into.

If you started with a company when you were in your early 20s, you might have 30 years or more invested with the same company and only be in your early 50s. Some companies even offer to sweeten your retirement incentive by adding years of service to your situation so that you qualify for a higher level of retirement income. This presents an interesting dilemma. Should you retire or keep working? This decision naturally depends on your particular circumstances, but some things to consider are as follows:

➤ Can you afford to live on the pension you receive from the company? You do not qualify for Social Security until age 63, so don't expect that money for a while.

➤ What benefits are transferred to you as part of your retirement? In particular, is health care coverage transferred, for how long and at what premium rate? What about life insurance and disability coverage? Are they also offered and at what premium rate?

➤ How is the severance package paid? Is it paid as a single lump sum, or is it paid out over a number of years? You might want to roll the money into a tax deferred investment vehicle after you make sure that you have enough to live on. Otherwise, you might need to make an early withdrawal from the account that incurs stiff penalties.

➤ Is it possible for you to take early retirement and still work for the company as a consultant or other type of employee? Many people have retired and then gone back to work for the company at a much higher rate than they made as an employee and with more flexibility. Strange but true.

➤ Is this a special opportunity that doesn't come around very often? Even more importantly, if you don't take the offer, are they going to lay you off ("downsize") anyway? Downsizing usually does not come with a major severance attached. Keep your eye on the money and take the course that is financially right for you. Work the numbers.

➤ What are you going to do with yourself if you retire? Many people get their retirement income from their old company and then turn right around and go back to work. These folks basically get paid twice. Now this is a way to create wealth. Pay your bills with one income and invest the other. That boat is starting to look more reasonable all the time isn't it?

➤ Do you feel that you are being squeezed out of the company because of your age and income level? If so, you might have a legal dispute with the company. Talking to an attorney familiar with age discrimination suits is probably a good idea to see if your instincts are correct. I suggest not telling the company that you talked with an attorney until you really have. No reason to lead with your chin. Legal guidance is your best option if you find yourself in this unfortunate set of circumstances.

Early retirement can be a great thing, and most people I know who took early retirement have found productive ways to use their newfound freedom. If you run the financial numbers, you might just find that your after-tax income, with all applicable expenses either added or deducted, might not change as much as you think. Plus, if you could have an after-tax income as a retired person that is 75% of your working income, would you take it? I would, because I am making 75% of what I made as a working person but never have to go to work. This must be what is meant by the good life.

Preparing for Aging Parents

As you age, your parents also age. If you are all lucky, your parents stay healthy, independent, and productive until they pass away. This is everyone's wish, and for many people, life turns out just this way. We also all know, however, that life is full of surprises, and these surprises can put parents into positions where they cannot take care of themselves. Dealing with these situations usually requires some level of intervention on the part of the children and other relatives.

Perhaps the most important thing that you can do with a parent is to discuss this possibility before it actually occurs. None of us wishes for a parent to become incapacitated, but we also all know that it can happen. Knowing the parent's wishes helps tremendously in determining the proper course of action.

There are a number of alternative actions that can be taken depending on the specific circumstances involved:

➤ If the parent has long term care coverage, a nursing home might be an affordable and personally acceptable option. (See Chapter 17 for additional information on long-term care coverage.)

➤ If the parent comes to live with you, you have a few options available. First, Medicare and any supplemental health care insurance your parent had should cover in-home care. Paying the premiums now becomes your responsibility, so make sure that it is done properly.

➤ Your parent might have a substantial portfolio saved that can be used to pay expenses. If your parent can make financial decisions, then getting money from the portfolio should be no problem. If the parent is not able to make responsible decisions, you might have to obtain legal control over these investment accounts. This is a long process if done after the fact, so try to work this out with your parent before something happens. Keep the lawyers from making a fortune off of your misfortune. In truth, this is also in the parent's best interest because lack of funds might interfere with getting the required healthcare. (See Chapter 23, "You Can't Take It with You, So Plan Your Estate Now," for additional information about durable powers of attorney and other estate planning topics.)

➤ If your parent is a U.S. citizen or a resident of Canada, Mexico, or the United States; has income of less than $2,650; does not file a joint tax return; and pays less than half of his/her support with you paying the rest, you can claim this parent as a dependent. It is strange to think of your parent as your dependent, but it can happen. Having an income of less than $2,650 is pretty tough when your consider interest income, so you are probably not able to take this deduction, but know that it is there if applicable.

➤ Medical expenses that you pay on your parent's behalf that are in excess of a 7.5% floor are tax deductible even if the parent has income of more $2,650. The parent must meet all other dependency requirements. Also, paying a parent's medical expenses directly to the health care provider does not constitute a gift to the parent, which means that the parent does not have to pay tax on the payments that exceed the gift threshold, which is currently $10,000.

➤ Finally, come to grips with the fact that you may now have to keep your parent's legal and financial affairs in order. This means filing tax returns, paying bills, handling investments, and dealing with other family members. This can be a substantial responsibility and one that is more easily administered if you, your parent, and other family members have discussed it before anything happens.

Hopefully your parents are never in a position where they are dependent upon you for their care. But it can happen. Take the time, in advance, to get things worked out and be thankful if you never have to use this information. Being a little paranoid on this point is time well spent for all parties involved.

What if Your Kids Don't Leave?

For any number of reasons, some children never leave home or end up moving back in with their parents when hard times come along. As a parent, you are hard pressed to say "no," especially if there are grandchildren involved. But their moving back in can have an impact on your financial situation in either a positive or negative way. If your child pays a portion of the rent, you might be appreciative of the extra company. If the child is not able to work for some reason, you might become the sole provider for a household that now has another person. It pays to know some of your financial and legal options. I'll leave the personal options up to you and your conscience.

➤ If the financial arrangements work out so that your child is a dependent from an IRS point of view, you should take the dependent deduction. If your grandchildren also qualify as dependents, take the deduction for them as well.

➤ If you rent a room to your child, you have rental income to declare on your taxes. This makes your house a rental that may have depreciation and expense deduction benefits associated with it.

➤ Keep your finances separate from your child's. If you don't and you have a child with a spending or gambling problem, he/she could lose your life's savings for you without even knowing it. This may sound heartless, but an ounce of legal separation in this regard can save you years of under-financed retirement.

Most of the other issues related to a child moving back home are of a personal nature to be worked out between you and your child.

The Least You Need to Know

➤ Have a retirement checkup at age 45 to allow enough time to make corrections, if needed.

➤ Take early retirement if it works out financially and personally to your benefit.

➤ Find a hobby that you love before you retire so that retiring is simply a transition from a job to a hobby and not into a complete lack of direction.

➤ Medical treatment obtained outside of the United States is not covered under standard Medicare.

➤ Parents can become dependents under the right financial conditions.

POVERTY 0 0 0
YOUR LIFE 0 1 2

Chapter 3

Keeping Score with Accounting

In This Chapter

➤ The importance of managing your finances

➤ The effect of time on your financial situation

➤ The value of interest income

➤ The dangers of inflation

➤ Assessing your current situation

It really is pretty amazing to look back on what $500 bought in 1963 and what it buys today. Granted, most people didn't earn as much back then as they do today, but the grim fact is that everything continues increasing in price. If wages don't increase in accordance with the price increases, you feel as if you are financially moving backward even though your annual income keeps increasing.

This chapter introduces several concepts related to time and money management. In addition, you learn techniques for judging your financial batting average. Like it or not, the value of things change over time and so does the value of your money. Playing any game means knowing the rules. Knowing these financial rules increases your odds of winning the time-honored competition of financial gain.

Keeping Financial Score

Life, and money management, is a game. As with any game, keeping score is a way of determining your level of performance. Following are a few criteria for a successful financial life that I have heard from a few colleagues and friends:

➤ "He who dies with the most toys, wins." Well, how do you afford the toys?

➤ "My descendents won't retire off of my estate." Well, how do you plan your finances so that you don't leave anything behind?

➤ "I want to retire at age 55 so that I can finally enjoy my life." Well, how much do you need to put away annually to ensure that you reach this goal? (Oh, by the way, I suggest you start enjoying your life now just in case you don't make it to age 55.)

Financial management is critical to achieving any one of these diverse goals, and most any other goal you can come up with. That is, unless you are so wealthy that it just doesn't matter. (Raise your hand if you are in that category and please call me so that I can get to know you better.)

Just as a company must track its financial performance to determine its economic health, so must an individual or family. This might not be obvious at first glance, but valid direct financial comparisons can be made between a company and an individual.

➤ Companies derive their income from producing products or services that turn into income when they are sold.

You produce a service (your time) that is turned into income when you sell it to your employer.

➤ Companies incur both fixed and variable expenses in the process of standard operations.

You incur fixed expenses (for example, your mortgage) and variable expenses (for example, college tuition for each child) in the process of living your life.

➤ Companies have a worth that is based on what it has of value (assets) minus what it owes (liabilities).

You have a worth based on what you own (your house, car, and so on) minus what you owe (mortgage, credit cards, and so on).

Get the point? You and a company have a lot of financial similarities. Companies take financial tracking very seriously. They have entire departments that look for ways to optimize the amount that the company makes over the course of a year. These departments also look for ways to turn what the company is currently worth into a more valuable company next year.

If companies, who live to optimize their profits and value, make a concentrated effort to manage their finances, why should less be required of you?

If you just got that point, you just changed your relationship with money. You also greatly improved your likelihood of achieving financial comfort and possibly financial wealth.

You have nothing to lose by taking your finances seriously. Carefully tracking your finances can be one of the most important decisions you ever make for the following reasons:

➤ It means college for your kids, or even for you.

➤ It means insurance when you need it and, unfortunately, even when you don't.

➤ It means enough money to take those vacations you always dreamed of.

➤ It means owning that summer/weekend cottage that allows you to truly get away from the bustle of daily living.

➤ It could enable you to work less, lower your stress level, and possibly prolong your life.

In short, keeping financial score with Quicken, combined with the procedures discussed in this book, enables you to keep your eye on the financial ball and best ensures that you hit a home run in the form of the financial freedom to live life as you desire, when you desire.

Just reading this book is a good start, but you also need to take action. Don't just dream about your financial freedom. Learn the basics, which aren't very difficult, and then apply them to your life.

When It Costs to NOT Do Something

Financial people often sound like they live in a different world from the rest of us. They talk about "the time value of money" and "opportunity costs" as if this jargon is more than a figment of their imaginations. It turns out that financial management has a few rules that are a lot like gravity in that they apply no matter where you are, and there is really no getting around them.

One rule is that a dollar today does not buy the same as a dollar next year. In general, next year's dollar buys less. This is due to inflation, which is covered in the next section, "When Is a Dollar Not a Dollar?"

QuickTip

When you borrow money, you pay interest expenses on the amount you borrow. When you have money, you gain interest income on the invested money.

Another rule is that a dollar invested today has some type of interest rate applied to it, so the same dollar has earned additional interest money by next year. For example, investing a dollar at a 12% annual return means that this dollar earns 12%, or 12 cents, over the course of the year. (Calculated by: .12 × $1 = $0.12, or 12 cents.) This same dollar left for another year at 12% earns 13.44 cents since the 12% is earned on $1.12 instead of just $1. (Calculated as: .12 × $1.12 = $0.1344.) Continue this process out for 5 years and you find that the dollar invested today at 12% interest rate becomes worth $1.7623. Multiply 1.12 times itself five times to prove to yourself that this is true and verify your calculations against those shown in Table 3.1. This is referred to as compounded interest in that next year's interest is based on interest earned last year, or is compounded year-after-year.

By the way, this also means that $10,000 invested in an account earning 12% per year is worth $17,623 at the end of five years. Now that buys a pretty nice vacation to Hawaii, don't you think?

Table 3.1 Account Balances Earning 12% Compounded Interest over Five Years

Investment	Interest	Earnings	Ending Balance
$10,000	12%	$1,200	$11,200
$11,200	12%	$1,344	$12,544
$12,544	12%	$1,505	$14,049
$14,049	12%	$1,686	$15,735
$15,735	12%	$1,888	$17,623

Talkin' Money

Opportunity cost is the amount of future earning potential that you gave up because you took one action instead of another. This is not always bad even though it sounds that way.

It should now be pretty clear that interest income is a good thing. So how can it cost you NOT to do something? Check this out.

Assume that you have the chance to put your money into an account paying 12% interest per year, but choose to leave it in savings account paying 3% per year. This means you are losing 9% interest income a year. It can be that simple.

Should you automatically move your money to the higher account? The answer is no. The 12% account pays a higher rate of return because there could be a higher likelihood of losing money in that account. (See Chapter 18, "Taking Risks Doesn't Mean Betting the Farm," for more information.)

If you are willing to take that risk, move the money. If not, leave it where it is, understanding that you are giving up potential income by not having taken advantage of the 12% account. Economists call this the "opportunity cost" of not placing your money into the higher yielding account.

By deciding to leave your money where it is, your accounts are still growing by 3% per year, meaning that you're not losing anything from your initial investment.

You're just not making as much on your investment as you could earn if you were willing to take a bigger risk.

Taking this topic to a more tangible level, assume that you have $10,000 that you feel is your "risk money" in that if you lost it you would hurt a little, but the loss wouldn't be catastrophic. Also assume that this money is sitting in a 3% account earning $300 per year (.03 × $10,000 = $300). This means that this money earns $1,593 over the five-year period. Once again, prove this $1,593 gain number to yourself as a practice exercise by multiplying (10,000 × 1.03 × 1.03 × 1.03 × 1.03 × 1.03) – 10,000 = 1,593.

Talkin' Money

Risk money is money used for higher risk investments because losing this money won't put your lifestyle and/or financial security at risk.

Now assume that you have access to a higher-risk account paying 12% but have just been too lazy or busy to move the money over. You know from the prior exercise that $10,000 invested in an account paying 12% per year earns $7,623 over a five year period. Your lack of action costs you $6,030 in earned interest over a five-year period. This is calculated by taking the amount you could earn if you were to move the money ($7,623) minus the amount you are currently earning by leaving it where it is ($1,593).

Using financial jargon, your opportunity cost over the five year period is $6,030. This opportunity cost may not feel like a real money loss today, but it probably will when you look back in five years.

Would you make a simple phone call if you knew that it would make you more than $6,000? Probably. Think about it.

Voice of Experience

Remember that you never want to invest money you can't afford to lose in a high interest bearing account without understanding that the higher interest rate means that you are rolling the dice at some level. It would be a real drag to lose your house, car, and other daily essentials simply because you feared regretting the opportunity cost five years from now. Balancing risk and reward is a tough highwire act for all investors.

When Is a Dollar Not a Dollar?

Inflation is another of those financial principles that works like gravity—it affects everyone. This section takes a closer look at the impact of inflation on your daily life and how you should consider the effects of gravity when making financial decisions.

Inflation means that a dollar today buys less than it did a few years ago. By the same token, inflation also means that a dollar today buys more today than it will a few years into the future (something many people never think about).

Deflation means the opposite of inflation, where a dollar today buys more than it did five years ago. Deflation doesn't come along very often, but it may appear in our lives if the Asian financial turmoil has a negative effect on U.S. exports. This might result in a glut of domestically produced products that can't be sold overseas, which could well mean a price drop to increase demand and reduce the amount of product manufacturers have in their warehouses.

If you aren't sure about the effects of inflation, think about a pack of gum that cost a nickel in the 60s (if you remember back that far) and that now costs between 75 cents and a dollar, depending where you buy it. Or think about a new car that cost $2,000 in 1965 and that now costs more than $15,000. Look around and you see that a dollar today does not buy as much as it did 10 years ago.

Talkin' Money

The time value of money refers to the buying power fluctuations of money over time based on the combined effects of interest and inflation rates.

Of course, there are exceptions to inflation, such as household electronics (stereo equipment, for example) and computers. Two hundred dollars today buys a lot more electronic capability than it did 10 years ago. Take, for example, a typical PC that could cost less than $1,000 today. A PC with far less than half the power and speed would have cost more than $3,000 just a few years ago. Other than that, you should find that this decreasing purchasing power rule holds true, especially when considering homes, cars, vacations, groceries, clothing, and entertainment.

Economists call this effect inflation, and it is factored into something else called the time value of money.

The same item that you can purchase today costs more in the future or, said another way, it takes more dollars to buy the same item five years from now. Because it takes more dollars to buy the same item, the dollars themselves must be worth less in the future than they are today.

Inflation has traditionally run in the 4% per year range, but it has run under 2% for the past few years, and some think it may actually go negative over the next few years.

Anyone who lived in the mid-1980s with both high mortgage and inflation rates understands what happens when your income buys substantially less every year. Things were out of control and you worked like crazy to just make ends meet. There are countries in the world that struggle with 100% inflation per year, or more. Imagine that a loaf of bread that costs $1 today would cost $2 the same time next year!

The good news for the United States today and probably until sometime into the next decade is that inflation should not be an important factor in our lives.

QuickTip

It is usually best to buy during a period of high inflation, because a stereo that costs you $150 today might cost you $165 after a year of inflation. On the other hand, it is usually best to put off buying during a period of deflation because that same $150 stereo might only cost you $135 after a year of deflation.

How Much Did You Really Make?

How much did you make last year? I know a guy who made six figures but can't afford to buy lunch. I know another female friend who makes nowhere near six figures, yet always has enough money to pay her way. Who is better off? I think it's pretty obvious.

What you make comes down to a very simple equation: subtract what you spend each year from the amount you earn each year. What is left over is what you made. If the final number is positive, then you actually made money. If the final number is negative, then it cost you money to get through the year.

Financial people track annual income performance using a formal report called an Income Statement. An income statement simply subtracts your expenses from your income to determine your net income. A simple income statement is shown in Table 3.2.

Table 3.2 Using an Income Statement to Figure Your Income

Income Items	
Salary Income:	$35,000
Interest Income:	$ 2,300
Total Income:	$37,300

Expense Items	
Income Taxes:	-$ 9,800
Mortgage Payments:	-$ 7,200
Car Payments:	-$ 5,100
Utilities:	-$ 1,800
Vacation:	-$ 2,500
Living Expenses:	-$ 9,600
Total Expenses:	-$36,000
Net Income:	$ 1,300

The basic procedure for calculating how much you make, spend, and keep in a year is as follows:

➤ Add up all sources of income for the year. This typically includes items such as salaries, rental income, interest income, dividends, alimony, royalties, and child support. Any item that involved someone giving you money should be added to this list.

➤ Add up all expenses that you pay during the year. This typically includes rent payments, mortgage payments, car payments, utilities, food, insurance, phone, tuition, federal taxes, state taxes, property taxes, charitable donations, and any other item where you give money to someone else.

➤ Subtract the expense total from the income total to determine your net income (refer to Table 3.2 for an example).

If a person makes a lot of money and has very high expenses, he might not be able to buy lunch without charging it, which only makes his situation worse. A lower income person who does not spend much can actually retain more of his or her income at the end of the year and be better off financially than the person making more money.

QuickTip

You might hear people talking about cash and accrual accounting and how important they are when considering finances. This is true, but these terms aren't really applicable to you as a standard consumer. By default, you are on a cash basis of accounting, which means that you track expenses and income when you either transfer money to someone else, or when someone else transfers money to you, respectively.

Accrual accounting applies when commitments are made, not when the money actually changes hands. We treat everything in this book on a cash basis of accounting, so don't get thrown off track if you come across this accounting terminology.

Wealth is a relative term, because you can have a lot of income and still not be wealthy. I suggest that you consider another definition for wealth. When your income exceeds your total expenses making your net income a positive number, you can consider that leftover wealth that you've attained. The net income may be large or small, but in either case you made money for the year. That net income can be invested and can start earning you money based on the earlier interest income discussion. But, if you never have a positive net income, you can never start investing, which means interest never begins to build up in your accounts.

Talkin' Money

Cash accounting tracks income and expenses when money actually changes hands, whether by cash, credit card, or check.

Accrual accounting tracks income and expenses when liabilities are incurred.

In this situation, you live from year to year always wondering whether you have enough money to pay your bills. Not only is this no fun, it can be financially disastrous if you lose your income. Without a financial reserve built up over years of positive net incomes, you are not able to pay bills without credit. Credit solves the short-term problem, but can be the final straw on a weak financial back if the loss of income lasts for more than a few months.

So, my recommendation to you from this section should not sound like rocket science:

➤ Arrange your life so that you always earn more money (after taxes) than you spend.

➤ Be disciplined about investing the net income as either a handy cash reserve for rainy days or as money that you use for investment purposes. This means that you may have to increase your income or decrease your expenses, either option may involve a lifestyle change.

➤ Know that the lifestyle change happens anyway if you continue with a negative net income because you eventually are not able to pay your bills. At least by increasing your income or decreasing your expenses, you control when the changes happen and preserve your credit rating.

How Much Are You Worth and Why Should You Care?

You probably know that making more than you spend is a good idea. There is no mystery here. A probable next question might be how this positive net income eventually turns into a nest egg that provides psychological comfort and eventually real wealth. Tracking the wealth building process is the focus of this section.

Talkin' Money

Net worth is the difference between the value of what you own minus the value of what you owe.

Every year magazines publish the names of the wealthiest people in the world. Have you ever thought about what this means? How is this wealth determined? It is assessed by calculating the net worth of the people involved.

Even the poorest monk owns something, whether it is a robe, slippers, or a small travel pack. You probably own a car, house, furnishings, a savings account, checking account, and other items such as a retirement fund at work. These items are called assets in accounting lingo. Think of anything you own that has financial value of any kind as an asset.

Financial people track assets, liabilities, and net worth on a report called a balance sheet. A typical balance sheet shows the things you own, or your assets, on the top. Below the assets is a listing of everything that you owe, or your liabilities. At the bottom is the result of subtracting the liabilities from the assets, which is the net worth. A typical balance sheet is shown in Table 3.3.

Talkin' Money

Assets   Things of value that you own. Typical assets include houses, cars, furnishings, and bank accounts.

Liabilities   Things on which you owe money. Typical liabilities include mortgage loans, car loans, student loans, credit cards, and unpaid taxes.

Net worth   The total amount of assets that you own minus the total amount of liabilities that you owe. You build wealth when your net worth is positive.

Balance sheet   A standardized financial statement that shows what you own, what you owe, and the difference between the two, called your net worth.

Table 3.3   A Simple Balance Sheet

Asset Accounts

Bank Accounts	$ 24,000
House	$135,000
Car	$ 18,000
401(k) Account	$ 47,000
Total Assets	$224,000

Liability Accounts

Mortgage Loan	$ 76,000
Car Loan	$ 7,600
Credit Cards	$ 4,450
Personal Loan	$ 1,200
Total Liabilities	$ 89,250
Net Worth	$134,750

The balance sheet includes financial items, such as 401(k) plans, bank accounts, credit cards, and loans. It isn't only major physical items such as your house and car. Also, the balance sheet doesn't indicate whether this person makes money each year or not. It only indicates accumulated wealth. This wealth could have come from an inheritance, winning the lottery, or other lucky activities. For most of us, it must come from a consistent, positive net income that happens over a number of years.

This statement also shows the account values on a particular date. Income statements track flows of cash in and out of accounts. Balance sheets track the value of an account on any particular day after the income statement flows have been tallied.

Enough about accounting. How do you typically use a balance sheet?

➤ Verify that your net worth is positive and increasing from year to year.

➤ Create a plan to increase assets and decrease liabilities, if net worth is negative. This may involve selling certain items to pay off debts that are at high interest rates or earning more net income so that larger payments can be made on liabilities, which eventually reduces them.

➤ Verify that you have enough ready cash on hand, and that all your assets are not in fixed assets, such as furniture and houses, that cannot easily be changed into cash for emergency purposes.

We return to the balance sheets and income statements throughout the book. It is difficult to track your financial performance or to discuss strategies without referring to asset, liability, income, and expense accounts. Quicken makes a lot more sense if you get this simple terminology. In addition, you do a better job of managing your finances if you understand the jargon.

Quicken Makes Accounting Pretty Painless

I keep talking about how cool Quicken is and why you should be using it. You are now ready to understand some of the major benefits associated with using Quicken. The folks at Intuit who developed Quicken have done a great job of creating a software package that does accounting for you while insulating you from much of the accounting complexity.

A major benefit of using Quicken is that it easily and quickly creates income and balance sheet statements for you, using your entered data. You can even graph the net income and net worth values over various periods of time.

These reports are valuable for determining your financial position, and they also add credibility should you have to convince someone else, or a bank, to lend you money. Financial people like financial reports for all the reasons discussed in this chapter. Get your information into Quicken so you can determine where you stand financially and what is needed to get your net income and net worth into the positive number category. Then track your performance as you move toward your financial goals. (See Part 2, "Getting It into the Computer," for the details associated with entering your data and getting reports.)

Think of yourself as the player, the bookkeeping as the scorekeeper, and Quicken reports as the game results listed on the scoreboard.

The Least You Need to Know

➤ Money and items change value over time.

➤ A positive net income and net worth are a must if you plan to build personal wealth.

➤ Tracking your financial position keeps you from getting into a precarious spot.

➤ Quicken makes financial data entry and report generation quick and easy.

➤ Computer reporting of your financial situation makes it easier to get loans and pay your taxes.

Chapter 4

Book It with Bookkeeping

In This Chapter

➤ Automating mistakes just makes them happen faster

➤ Personal finance management is too complicated for any software package to anticipate all possible transactions

➤ Understanding simple bookkeeping rules gives you the best chance for getting your accounting data accurate

➤ Accurate historical expense data enables valid budget creation and tracking

➤ Prepare in advance for next year's taxes

If you have never taken a course in bookkeeping, you might be wondering whether the bookkeeping aspects of working with Quicken are going to be overwhelming. Take a deep breath, relax, and let me assure you that this is not the case.

Professional bookkeeping can get incredibly complicated when you're involved with all the details and circumstances associated with a large corporation. Individual bookkeeping, on the other hand, doesn't have to be that hard. Quicken easily handles the needs of the basic consumer and is more than adequate to manage all your personal finance records. The degree of bookkeeping knowledge that you need to keep Quicken up and running certainly is within your grasp and skill.

But, you need a few more tools to help you make the right financial decisions, which is something that Quicken can't do for you. That's where this book comes in. This book is an attempt to give you all the details you need to make good financial decisions.

It also helps you with some of the jargon you need to understand along the way. Armed with this book and Quicken, you are taking the first step to skillful personal finance.

Remember that lenders give money to people, not reports. The more you know about financial management in general and your financial situation in particular, the more credible you appear and the more likely you are to succeed when borrowing money.

Debits and Credits and Bears, Oh My!

Quicken does a great job of insulating you from the Byzantine world of bookkeeping. In particular, it protects you from the infamous debit and credit. So what is this debit or credit? Simple. Think of any bookkeeping account as having two columns—left and right. It would be way too simple to call them that because that would take away the mystery. Instead, they call the left side the debit column and the right side the credit column. That's it. Debit means left and credit means right.

QuickTip

Quicken rarely uses debit/credit terminology and instead refers to increasing or decreasing the balance on an account. Remember that these debits and credits are still happening in the background as you enter your data, regardless of Quicken's terminology—or my left and right terminology, for that matter.

Now, the implications of a debit or credit are dependent on the type of account into which the debit or credit is being applied.

Accounting uses asset, liability, revenue and expense accounts. Quicken also tracks your accounting information using these types of accounts. See "Keeping Score with Accounting," in Chapter 3, for more information on the different types of accounts.

Entering a number into the debit column of an asset account, increases it. Entering a number to the debit column of a liability decreases it. To make it worse, a debit to an expense account increases it, where a debit to a revenue account decreases it. This is known as double entry accounting.

Double Entry Accounting

Double entry accounting says that the total amount of debits added for a transaction must equal the total amount of credits for the same transaction. For example, if you take $45 from an asset account, such as your checking account, you are crediting (decreasing) your checking account by $45. You now must create debit entries that equal $45. These debit entries could be to an expense account, such as one you may have for your telephone expenses. Making entries in both accounts (in this case your checking and telephone accounts) results in a double entry.

It's also possible to split the $45 over multiple accounts as long as the total amount of debits equals the total amount of credits.

As for you and your accounting, don't get discouraged, because Quicken hides all this by handling the proper entries for you after you enter your initial data, meaning that Quicken makes the second entry for you. I've introduced the double entry accounting requirement simply to provide you with a foundation for understanding the rationale behind some of Quicken's data entry procedures.

Setting Up Checking, Savings, and Money Market Accounts

Just as the foundation provides the basis for building a house, the accounts provide the foundation for bookkeeping data entry. Without the asset, liability, expense and revenue accounts, there would be no place to store the data.

By the way, these accounts must be created whether you use Quicken, MS Money, or simply a paper and pencil manual tracking system.

The following are a few rules that apply to everyone when creating accounts:

➤ If you own anything of value, such as cash, a house, a car, or things that people owe you, you need to create asset accounts.

➤ If you owe anything to others, such as the car loan, mortgage, credit cards, or student loans, you must create liability accounts.

➤ If you have any type of income over the year, whether from salary, interest income, dividends, or other sources, you must create revenue accounts.

➤ If you pay others for living expenses, such as groceries, utilities, insurance, or telephone, you must create expense accounts.

It doesn't matter who you are, or what you do. When you pull money out of your checking account, that money goes to pay down a liability (decrease a loan), to increase an expense (pay the phone bill), or a combination of both. When you add money to your checking account, you must increase a revenue account (increase your payroll account), increase a liability (take out a loan), or a combination of both. For example, you could deposit $1,500 (debit) into your checking account where $1,000 was revenue from your paycheck (credit) and $500 is liability from a loan (credit) that you just took out from a bank.

Voice of Experience

It may seem to you that I spent a lot of time on this topic, and if you are bored, I apologize. I have found over my years of using Quicken that all situations cannot be handled automatically, and an understanding of the basic relationship between the accounts and double entry accounting has kept me from making errors that would have been very confusing later. Hang in there because you are almost done with the tough stuff.

Covering Your Assets

Most red-blooded Americans own stuff. That is one of the joys, or curses, of living in a free market country. Keeping track of, and paying for, all this stuff is another question. "He who dies with the most toys, wins." Tracking your assets is how you keep score.

Take a look at the following partial list of typical assets:

Checking account

Savings account

Money market account

Cash

House

Car

Furnishings

Jewelry

Artwork

Boat

Recreational vehicle

Retirement plans

Loans that people owe you (receivable)

Under each of these categories may be a number of items that are important to you. For example, furnishings probably includes your sofa, chairs, dining room set, TV, radio, kitchenware, and other items you have around the house.

Jewelry is tracked separately because you probably want to specially insure these items; a running tally of all jewelry items ensures that you have enough coverage. Otherwise, the jewelry items would be buried in the Furnishings account and might be overlooked. Artwork is a separate category for the same reason.

The value that you place into these accounts is dependent upon what you paid for it at the time of purchase if you plan to track the book value of the assets. Some people set the asset value based on its current market value, which might have increased substantially since its purchase. This is usually true for houses, fine art, and other collectible items.

Assume that you just opened a checking account with your local bank. See the following simple example of how your checking account handles transactions. Most likely, you've been doing this for years without understanding the double entry system behind the scenes.

1. You open the account by depositing a paycheck. (In this example, the paycheck is for $2,000.)
2. The checking account asset balance increases by $2,000.
3. This action also increases the Salary revenue account by $2,000, which keeps double entry accounting in check. Remember that this is a debit entry to your checking account because you increased the value of an asset and a credit entry to your salary account because you increased the amount of a revenue account.
4. Next, you write a rent check for $600 to your landlord.
5. This action decreases your checking account by $600.
6. The rent expense account is increased by $600—once again keeping double entry accounting in check. Keep in mind that this is a credit entry to your checking account because you decreased the value of an asset and a debit entry to your rent account because you increased the amount of an expense account.

It should now be obvious that keeping all the numbers in the correct columns is important. Without the structure, all financial data would appear different and a third party, such as your banker, wouldn't be able to understand the particulars of your financial situation. So far, you have only dealt with the asset accounts. The following sections introduce you to the common liability, expense, and revenue tracking storage locations.

Voice of Experience

The check recording register that you get from your bank can be confusing if you look at it in light of the checkbook example just outlined. My register shows a written check as a debit (−) and a deposit as a credit (+). This jargon appears to be the opposite of what I just presented to you, and it is if you look at it from your side, but it matches perfectly if you look at it from the bank's side.

When you put your money into a checking account, the bank actually creates a liability account with your name on it for the amount of the account balance, which in this case is $2,000. A credit is used to increase a liability account, and a debit is used to decrease a liability account. So, what you see on your check register is bank-oriented terminology, not people-oriented terminology. Don't let it throw you. Simply think in terms of increasing and decreasing the account, and let the debits/credits work themselves out.

Monitoring What You Owe with Liability Accounts

When you take out a loan for $5,000, you become liable for paying it back. You have increased your financial liability by taking out the loan. Typical liability accounts include those in the following list:

House mortgage loan

Car loan

Credit card balances

Tax payments

Personal loans

Student loans

Tuition loans

Retail store credit lines

Bank lines of credit

Equity loans

You might notice a correlation between the liability accounts and the asset accounts. Many of the major assets that you purchase, such as your house or car, also have a loan associated with them. The loan amount is usually less than the dollar amount of the asset because a down payment of some type is generally required, meaning that you should start out owing less than the value of the item you've purchased.

For example, assume that you purchase a house for $150,000 and 20% down payment ($30,000) is required. The loan amount secured by the house itself is calculated as $150,000 – $30,000 = $120,000. Tracking these transactions requires a $120,000 increase in loan liabilities, a $120,000 increase in house assets, a $30,000 decrease in the cash assets, and a $30,000 increase in house assets. Double entry accounting is again preserved, and all transactions are accounted for (no pun intended). Also, the cash portion of the transaction reduces one asset and increases another, which indicates that you can perform double entry accounting entries within the same group, such as within liabilities or within assets.

Every time you take on a new debt, you must create a new liability account. This can be a credit card or a student loan. If you purchase an item with your Visa credit card, such as a new TV, you increase the Furnishings asset account while also increasing your Visa liability account.

QuickTip

Asset and liability accounts appear on the balance sheet and are used for calculating your net worth.

Tracking Expenses and Income

The final two areas that need consideration are income and expense accounts. These accounts track how much money came in and how much went out over a period of time.

You consistently find that you have far fewer income accounts than you have expense accounts. If you think about this, it makes a lot of sense. You probably work for a single employer during the year and have a single paycheck. This gives you a single source of income. But, you probably write checks to what may seem like every-one and her sister for things such as telephone, utilities, loan payments, mortgage payments, food, eating out, and numerous others.

The following is a list of typical income accounts:

Your salary

Your bonuses

Spouse's salary

Spouse's bonuses

Interest income

Dividend income

Gifts received

Rental income (if you own rental property)

Creating the income accounts is not too complicated, but allocating the various items associated with your paycheck can be very complicated. Take a look at your paycheck and notice that you have various taxes taken out, payments for medical insurance, payments for life insurance, deposits into retirement plans, and other specific items. Making sure all these accounts are created properly and with the proper amounts applied can get complex, and Quicken takes care of it for you.

Quicken has an automated tool to use to set up the proper accounts and apply the proper amounts. This **Paycheck Setup Wizard** is located under the **Features** menu, **Banking**, **Set Up Paycheck** option. Follow the wizard's instructions to easily and accurately set up your paycheck allocations. After you become confident with Quicken, you can establish these transactions on your own if you feel the need to exercise your knowledge, but use the wizard when first starting out. (See Chapters 6, 7, and 8 for additional information about setting up Quicken categories and accounts.)

Expense accounts track where your money is spent. You generally have a lot of these, and you can add as many as needed to track your expenses into the smallest level of detail, if so inclined.

The following are typical expense categories:

Mortgage interest

Food

Rent

Utilities

Telephone

Eating out

Vacations

Tuition

Books

Clothing

Insurance

Gasoline

Credit card interest

Other interest payments

Postage and shipping

Taxes of all kinds

Medical payments

Expenses are often grouped under a major heading, such as Insurance. Under Insurance you might create subcategories, such as Medical, Automobile, Homeowners, Artwork, Jewelry, Life, and other insurance types so that you can track how much you pay for each. Otherwise, the amounts are recorded under the main Insurance category, and the amount spent on each of these individual insurance areas must be extracted and summed to get the desired information. Setting up the main and subcategories from the beginning makes later use of the entered data easier and more meaningful. (See Chapter 6, "Quicken from 20,000 Feet," for details regarding the definition of categories and accounts.)

When tracking payments into liability accounts and expense categories, you need to be aware of how principal and interest portions of your payments are tracked. For example, assume that you make a mortgage payment for $1,000, where $150 goes to paying off the principle loan amount and the $850 balance goes to mortgage interest expense. You must decrease Checking by $1,000, increase Mortgage Interest expense by $850, and decrease Home Loan by $150. (See Chapter 10, "Lend Me Your Ear...," for additional information regarding loans and the relationship between principle and interest payments.)

Congratulations! You have made it through the worst part of learning accounting and bookkeeping. These few pages were not designed to make you accounting gurus, but only make you conversational with what happens when the data is recorded. Quicken does most of this for you, but it still requires occasional intervention on your part for those special cases that Intuit didn't anticipate.

Setting a Budget That You Can Live With

You've now got blisters on your fingers from all this account creation and data entry. Now what? Good question, and I've got a good answer for you.

Take a look at what you made last year and what you spent. How did you do? Did you have any money left over at the end of the year, or was your net income a negative number? How much did you spend as listed in the various expense categories? Do any of the numbers surprise you? If so, you might want to take a closer look at that category to verify that there aren't any mistakes and to see if there were individual expenses that sent the total amount through the roof.

It is great to finally get your historical information under control, because it gives you a snapshot of how your money was spent over the last year, for instance. Unless last year was unique, you can pretty much assume that next year will cost you the same amount, which enables you to start planning for it today.

This is called budgeting and it is a critical process if you plan to save money and you are on a tight income.

Assume that you spent $1,300 last year in eating out expenses, which comes out to around $108 per month. You can start tracking your eating out expenses on a monthly basis, compare what you pay to what you have budgeted, and determine whether you need to eat out less to keep to your budget goals. Setting and tracking budget goals ensures that you do not unconsciously spend yourself into a negative financial position.

Flow Compared to Balance

If you are like most people I know, the fury of activity that appears in your daily life occupies most of your attention. You primarily worry about having enough money to pay your bills. Worrying about account balances is a secondary thought if the bills are paid and you made it through another month.

This is a strong focus on managing the income statement, because you are focused on how much income you have and how much is left over after expenses are paid. This is important, but it ignores the asset tracking that is so important to accumulating wealth.

Income statements are a measure of financial flow over a period of time. Income flows in and expenses flow out. The left over amount is the net income. If you spend it, it becomes an expense and no wealth is accumulated.

Your net worth is determined at any given point in time, usually assumed at December 31 for most individuals. This is not a flow measurement. It is a measurement of the balances that exist in your asset and liability accounts on that day. There is no measure of how the money got there or how much was spent, only how much is left over on December 31.

Tracking net income is critical because without a positive net income, there is no way to accumulate wealth. A zero or negative net income means that you are way too busy trying to pay your bills to worry about increasing your net worth. Tracking an increasing net worth best ensures that you have enough financial power in retirement to keep you comfortable when the traditional income stream disappears.

Tracking income is also essential for tax planning, because you pay taxes on your income after all acceptable tax deductions have been subtracted. Tax planning is particularly important for you self-employed folks or those of you who own rental property. (See Chapter 9, "Planning for the Tax Man," for detailed information regarding account setup and tax preparation.)

Think of your net income flowing into your balance sheet asset accounts, increasing your assets while not increasing your liabilities. In short, you create wealth by increasing your assets while not increasing your liabilities. Measure your improving net worth by comparing last year's bottom line with the current year-end total. If the net worth figure increases, life is good and you are accumulating wealth. If the figure decreases, then you are spending your cash reserves in a way that does not contribute to your long-term goal of financial independence and a secure retirement.

Make sure that you review Part 2 of this book, "Getting It into the Computer," so that you set up Quicken in a way that is right for you and your financial needs.

The Least You Need to Know

➤ Understanding basic accounting terminology makes Quicken operation easier and more accurate.

➤ Double entry accounting is your friend and completely hidden with Quicken.

➤ Net income flows must remain positive to maintain a positive net worth and accumulate enough wealth for retirement.

➤ Plan your accounts and categories so that tax related information is easily extracted from the accounting records.

➤ Assets, liabilities, expenses, and income are all interconnected to ensure proper reporting of financial condition.

➤ Proper budget goal setting and tracking of adherence to those goals is very important to keeping your income and expenses on track.

Chapter 5

Maintaining Your Balance

In This Chapter

➤ Track the route your checks follow

➤ Learn how to avoid bounced checks

➤ Use your automated teller machine (ATM) card safely

➤ Learn how to manually balance your checkbook

➤ Use Quicken to balance your checkbook

Keeping your balance is very important when working on a tightrope and also when writing checks. Falling off a tightrope hurts and so does paying returned check charges and explaining to payees why the checks bounced. The simplest way to avoid explanations and charges is to keep your balance. I can't help you much with your tightrope routine, but I can help you with keeping your bank accounts in balance. Taking the time to read and digest this chapter saves you money and the embarrassment of having checks returned when you have the money to cover them.

Importance of Balancing Your Checkbook

You don't need an MBA or degree in finance to know that you can't spend it if you don't have it. If you don't accurately know the balance in your checking and savings accounts, there is no way you can really say that you have control over your finances.

You might be one of those lucky people who can leave an extra few thousand dollars in your checkbook to cover any amount you might be off. Of course you might be someone who runs their expenses so tight to their income that every penny counts. In either case, having a solid checking account balance is critical to not losing money.

Voice of Experience

Think about this. You could write a series of $5 checks that hit an account without sufficient funds and pay 4×$25 = $100 to the bank for either covering or returning the checks. Having this very situation happen to me taught me the value of balancing my checkbook.

For those of you with a lot of money, you should realize that you make little to no interest income off money in your checking account. If you have an extra $2,000 sitting in a checking account that bears no interest, instead of a money market account that bears 6% interest, you are throwing away $120 per year in interest income simply because you cannot work with a balanced checkbook.

If you are the person with a tight budget, you cannot afford to bounce checks, because if you are off by several hundred dollars, the returned check fees can burn up a $100 before you blink. Most banks charge a $10 to $25 fee for covering or returning a check written on an account with insufficient funds.

Balancing your checkbook is a necessary early step to getting your finances under control. I say this completely aware of how confusing this process can be. A good friend of mine had her MBA from a good school, but could not balance her checkbook. I thought this strange until I learned that it was tied in with other emotional issues, as is true for so many of us when it comes to our dealings with money.

Work your way through this chapter and convince yourself that balancing your checkbook is good for the soul and also good financial management. It really isn't hard and Quicken makes it even easier.

Understanding What Goes On with Your Checkbook

Balancing a checkbook is really an easy process after you understand the timing of events and the purpose for each of the items recorded on your bank statement.

First, know that any money deposited into or removed from your checking or savings account is recorded on the statement. Also know that writing a check for $100 does not immediately take $100 out of your account. It eventually is removed, but only after a certain amount of time has elapsed. The same is true for a deposit, but more about that in a later section.

Tracking a Check from Your Checkbook to Your Account

Assume you write a check to Jerry's Shoes for $50. The following is the process by which the check becomes money in the Jerry's Shoes account:

1. You write a check for $50 with Jerry's Shoes shown as the payee or entity intended to receive the money. Hopefully, you also record the $50 check in your handwritten check registry and note the purpose for the expense. Those of you who use check carbons may think that you don't need to record the check in the register. Just know that it is easier to find a check in a register than having to thumb through dozens of checks to find the right one.

2. The check is presented to the cashier who obtains additional information that confirms you as the owner of the account. He then rings up the sale and you walk out with your shoes.

3. Jerry's Shoes makes a deposit into its bank account that evening. This deposit includes your check, some cash, and other checks from other patrons.

4. Jerry's bank receives the deposited check and adds it to Jerry's account balance with a little asterisk attached to the check that indicates that no money has actually changed hands yet. Only a commitment on your behalf to pay the $50 exists.

5. Jerry's bank then presents its batch of checks to a central clearinghouse that presents a request for $50 from your banking account.

6. Your bank then either pays the $50 or sends the request back saying that your account has insufficient funds. If your checking account does not have enough money on deposit, your bank might take money from your savings account to cover the check and charge you a fee for the service.

7. Jerry's bank receives the $50 from your bank and removes the asterisk from your check. The money has now actually changed hands.

Notice that this procedure assumed that Jerry's Shoes instantly deposited the check the day your wrote it. What if the check is mailed to a smaller company on the other side of the country that only processes its checks once a week on Friday. Assume that you wrote your check on Tuesday, mailed it on Wednesday, and that

QuickCaution

The reverse process is also true for checks that you deposit. Banks often put a deposited check on "bank hold" pending the presentation of the check to the issuing bank and receipt of the deposited check dollar amount. Your bank doesn't know if the deposited check is good and does not let you write checks against the deposited amount until the check clears. This may take a few hours to a few days depending upon your bank, who wrote the check, and the respective geographic locations. Government checks are almost always immediately accepted because they come from the government.

The deposits may take longer to clear than the checks you write. If you write checks against these deposited funds before the deposited checks have cleared, you might have bounced checks on your hands even though you deposited enough money to cover the checks.

small company received it the following Monday. It will sit at their site until Friday when it is deposited. The banks then take some time, perhaps a few days, to process the requests. This means that a check for $25 that you write on Tuesday might not actually cause the $25 to be removed from your account until two weeks later.

This is why you can write a large number of checks that drop your checkbook register balance to, say, $250 but the bank shows your balance as $1,500. The $1,250 in checks that you wrote have not yet made their way through the mail, payee, and bank transfer process. When the sequence is completed, the money is drawn from your account and your bank balance eventually drops to $250.

A Close Look at a Bank Statement

Coming back to your bank statement, it is now clear that the bank statement reflects only the deposits and withdrawals that made it to the bank before the statement was issued. Assume that you wrote 10 checks, numbers 1001 to 1010, and mailed them all on the 27th of the month. Some might go to local payees where others might go to payees in other states. Assume also that the bank issues its statement on the 30th and that all checks but numbers 1006 and 1008 were received. There is no way for the bank to know the amounts of these two checks, so there is no way for the bank to show a balance that matches the one in your checkbook register. It is your job to reconcile the difference between the amount shown on your checkbook register and the balance amount shown by the bank statement.

Voice of Experience

I know people who determine the amount of money left in their checking account by calling up the bank and asking for the current balance. They then write checks for a total equal to or less than of the amount given to them by the bank. Do you now see the fault in this approach? You have probably written checks that the bank doesn't know about, which means you could be spending the same money twice. At some point, people who follow this practice pay overdraft fees.

Talkin' Money

Balancing a checkbook is often called reconciling your checkbook because you must account for, or reconcile, any account balance difference that exists between your check register and the bank's account balance. Quicken provides excellent tools for reconciling your back accounts.

A bank often pays a check that is presented against an account, even if the account does not have enough money in it, as long as another account owned by that account owner has enough to cover the presented check. You are charged a fee for this service, which is called an overdraft fee. These fees are a drag to pay, but this procedure is much better than explaining to someone why the check was returned for insufficient funds. Pay the fees and start balancing your checkbook properly. Be sure to record any overdraft fees in your Quicken register as a checking debit or your account does not balance.

The following are some of the items that appear on a typical checking account statement and their meaning:

➤ The beginning balance is the account balance at the beginning of the accounting period, usually the prior month. Notice that the statement's beginning balance is actually the ending balance for the prior statement.

➤ The ending balance is the amount of money left in the account at the end of the accounting period after all deposits have been added and all presented check amounts have been withdrawn along with any applicable fees.

➤ The statement period is the time interval covered by the statement. It usually covers a month for a personal checking account and may vary a little depending on the way weekends fall at the beginning and end of the month.

➤ Deposits are money amounts put into your checking account during the statement period. They are usually comprised of interest earned on the account, if applicable, paychecks, and other checks that you deposited. Deposits increase the account balance.

➤ Withdrawals are money amounts taken out of the account during the statement period. Withdrawals decrease your account balance.

➤ Checks paid lists the number of the checks presented for payment, the date that the check was presented, and the amount of the check. The checks are normally listed in numerical order with gaps in the number sequence somehow indicated to let you know which checks in the sequence were not submitted during the statement period.

➤ Electronic withdrawals are money amounts taken from your checking account where no check was involved. These types of withdrawals can include ATM cash withdrawals, purchases made using a debit card (which instantly removes the money from your checking account), and pre-authorized automatic withdrawals, such as for mortgage or utility payments.

➤ The Daily Account Activity section shows the transactions that happened on specific days within the statement period, the type of transaction involved, its tracking number, whether it was a deposit or withdrawal, and the account balance after the transaction was completed. This is the most detailed level of the statement, whereas the others are less detailed.

➤ Notice that the tracking number shows either the check number involved, the deposit reference number, or the ATM location where money was withdrawn. These numbers become important if you have questions about any of the transactions and ask the bank to research what really happened.

You now have a clear picture of the information contained on your checking account statement. But you still have not reconciled your bank statement with your personal check register. That is your next step.

Balancing It to the Penny Is Good for the Soul

Place your bank statement in one hand and your handwritten check register in the other. Which is heavier? If they feel about even, your account is balanced. Not! There is a little more to it than that, but not much. Your bank statement might contain an Account Balancing Section that leads you through the steps needed to determine your balance. If you're not sure what I mean, look carefully at your bank statement. You should find that your banking institution provides the steps needed for balancing your accounts, although often in a cryptic format.

QuickTip

Quicken provides a cool way of balancing your checkbook, but the tool doesn't make much sense unless you understand the concepts behind balancing. Hopefully, this is the last time you ever manually balance a checkbook. See Chapter 7, "Quickening Your Bills," for details about checkbook balancing.

If your bank does not provide this help or if the instructions aren't clear enough, follow along with these next simple steps that are also shown in the following table:

1. At the top of a sheet of paper, write the period ending balance of the statement you received from the bank. This is what the bank believes to be your current account balance. Assume, for this example, that the account balance is $3,500.

2. Under the number from line 1, enter the total dollar amount of deposits that you made to your account that did not show up on the bank statement. Assume for this example that the deposit amounts not shown total $1,500.

3. Total lines 1 + 2 and write this total number next on your sheet. For this example, the amount is $3,500 + $1,500 = $5,000.

4. Total all checks, ATM withdrawals, automatic withdrawals, or other transactions that took money out of your account that did not show up on the bank statement. Assume for this example that the amount is $1,900.

5. Subtract the amount from line 4 from the amount in line 3 (line 3 – line 4) to get the current balance of your account. This number should equal your hand-written check register balance, or something is wrong. In this example, the balanced amount is $5,000 – $1,900 = $3,100.

(1) Period Ending Balance:	$3,500
(2) Total Unrecorded Deposits:	$1,500
(3) Sum of Lines 1 + 2:	$5,000
(4) Total Unrecorded Withdrawals	$1,900
(5) Account Balance (line 3 – line 2)	$3,100

If this is a little confusing, try this explanation:

1. Step 1 shows the account balance after the bank removed the money associated with all presented withdrawal transactions and deposited the money associated with all presented deposits during the statement period. If the check or deposit was not presented during the statement period, it does not show up on this statement.

2. Step 2 adds all deposits that you know about that the bank doesn't know about, for some reason. These deposits usually don't show up because you made the deposits after the statement period ended. If a deposit you made in the middle of the month does not show up on the statement, you should contact your bank to track it down.

3. Step 3 adds the amount of money that the bank knows about with the total deposits that you know about. This would be the current account balance if no other money had been taken out since the end of the statement period and all prior withdrawal transactions had been accounted for.

Talkin' Money

A transaction is referred to as cleared when it appears on the bank statement. The implication is that the transaction cleared the bank and applies to both deposit and withdrawal transaction types.

4. Step 4 tallies the total withdrawals that the bank doesn't know about. This number might include checks that you wrote several weeks ago, that have still not been presented to the bank for payment. Some people are just slow. It definitely includes checks written and other withdrawals made after the end of the statement period.

5. Step 5 sums it all up to give you a valid balance by subtracting the outstanding withdrawals from the amount shown in step 3.

It is a great feeling to have your personal account register balance exactly with the bank's account statement. It is hard to explain why it feels so good, but it really does. Try it some time. You'll like it.

But what if it doesn't balance. Something is out of whack, and you must find the error(s) or your account remains out of balance. The following are a few tips:

➤ First, check your math. It is easy to make an addition or subtraction error. So, check your math first to make sure that the totals are mathematically correct.

➤ Verify that all bank charges appearing on the statement have been recorded into your handwritten register. It is easy to not include charges for returned checks, printing new checks, automatic withdrawals, overdraft fees, and other items that do not pass through your checkbook.

➤ Verify that all ATM charges have been recorded in your handwritten check register.

➤ Look at the dollar amount by which the balance doesn't agree. Look for transactions that equal that dollar amount in either the bank statement or your handwritten account register, and then verify that the other contains the same transaction. Sometimes you are lucky and can catch it this way.

➤ Verify that you and the bank are working with the same beginning balance. This can be a particular problem if you decide to start balancing your checkbook after having had it open for a while. You must have a valid beginning balance that matches the banks or you never reconcile properly. When in doubt, assume that the bank is right and make your account balance match the bank's.

Provided that you keep careful records and balance your account regularly, your accounts should balance with your bank statement from that point forward.

➤ Verify that the amount you entered for a check or other transaction matches the amount entered by the bank according to the statement. This is tedious work, but it has to be done to get an accurate balance.

➤ If your handwritten register balance is larger than the bank's, there is a strong chance that you did not include certain automatic withdrawals. Verify that all automatic transactions shown on the statement are also listed in your check register.

➤ If your handwritten register balance is smaller than the bank's, there is a strong chance that you did not include a bank deposit in your handwritten check register. Once again, make sure that all deposit transactions match.

I encourage you to verify your beginning register balance at the time you decided to start balancing your checkbook. Some people use the bank statement's ending balance as their starting balance, which is probably not correct. You must account for all transactions that affected your account within the statement period and use that balance. Otherwise, your numbers never match and are always off by a transaction amount.

Beware of ATM Charges

The Automatic Teller Machine is a great convenience, but it can also be a nuisance when trying to balance your checkbook. It can also be expensive because some ATM transactions may cost as much as $2 per transaction if you do not use the proper teller machine type. If the transaction costs you $2 and you only withdraw $40, you are paying a 5% transaction fee to get at your own money. This just seems fundamentally wrong to me, and I do everything in my power to avoid using teller machines that charge a fee. But, when you need the money, an ATM is hard to beat.

Tracking ATM transactions is especially tricky if you have multiple people making ATM transactions, because one party can increase/decrease an account balance by hundreds of dollars without the other party's knowledge. This situation has "bounced check" written all over it. Try these steps to keep ATM transactions under control:

➤ Place all ATM receipts in a central location where the keeper of the checkbook can easily find them.

➤ Immediately notify the keeper of the checkbook of any ATM transaction and give him or her the receipt. This way the account balance can be tracked and maintained.

➤ Leave a certain amount of balance in your account as a "slush" fund to accommodate those times when an ATM withdrawal is done without the other person's knowledge.

➤ Use your credit card for most purchases and budget a certain amount of monthly cash per person. This minimizes ATM card usage, which minimizes fees and avoids overdraft charges. You must immediately pay off your credit card balance with this approach or finance charges eat up all your ATM savings.

➤ If you make a deposit at an ATM machine, make sure that you get a printed receipt of the deposit. This may sound a little paranoid, but how would you ever prove that you made a deposit without the receipt? You're better off erring on the side of caution than to lose or delay a $4,000 deposit due to ATM network error.

I love the convenience provided by an ATM machine, especially when traveling in a strange city. Cash is important; however, traveling with too much money on you is not only potentially dangerous but you can easily lose it. I used to travel only in places where I could cash a check, but I don't need to worry about that any more due to the ATM network. As a final backup when traveling internationally, I always carry $500 to $1,000 in travelers checks to cover those times when an ATM is not available. It is a very lonely feeling to be in a foreign country where you don't speak the language and not have any cash money.

How Quicken Helps to Provide Trusted Balances

Looking at the bank balance procedure, you see that the process is pretty simple. The difficult part is making sure that all the data is in your checkbook register. After the data is entered, it is a simple matter of tallying up the cleared transactions and those that the bank doesn't know about yet and coming up with an account balance. Quicken makes this process pretty simple through its account reconciliation features. (See Chapter 7 for specific information on balancing a checking account.)

Account reconciliation is accessed by selecting the **Features**, **Banking**, **Reconcile** menu options. Follow the instructions from that point forward.

Quicken makes it simple to enter the various account maintenance transactions associated with accounts such as finance charges, interest income, dividends, bank charges, automatic transactions, and others. Working within the Quicken account structure takes a little getting used to, but it is well worth it after you get up and running.

The Least You Need to Know

➤ Your account balance does not actually decrease the instant that you write a check.

➤ Your bank balance and your actual account balance are almost never the same due to transaction processing delays.

➤ Some deposits are held at the bank for a few days until cleared, which can cause bounced checks if you are not careful.

➤ Balancing your checkbook is a critical part of getting your finances under control.

➤ Using the Quicken account reconciliation features make account balancing easy and quick.

Part 2
Getting It into the Computer

This part introduces you to Quicken and shows you how to get your financial information into the computer. After your data is in the computer, you can quickly create the financial reports needed to gauge how you are progressing on your financial trip to security. Learning the Quicken operations presented here will pay off for the rest of your life.

Chapter 6

Quicken from 20,000 Feet

In This Chapter

➤ Install Quicken for maximum feature availability

➤ Set up categories and accounts that are right for you

➤ Simply define budgets that match your specific spending history

➤ Automatically set up an Internet connection

➤ Learn where to go to get additional help

We all have those things in our lives that we know we should do and don't. From working out every day to changing the oil on your car every 3,000 miles, none of us ever does all the things we *should* do. Using your computer for financial management most certainly falls into this category, too.

If you have the Quicken software and have not yet installed it on your computer, it is about time that you did. You can put off that morning jog for a while, but you have already spent the money for the Quicken software, and it would sure be a shame to see it go to waste.

Work your way through this chapter and get started on your way to automating your finances and starting your financial planning process. You might even lose weight as your metabolism increases from the added excitement of knowing where your money is spent.

Getting Started with Quicken

Every software package has a learning curve associated with it, and Quicken is no exception. Just as learning a foreign language takes time, so does learning a software package. Be patient with yourself and get started by following my instructions. First you install Quicken, and then you set up accounts and categories. Finally, you create your first transactions. This is important information, and you are well-served by completing this section.

QuickTip

For purposes of this book, I assume that you understand the operation of Windows 95/98 and are familiar with the operation of the Windows Explorer.

Installing Quicken

Just as that treadmill machine never does you any good until you get on it, no software package does you any good until it is installed on your computer. The installation of Quicken is very straightforward and should cause you no trouble at all.

You can install Quicken from either CD or floppy disk. You find that the CD version not only installs faster but also contains multimedia information that is not available when installing from a floppy disk.

Though the options on your screen might vary slightly, depending on what version of Quicken you are installing, the following steps give you enough information to install your new software.

Follow these steps to perform a Quicken installation:

1. Insert the Quicken CD into your CD drive. The installation should begin automatically. If **Setup** doesn't start automatically, click **Start**, **Run**. At the dialog box, type D:\Install, where D: is the drive letter associated with your CD drive (which might be different on your machine) and press **Enter**.

QuickTip

When installing from floppy disks, insert the first disk, click **Start**, **Run**. At the dialog box, type A:\Setup (where A: is the drive letter associated with your floppy drive) and press **Enter**. Simply insert the other floppy disks as requested by the setup routine. Otherwise, the procedure for installation from floppy is almost identical to the steps outlined for CD installation.

2. Quicken presents you with a number of windows related to copyright licensing. The Quicken Setup program also prompts you to close any open programs before continuing with the installation. Accept the default settings for the next set of dialog boxes, unless you must install Quicken to another drive due to space limitations.

3. When the Type of Installation window appears, you need to choose whether you want to perform an **Express** or **Custom** installation. Click **Next** to move to the following screens.

QuickTip

The Canadian version installation includes special Canadian accounts such as the Quebec Pension Plan and Old Age Security. The U.S. version includes special accounts related to the United States, such as Social Security. Dates are also recorded differently between the two versions, so pick the installation that is right for you.

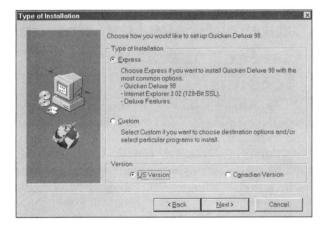

Choose between Express (default) and Custom installation.

QuickTip

Accept the **Express** installation type unless you specifically do not want to install certain components such as the Web browser for non–Internet connected systems, or unless you need to change the default location drive and folder location into which the files are installed. Accept the default settings for the screens that follow, until the Summary screen is shown.

QuickCaution

By not choosing to install a Web browser, you limit the online features available to you through Quicken, such as some online banking options and investment tracking. If you do not have an Internet connection and do not plan to add one right away, feel free to skip the Web browser install for now. You can always go back and install it later.

QuickTip

If you have problems with your installation, call Quicken Tech Support at 1-520-618-7101 or connect to the Intuit Web site at www.intuit.com for help with installation problems.

4. Quicken displays a summary of your installation preferences. You are given the option to accept the preferences and continue with the installation or to change the installation setup. If you choose to change the setup, simply click the **Back** button until the proper window appears.

5. If the installation of Internet Explorer was one of your selected options, Quicken asks whether you want to proceed with the installation. Click **Yes** or **No**, depending on whether you want to install Internet Explorer.

6. After installation is completed, Quicken notifies you that you must restart the system to have the new software function properly. Click **Yes** to restart now, or click **No** to manually restart at a later time. Remember that you must restart for Quicken to function properly.

Automatically Defining Your Categories and Initial Account

There are people who like to control everything, and I say "great" to these folks if they have that much time on their hands. I, on the other hand, let the computer do things that are pretty simple and require a lot of tedious data entry. Creating standardized categories is one task that requires little creativity and lots of typing. Quicken can do a lot of that for you, if you let it. So, get your Quicken version up and running and get ready to create your initial categories and account.

To start Quicken, simply click **Start**, choose **Programs**, point to **Quicken**, and select your version of Quicken (such as **Quicken Deluxe 98**).

The first time that you start Quicken, it prompts you for information regarding your personal financial situation. This is an important step, and working your way through these steps saves you time later on. In essence, Quicken is trying to determine the best set of accounts and categories for your financial situation.

All your Quicken accounting information is stored either in accounts or categories. Accounts are used for tracking balance sheet items such as asset and liability information. Categories are used for tracking income and expense information. Your Quicken setup almost always involves more categories than accounts, because one major role of the categories is to subdivide your expenses into divisions that can be totaled to provide the desired expense information. For example, you can use Quicken to total your utility expenses, medical expenses, even your late night pizza cravings. Quicken makes the creation of categories easy by defining several standardized groupings that meet different typical use needs. The possible combinations are as follows:

QuickTip

By the way, if you are upgrading from an older version of Quicken, your old data is converted to the newer format. Quicken does not need to ask you questions about your desired account/category setup when converting your old files, because the old files contain this information.

➤ Standard categories that apply to all situations

➤ Categories for married people

➤ Categories for those who have children

➤ Categories for homeowners

➤ Categories for those who own a small business

You need different sets of categories for different living situations because the tracking requirements change. Start with the appropriate set of Quicken-generated accounts, and modify them from there. Any or all of the selected category combinations can be selected.

QuickTip

You can create a new Quicken file by clicking **File**, **New**, checking the **New Quicken File** option, and clicking **OK**. You then designate the location and name of the file and click **Categories** to display the various category combinations. You can select any or all the provided selections. Click **OK** and then **OK** again to create the new file with your designated categories that is stored under your specified name and in your specified location.

Creating Your First Account

After you are through choosing your desired category groupings from the standard categories provided by Quicken, as you did in the last section, you are prompted to create your first account. For this example, we start with a checking account because this is most likely the place you want to start. If you'd like to follow along, grab your checking account statement and let's get started.

1. Select the **Checking** option if not already checked, and click **Next**.

Select the account type you want to create.

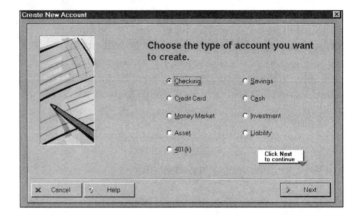

2. Enter the **Account Name** that you want to use when referring to this account, such as First Bank Checking, and define the optional **Description**. Click **Next**.

3. Select **Yes** if you have your last checking statement. If you want to start from the beginning of the year, which is recommended, use your December statement from the prior year. Otherwise, click **No** to indicate that you do not have your last statement. Then, click **Next**. If you do not have your last statement, Quicken assumes that this is a new account and displays a dialog indicating that the starting balance is set to $0, which is proper for a new account. Step 4 is skipped under these circumstances, and you move directly to step 5.

4. Type the **Statement Date** and **Ending Balance** for the statement month selected. Click **Next**.

5. Click **No** if you have not yet enrolled with an online banking service, which is probably the case when first installing. Click **Yes** if you are already set up and you are led through online setup. If this is your first time using Quicken, click **No**. You can always set up online banking later.

6. A Summary dialog box displays the information associated with this account.

7. Click the **Info...** button to enter additional information regarding this account. It is a good habit to enter this account information when the account is created because other Quicken features, such as the Emergency Records Organizer, use the information. Click **Next** when done to finish creating your first account. Don't click the **Online** features unless you are already set up for online banking

with your financial institution. See Chapter 8, "Banking Anytime—Day or Night," for additional information about setting up an online account.

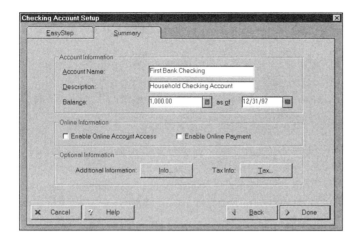

Account information is displayed on the Summary tab.

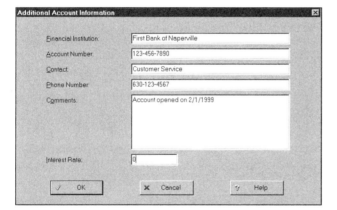

Click the Info... button to enter additional information.

QuickTip

The **Tax** button is used to associate tax payment information with this account. This topic is covered in detail in Chapter 9, "Planning for the Tax Man."

Congratulations. You have set up your Quicken checking account. The next section takes a detailed look at setting up other accounts and categories.

Creating Custom Accounts and Categories

QuickTip

I chose all category options when doing my installation, so don't worry if your account and categories don't exactly match mine.

You are really like nobody else. You can debate the good or bad aspects of this with your friends and family. Financially speaking, no standardized set of accounts and categories ever really fit the intricacies of your financial life. Only you really understand those intricacies. Fortunately, Quicken lets you take over when you need to.

In this section, you review the accounts and categories that Quicken automatically set up for you during installation. You then look at ways of creating your own custom accounts and categories. You first create accounts and then create categories.

Customizing Your Accounts

Quicken does a great job of creating a starting group of categories, but does not create accounts. That is your job and must be done manually.

Reviewing your established accounts is simple. Press **Ctrl+A** to display your existing accounts, as shown in the figure. Your accounts listing is empty at this point except for the account created in the last section.

Each of your Quicken accounts appears in this window.

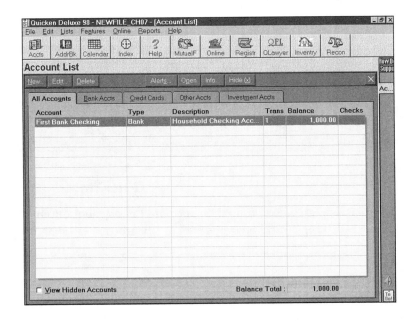

The tabs enable you to display your accounts by group—all, banking, credit card, investment, or other. These group headings also appear as options when creating a new account. For this reason, it is important to designate an account as a member of the proper group.

QuickTip

The QuickTabs are available at any time from within Quicken and are controlled from within the **Edit** menu's **Options**, **Quicken Program**, **QuickTabs**.

There are two sets of tabs with the general Quicken window. The tabs at the right of the window, called QuickTabs, open the general information windows that deal with categories, accounts, or other major Quicken features. The tabs at the top of the window activate subsets within the activated QuickTab such as the Bank Accts subgroup as part of Accounts. (In some versions of Quicken, these tabs are contained under the **Options** button found on the button bar.)

The X in the upper-right corner of the activated QuickTab is used to close the QuickTab. The button bar within each QuickTab displays various buttons that activate features associated with the activated QuickTab. These buttons typically include **New**, **Edit**, **Delete**, and others related to creating new accounts, editing the existing accounts, or deleting existing accounts. A **Balance Total** is displayed in the bottom-right corner of the accounts QuickTab, which is a simple way to tally account totals such as those associated with bank (cash) accounts.

The bulleted list below not only helps you create a new account, but also edits some of the properties associated with the account. Any account type can be created using the procedures that follow:

➤ Click **New** to invoke the New Account Setup Wizard, which you saw when performing the initial installation. This process is used to create any asset or liability account. Follow the wizard screens to easily create accounts. For now, click **Cancel** to stop this process.

➤ Highlight an account, such as **First Bank Checking**, and click **Edit**. The general information associated with the highlighted account appears. Click **Cancel** to return to the Accounts view.

➤ Click **Info** to add more detailed information regarding this account, such as the institution name, address, and so on. Click **Cancel** to return to the Accounts view.

➤ Quicken enables you to set up various alerting criteria that Quicken should use when determining whether an account has reached a level where you should be notified. When a specified criteria is met, such as a checking account with a balance below the alert criteria, a message appears on your screen. Click **Cancel**. The Alerts… feature is not included with all Quicken versions. In some versions of Quicken, you may need to set up alerts by choosing the **Features** menu, **Reminders**, **Alerts** options.

Creating and Using Custom Categories

Categories are used for storage of income and expense related items. Salaries and dividends are typical income categories, whereas interest and utilities are typical expense categories. To display the category listing at any time, simply press **Ctrl+C**. Typical expense categories include Telephone, Utilities, Life Insurance, Car Insurance, Groceries, Vacations, and any others that are needed to track your accounting expenses. Typical income categories include Salary, Bonus, Interest Income, Dividend Income, and so on. These are all income-statement-related tracking categories.

Setting up categories is easy, as you see in this section. In general, using lots of categories is better than using just a few because creating a detailed list of categories allows you to track your expenses at a much more detailed level than is possible with only the few categories automatically created with the Quicken installation.

For example, Utilities is a general category that could include electric, gas, phone, and water. If all expenses are allocated to this same category, finding the amount spent on Electricity for a given period can be tricky.

If, on the other hand, you created several subcategories under the Utilities main category, such as Electricity, Gas, Water, and Phone, the Quicken reports automatically total this information by category. Try not to go overboard with the level of detail, or you could end up with categories that track the number of size 8 shoes you bought.

Press Ctrl+C to review the categories you've created.

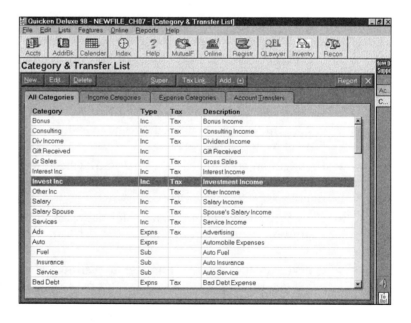

Categories are grouped according to whether they are Income, Expense, or (Account) Transfers and Tax-Related. Income and Expense are self-explanatory. Depending on your Quicken version, these groups are accessed either through selecting the proper tab, or by clicking **Options** and selecting the desired category grouping.

(Account) Transfers are transactions where money is transferred from one account to another and not directly from an account into a category. A typical account transfer transaction would transfer money from your savings account into your checking account. No money was actually spent or received with this transaction. It was simply moved from one Quicken account into another.

Categories can be related to each other where one or a group of categories are subordinate to a main category. Take a look at the Auto category and you see that there are three subcategories (Fuel, Insurance, and Service) listed under it. Subcategories are indicated by a **Sub** designation in the **Type** column. This grouping by subcategory means that reports list the Auto main category, with a total, and then list the totals for the subcategories contained underneath.

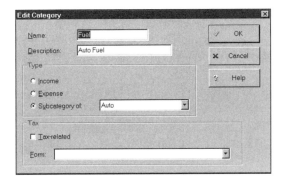

Defining subcategories to group specific expense and income items.

Highlight the Auto: Fuel subcategory, and then click the **Edit** button to display the dialog shown in the figure. The subcategory designation is specified by the Subcategory of: settings contained within the displayed dialog box. The main category must first be created before subcategories can be added to it. For more information about the tax section of this dialog box, see Chapter 9.

The button bar displayed at the top of the Categories QuickTab contains a number of command buttons that perform various category-specific functions:

➤ **New**   Used to create a new category, whether income, expense, main, or subcategory. Click **New** and fill in the required information for the category you are creating.

➤ **Edit**   Used to edit the properties associated with the category highlighted just before clicking **Edit**. Changes made in the Edit screen are adopted by the category.

➤ **Delete** Used to remove a category. This is dangerous business when working with categories that have information, so Quicken won't allow you to delete a category that contains transactions.

➤ **Super** Used to define a supercategory, which is a special category that cannot contain transactions that are used to group other, real categories. For example, adding existing categories to the already existing Discretionary supercategory that contains all categories associated with discretionary spending is a great way to track money that you do not need to spend. The supercategory dialog box enables you to create your own supercategory to which you can attach real categories. Some versions of Quicken refer to a 'super' category as a category 'group,' which is created under the **Options** button by clicking **Assign Category Groups**.

➤ **Tax Link...** Used to associate a given category with a specific tax form and line item. This is covered in detail in Chapter 9. Some versions of Quicken use the **Options** button's **Assign Tax Items** option to define tax-related associations.

➤ **Add...(+)** Used to transfer categories from the predefined Quicken category groups into your specific Quicken setup. You might not have included all categories in your setup. This is an easy way to take advantage of the advance work done by those folks at Intuit. Some versions of Quicken require that the user click the **Options** button's **Add Categories** option to create additional categories.

➤ **Report** Used to print a report that contains all transactions included in the highlighted category. This is the easiest way to print out category transactions.

Category setup is critical to effective and efficient use of Quicken. The level of detail you can extract from your Quicken data is only as detailed as your accounts and categories. Spending the time up-front to get your categories right saves you a lot of time later when reporting the information.

Accessing Help

Like everything else in life, people differ in their perspective on things. Views about the effectiveness of the Quicken Help features are divergent. Some love it because it is heavily practical-use-oriented because a number of examples explain the relationship between accounting theory and Quicken features. Others dislike it because it just doesn't contain enough software feature detail. You should judge for yourself by clicking **Help** and **Overviews** to walk through various multimedia clips about Quicken operation and use. Some versions of Quicken require that the CD be in the CD-ROM drive for these clips to run, so verify this requirement for your particular version. After the **Overviews** start, follow the screens just as with a browser.

The following are some things to keep in mind when using the Quicken Help system:

➤ Pressing **F1** opens the portion of Help that pertains to the window you currently have open.

➤ Clicking **Show Me** in any of the Help windows activates a multimedia presentation related to the displayed topic. Once again, the CD must be in the CD-ROM drive for these clips to run properly. This feature is not available in all Quicken versions, so verify its inclusion with your particular version. If not provided, try pressing **F1** to get the same help information as that provided under **Show Me**.

➤ Clicking **Help, Index** opens a standard Windows index of help topics. Simply type the topic of interest and let Quicken show the various help topics that pertain to your request. I have it on good authority, including my own experience, that Quicken's Index feature is one of the best. Get to know this valuable tool and use it as a starting point for answers.

➤ Click **Help, Product Support** for additional information regarding the operation of Quicken if trouble comes up. Phone numbers, Internet-based assistance, and procedures are all listed under this help topic.

➤ Some versions of Quicken include a **How Do I?** button that, when clicked, displays a series of topics that should be of high interest to most users.

Don't be afraid to look in the Quicken booklet and to use the provided electronic help for tips and other information regarding effective Quicken operation.

Creating Reports with Quicken

It is one thing (a potentially mind-numbing thing, at that) to enter hundreds of transactions. It is another to be able to sort through those transactions just to be able to see what you spend on medical bills in a year. This is another place where Quicken comes to your rescue. With Quicken, you can create reports showing just the data you want to see—from your net worth to the amount of money you spend on new shoes every year.

You regularly run reports to determine whether you are making money and whether you are increasing your net worth. Quicken makes running these reports a simple and easy process. For example, the Net Worth report is used to determine the success of your nest egg–building activities. The Cash Flow report tells you the amount of money that you made/lost during a specific time period. The various budget reports present comparisons between your actual income/expenses and your estimates as defined in your budgets.

Taking the time to review reporting procedures makes all your other Quicken work more valuable. Quicken provides numerous reports, and you are encouraged to familiarize yourself with all of them.

Using the EasyAnswer Reports and Graphs Tool

The simplest way to create a report is by using the EasyAnswer Reports feature, which is located in the **Reports** menu.

Quicken provides an easy way to create reports to help you manage your finances.

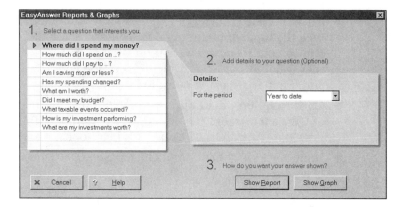

This dialog box, which is shown in the figure, makes report creation a snap. To create a report, use the following steps:

1. From the **Reports** menu, select the **EasyAnswer Reports** option.
2. Select the area of interest from the list on the left side of the dialog (such as **Where did I spend my money?**).
3. On the right side, set the parameters that are associated with the selection (such as **For the period: <Year to date>**).
4. Click **Show Report** to display a numeric report of the information.
5. Click **Show Graph**, if provided, to graphically display the selected data.

Play with the other reports provided and convince yourself that with only a few keystrokes, you can learn more about your finances than you ever knew before. This is where the fun associated with using Quicken really kicks in.

Using the Snapshot Tool

Another quick reporting tool that I really like is the Snapshot, which is also found under the **Reports** menu in earlier versions of Quicken but is not included in some later versions of Quicken. A snapshot can show you multiple reports onscreen at once. This is useful if you need to have access to summarized information from several sources at once or if you just like to look and see how much money you have stashed away at one time. Determine your favorite or most useful reports and set the Snapshot to display them every time that the Snapshot is activated. For example, one display quadrant can be configured to display a graph of expenses while another might display a graph of net worth. Simply click a few times to open the Snapshot and get a quick view of your finances.

Clicking **Customize** under the Snapshots display enables you to define the specific information displayed in each quadrant of the display. A wide variety of snapshot displays are possible, including the ability to create your own custom snapshot display quadrant type. The Snapshot feature is a quick, valuable tool that you are encouraged to learn.

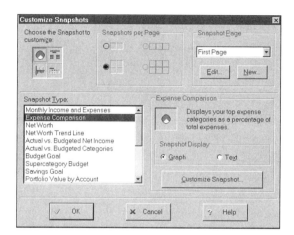

Customize the Snapshot display for speedy report generation.

The **Reports** menu contains a number of other standard reports, and you are encouraged to play with them to see the wide array of information they provide. The three reports that you absolutely want to get to know well are contained under the **Reports, Home** option. These three reports are as follows:

➤ **Cash Flow** The cash-basis equivalent of an income statement that shows your income and expenses for the period of time you define in the report.

➤ **Monthly Budget** Shows a comparison of your actual spending compared to your spending targets, or budgets. See the next section for more information on Quicken's budget operations.

➤ **Net Worth** Shows your net worth for a given date. This number represents the value of your assets minus what you owe (liabilities). This is the number you want to monitor on a regular basis because increasing your net worth is the ultimate goal of any financial planning program.

Quicken reports have a lot of power, and getting acquainted with their various customization features and data-sorting capabilities is time well spent.

Setting Budget Goals with Quicken

A word my wife has come to have a love/hate relationship with is the word "budget." Budgets make you review your expenses as compared to what you planned to spend. Throughout this book you are asked to project future incomes and expenses. Based on those projections, you determine the required income and expenses needed to meet your retirement and other financial goals. Without a budget you are relying on memory and luck to ensure that your financial goals are met. Through budgeting you can determine whether you have the money to buy those items you are considering.

81

Budgeting is accessed by clicking **Features**, **Planning**, **Budgets**.

Set up your budget goals with Quicken.

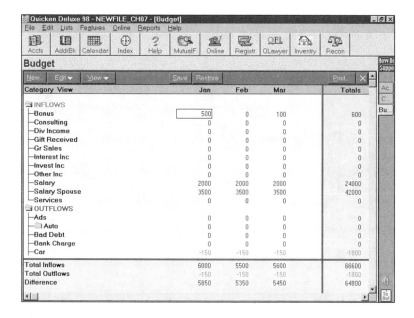

There are a number of different ways that you can enter your budget information depending on the form of your budget information.

Quicken starts you out with a budget scenario, called Budget1. You create additional budget scenarios by clicking **New**. (Some versions of Quicken require that you click the **Options** button, and then select **Other Budgets**, **Create**.) Then you need to set the name of the new budget and indicate how you want the initial budget numbers defined. You can have the new budget numbers entered by Autocreate, which estimates the budget from historical information; Zero-filled, which fills the new budget with zeros (not available in some versions of Quicken); or Copy Current, which uses the numbers in the current budget as the starting point for the new budget.

QuickTip

The multiple budget scenarios enable you to play with your budget numbers to arrive at the one you feel is right for you. This provides more flexibility and minimizes the likelihood of mistakes.

The various options for filling in the budget data are listed under the **Edit** button located on the button bar. Using these fill features greatly reduces the tedium associated with manually entering a large quantity of numbers. The primary automatic fill features are as follows:

➤ **Autocreate** Enables you to select a period over which Quicken should evaluate your actual income and expenses and enter its assessment of a realistic budget based on this assessment. Use Autocreate first if you already have historical data, and then modify the specific rows/columns as needed.

➤ **Fill Row Right** Copies a number entered in the far left column to the other columns in that particular row. This way, you can set the first month's budget for this particular row and copy it to the rest of the columns.

➤ **Fill Columns** Copies the entire column of numbers for the column selected to the other budget columns. This feature is handy for entering a single month's budget numbers, which are then copied to all others.

> **Voice of Experience**
>
> Another simple trick I use is to set the view to Years, and then enter my annual budget numbers for each category. When the view is then expanded to Months, you find that Quicken divided the annual amount by 12 and entered that pro-rated amount in as the budget for each category/month.

Quicken's Online (Internet) Services

Internet, Internet, everywhere is the Internet. And not a byte to drink. Well, Quicken is no different because it too wants you to use the Internet and for really good reason.

It has a series of very handy online features that enable you to quickly perform a number of activities from comparing insurance premiums, finding the right mutual fund, verifying mortgage rates, and ordering Quicken supplies to online banking. The more you get used to these automated features, the more you like Quicken. These various online features are covered throughout the book as they pertain to the topic under discussion. Keep your eyes open to learn the right time to use these tools. You must have a working Internet connection to use these online features.

It is important to know that these features only work with an already established Internet connection such as through a standard Internet Services Provider (ISP), America Online, or CompuServe.

Intuit has an established relationship with Concentric Network, which enables you to sign up for their Internet access service if you do not already have an ISP. Simply click **Online**, **Internet Connection**, **Setup** and follow the wizard to get your account established from within earlier versions of Quicken. Users of some Quicken versions need to click **Start**, **Programs**, **Quicken** and then select either **AOL & Internet Free Trial** or **Sign Up for Concentric Internet Access**. Follow the instructions displayed to set up your account. You must have a functioning modem installed on your system to establish an Internet connection.

This is the easy approach, but not necessarily the least expensive. At the time of this writing, Concentric Network provided one free hour of Internet connection per month and then charged $2.95 for each additional hour. This can really add up if you start to make extensive use of your Internet connection. Other providers connect you for under $20 per month and for almost unlimited connection hours.

The Least You Need To Know

➤ Quicken can be installed from CD or floppy, with CD being the preferred method.

➤ You must have an Internet connection for the online services to function.

➤ Accounts are used for tracking asset and liability transactions.

➤ Categories are used to track income and expense transactions.

➤ Quicken provides automated tools that speed up and simplify budget information.

Chapter 7

Quickening Your Bills

In This Chapter

➤ Getting the data into the computer so that you can start managing your finances

➤ Balancing your accounts keeps you honest and on track

➤ Quicken has tools to remind you of due bills so that you stay on time

➤ Data entry procedures that apply to all Quicken accounts

You can read this book and think that the information you see here could really change your life, but until you actually start using Quicken for your personal financial management, nothing has changed.

Your first step starts here with getting your bills into the computer. Quicken must have the information to work with, or it cannot provide you with the reports and analysis needed for valid decision making on your part.

Take the plunge. Start entering your bills and move on to writing checks in Chapter 8, "Banking Anytime—Day or Night." It makes the bill paying process a lot faster, more accurate, and it is actually pretty cool.

Entering Bills the Easy Way

I sometimes think that computers were created for people like me who dread the drudgery of financial data entry in general and hand writing checks in particular.

Quicken enables you to enter the data once into the computer, and then use that data to print your checks on your computer's printer, or even pay them electronically with no paper involved.

QuickTip

If you manually write your checks, you can use Quicken for recording and reporting on your income and expense information. I used the package in this way for years. I then took the plunge and started actually printing my checks from within Quicken, and I have never regretted making that move. Either approach is fine as long as you enter the information into Quicken.

Voice of Experience

I thought that setting up automatic check writing would eliminate the need for our standard checkbook. We automatically write between 20 and 30 checks per month for things such as the mortgage payment, utilities, credit card payments, and the car payment. My wife prefers to use handwritten checks to pay for her daily expenses, so she carries the standard checkbook around with her. That is her preference, and nothing is lost from a Quicken standpoint by going along with her. You both win and Quicken becomes the consolidation point for all information.

A few benefits derived from using Quicken to track your bills include the following:

➤ Historical finance information enables you to create a realistic budget and ensure that you stick to it.

➤ Tracking your money flow on a regular basis keeps you from overspending over a long period of time until you are in real trouble.

➤ Tax time is simpler because you already have your information collated on the computer.

➤ You also get greater peace of mind knowing that your financial house is in order.

➤ The Reminder features keep you informed of when bill are due, which keeps your payments on time.

➤ If you run on a tight budget, having an accurate checking and savings account balance is critical to avoid bounced check charges.

By the time you finish this chapter, you will be comfortable entering bills, recording deposits, recording credit card transactions, and balancing accounts.

Tracking Bill Payments with Quicken

Obviously, you must get your bill data into the computer before the computer can print out your checks.

This is really not too difficult as long as your accounts and categories are set up in a way that matches your personal needs. (See Chapter 6, "Quicken from 20,000 Feet," for more information on creating accounts and categories.)

To get started, simply enter your bill payments in your Quicken checking account(s). For example, entering a payment for your telephone bill requires that you enter the payee and the amount into the checking account register.

The following steps get you started:

1. Make sure that Quicken is open.

2. Open the **Accounts** listing by clicking the Accounts icon or pressing **Ctrl+A**. A display opens similar to that shown next. The contents of this window vary with your particular setup.

> **QuickTip**
>
> The steps used in this chapter apply to both Quicken 98 and 99.

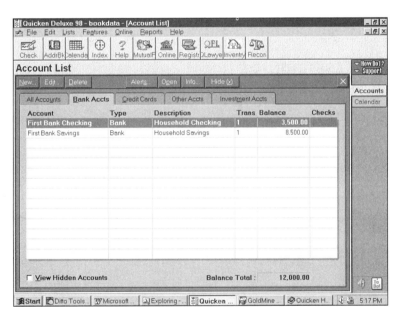

Click the Accounts icon to list and work with your accounts.

3. Click the **Bank Accts** tab to display all bank accounts that you have already created.

4. Press **Ctrl+W** or click the Check icon to open the **Write Checks** window shown next. Notice that the date is automatically filled in for you. Change the date, if desired, by simply clicking the date section and typing the desired date. Also notice that no check number is assigned at this point, because Quicken assumes that this check is for printing at a later date when the check number is automatically assigned.

Click the Check icon to enter payee address and account information while entering bills.

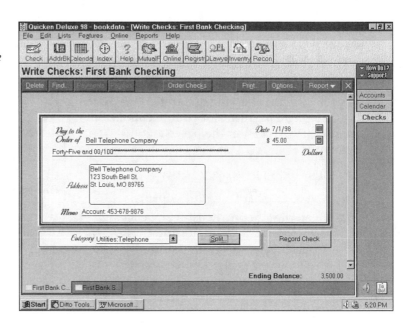

QuickTip

You can either set up the check to have a manually assigned check number or to be assigned one automatically by Quicken.

Manually assigned check numbers are used when manually writing the checks while entering the bills data. This ensures that the actual check number written from your checkbook matches the check number used by Quicken in the check register.

5. Click the **Pay to the Order of** section and type Bell Telephone Company (the payee); press **Tab** or **Enter** to move to the amount field.

6. Type the dollar amount (in this case, I've used $45.00) in the space next to the dollar sign and press **Tab** or **Enter** to move to the address field. Notice that the written amount field is automatically filled in for the amount entered in the amount field.

QuickTip

Automatic printing assigns the check number at the time of printing, which also ensures parity between the Quicken check number and the actual check number.

It is often advantageous to set up bills for later printing even when you manually write your bills and manually assign check numbers. Assume, for example, that you enter your bills all at once at the beginning of the month and then write the checks individually at later dates throughout the month. Some bills may be due at the beginning of the month and others in the middle. You enter all bills into the computer at the same time but with different dates. You then manually write the checks for those bills on their respective due dates entering the check number from your manual register into Quicken at that time.

7. Type the company name and address information into the **Address** section and press **Tab** or **Enter**. The address is very important information. It is printed on the check so that double window envelopes display the proper destination and return address information.

QuickTip

Quicken stores payee information such as address and memo (account number) information as a memorized transaction for automatic recall later. Entering this information now saves you from having to ever enter it again later.

8. Type the vendor account number information into the **Memo** field and press **Tab** or **Enter**. This memo prints out on the checks ensuring that the account number prints on all checks. Of course, you can type whatever you like in the memo box, but in this case, I suggest using the account number.

9. Click the arrow on the right of the **Category** field to display its list box. Select the desired category from the list. The **Category** field designates the internal storage location into which Quicken saves the dollar amounts you just entered. Remember that when the check is actually written, Quicken decreases the First Bank Checking account by $45, which means that some other account(s) must increase by a total of $45 or double entry accounting is violated. (See Chapter 4, "Book It with Bookkeeping," for additional information.) The categories selected determine the proper tracking locations. In general, categories apply to expense

items, whereas accounts apply to balance sheet items such as assets and liabilities. Although, accounts appear under the categories listing for internal transfer usage.

The bill amount can be applied to multiple categories by clicking the **Split** button to display a window that allows you to allocate portions of the amount to multiple categories. For example, the $45 bill could be allocated as $20 to a house telephone account and $25 to a business telephone account.

Use splits to allocate bills to multiple accounts or categories.

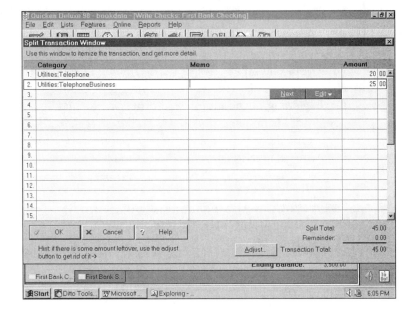

10. Click **Record Check** to finalize the data entry process and record the check into the selected checking account. A new bill appears waiting for data entry just as performed in the prior steps of this exercise.

11. Clicking the **X** in the upper-right corner of the **Write Checks** window ends the bill entry process. Make sure you don't click the **X** in the far upper-right corner, or accounts you close Quicken completely.

Entering Deposits and Miscellaneous Charges

Deposits and miscellaneous charges are added to any account from within the register screen for that account. Deposits and miscellaneous charges do not generally have address information associated with them. This means that you want to add the information directly to the register for the desired account instead of using the previously described procedures for writing Quicken checks.

Use the following steps to enter deposits and miscellaneous charges.

1. Open the target account's register by first pressing **Ctrl+A** to open the accounts view, then highlighting the target account, and finally pressing **Ctrl+R** to display the register associated with the highlighted account.

2. Notice that Quicken is ready to begin a new transaction at the end of those currently listed.

3. Type the **Date** of the bill and press **Tab** or **Enter** to move to the **Num** field. A listing of various options appears. Included in this list are **Deposit**, **ATM,** and **EFT**. **Deposit** is used for all deposits whether paycheck or dividend payments on interest bearing accounts, **ATM** applies to transactions made from an automatic teller machine, and **EFT** applies to electronic fund transfers such as automatic withdrawals for bill payments. **Print Check** is used when you intend to print the check at a later time, and **Transfer** is used to transfer funds from one account to another. **Next Check Number** automatically assigns the next check in the sequence, which is useful when entering data from your manual check register.

4. Select **Deposit**, **ATM**, or **EFT** as applicable. Notice that one of the options is **Next Check Num**, which is used when manually writing checks while entering bills. You can also explicitly type a check number into this field if you desire. Press **Tab** or **Enter** to move to the **Payee** field.

5. Type the **Payee**. Notice that if this is an already existing memorized transaction, Quicken automatically recommends payees based on the first few letters typed.

Voice of Experience

In general, when writing checks, pay attention to the bill date used. The bill date used can be very important depending upon the Quicken feature in use. For example, Quicken has an accounts payable report that uses the dates of entered bills to determine the payables dates and amounts. Payables is a valuable report to the individual as well as a business because it adds up everything that you must pay out shortly. It is accessed by choosing the **Reports, Business, A/P by Vendor** menu options.

QuickTip

After your bills are initially entered along with their associated address and account information, you probably find yourself entering bills from within the register instead of the **Write Checks** window. It is faster and easier to work with, but has no way to enter address information without changing to other screens.

6. Press **Tab** or **Enter** to move to either the **Payment** or **Deposit** amount fields, depending on whether the transaction removes money from or adds money to the account, respectively.

7. Type the proper dollar amounts and press **Tab** or **Enter** to move to the **Category** field.

8. Select the desired category from the list provided, and press **Tab** or **Enter** to move to the **Memo** field. Click the **Splits** icon (on the far right of the line) to separate the amount entered into several categories.

9. Type the information needed to trigger your mind about this transaction at a later date. Remember that this transaction looks just like all others in 6 to 12 months, so entering the memo information now is a good idea although it seems unnecessary today. Press **Tab** to move to the **Enter** icon or simply click the **Enter** icon or press **Ctrl+Enter** to complete the transaction. Repeat this process for all entered checks, and then click the **X** in the upper-right corner of the subscreen to close the register.

Miscellaneous charges such as overdraft fees and transfers to other accounts are entered following a similar sequence. The first few entries take some time because you have to enter the address and account information for each new payee. After you get over this initial hurdle, Quicken's memorized transaction retrieval features make bill entry a snap.

QuickTip

Quicken has a really cool feature that walks you through the process of entering your paycheck deposits. This wizard keeps you from having to deal with the complicated splits that typically accompany a paycheck by asking you some questions and then allocating the splits for you.

Look in the **Features** menu, highlight **Banking**, and then click **Set Up Paycheck** from the list. Have your paycheck stub ready and answer the questions presented by the wizard to make this process really simple and to ensure that all the accounts get set up properly.

Working with Other Quicken Accounts

You are now a wizard at checkbook bills entry, and if the only account you ever used was the checkbook, life would be great. However, you probably also use a credit card for buying things.

Basically, any type of transaction other than check writing is entered directly into the register for the active account.

Assume that you have a credit card named First Bank Visa, and you now want to enter charges made against this account.

1. First, the account must be opened and the target account must be highlighted from within the **All Accounts** or **Credit Cards** tabs. (Depending on the version of Quicken you use, you might use a tab simply labeled **Accounts**.)

2. Next, press **Ctrl+R** to open its register.

3. Enter the charges within this screen. By the way, selecting the credit card account as the **Category** when writing a credit card payment check from within a checking account automatically applies the amount to the credit card account. The credit card transfer transaction may be located at the bottom of the list as **Transfer to/from [*account name*]**, so keep looking until you find it.

4. Depending on your level of desired tracking detail, you can enter a transaction number into the **Reference** field when entering credit card data.

Reconciling Checking Charges

Balancing a checkbook might be right up there with getting a tooth drilled without painkillers, but it is a necessary evil. The automation aspects of Quicken are useless unless you keep your accounts in balance and can trust that the information displayed by Quicken is accurate and trustworthy.

Quicken makes balancing checkbooks a simple process, and it feels great when it congratulates you for having a perfect account balance. I encourage you to treat this like a game.

Quicken calls balancing an account reconciling an account. You must have a statement from your bank in either standard paper format or from an electronic update using the online capabilities discussed in the Chapter 8.

QuickCaution

The specific design of the account balance window looks different depending upon whether you have online banking activated or not.

Reconciliation is done in the following way:

1. First open the **Accounts** window.

2. Highlight the account to be reconciled and select the **Features**, **Banking**, **Reconcile** menu options. The **Reconcile Account** window appears.

The Reconcile Account window allows you to enter account balances needed to reconcile your accounts.

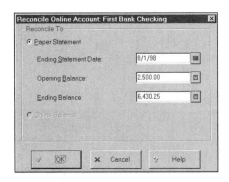

3. Enter the **Statement Ending Date**, **Opening** (beginning) **Balance**, and **Ending Balance** (used for the statement's last period ending) amounts. Any associated check charges or accrued interest are entered into these textboxes during the non-online reconciliation process.

4. Click **OK** to display the **Reconcile Bank Statement** window shown next.

Click OK to start the account reconciliation.

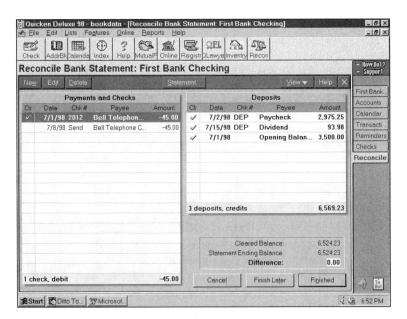

5. In the **Payment and Checks** portion of the window is a listing of all deductions made to the account. Click in the **Clr** column next to each transaction that has cleared the bank.

6. The **Deposits** portion of the window contains a listing of all additions to the account. Click the **Clr** column next to each transaction that has cleared the bank.

7. Notice that the bottom-right corner shows the difference between what the bank says is your account balance based on the bank statement and what your Quicken account says is the balance. When this **Difference** equals zero, you have a balanced account.

8. Click **Finished** when done balancing to have Quicken update the account contents so that reconciled items are noted as such and do not need to be reconciled in the future.

9. Congratulate yourself for having a perfect balance. Quicken does!

Creating Automatic Reminders

I don't know about you, but I sometimes get overwhelmed with all the detail in my financial life. Keeping track of Personal Identification Numbers (PINs) for all my various cards is difficult. Keeping track of my personal and business schedule is always an interesting juggling act. Paying bills at the various times that they are due during the month can be very difficult, and I used to incur late fees simply because I lost track of the various bill due dates.

Voice of Experience

This might sound a little silly at first, but I know people who had incredible financial problems who got themselves back to financial control simply by balancing their checkbook to the penny and then tracking their expenses, down to the penny, for two weeks after that. The theory behind this technique's success is that we spend a lot of money unconsciously, and really don't look closely at where it all goes. By performing the detailed account balance process and tracking your expenses, you start to see where your money goes and realize when you are either in trouble, or realize that you truly have the freedom to spend without worry.

Quicken helps in this area by providing the **Scheduled Transaction List**, **Reminder**, and **Billminder** features.

The **Scheduled Transaction List** is a listing of transactions that occur at specific times during the month, every month, on a recurring basis. Typical bills that fall into this category are mortgage payments, car payments, student loan payments, cable TV bills, and others. Each of these transactions is added to the **Scheduled Transaction List** to inform Quicken that you expect these bills to become due at the times specified when the transaction is set up.

The cool part of all this is that each time you start Quicken, it uses its **Reminder** feature to let you know that these bills are due. You can either choose to pay them at that time or put them off until later.

But what if you only open Quicken a few times during the month, which is my case? This is where the **Billminder** feature comes into play. It is linked with Quicken so that it knows about your scheduled transactions, and lets you know that you have bills to pay, just like the Reminders. But **Billminder** lets you know every time that you open Windows. So, even if you don't start Quicken, you are still notified that bills are due and need to be paid.

If you are the "out of sight, out of mind" type, this set of features keeps your bills in sight, and keeps your credit record on track.

First let's set up the schedules transactions themselves.

1. From the **Lists** menu, select the **Scheduled Transactions** option, or press **Ctrl+J**.
2. Click the **New** button in the **Scheduled Transaction List** window to create a new scheduled transaction item. The **Create Scheduled Transaction** window appears. (Depending on the version of Quicken you use, this window might have a different name.)

Click the New icon to create a scheduled transaction.

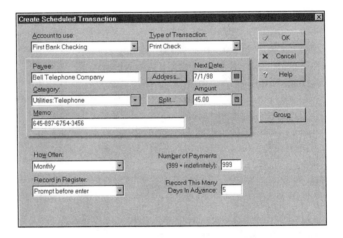

3. Select the account affected by the transaction from the **Account to use**: list box.
4. Select the **Type of Transaction**: from the list box, whether it is an online payment, a check to be printed, a deposit, or other payment type such as an inter-account transfer transaction.
5. Type the **Payee**, **Category**, **Amount**, **Address** (checks only), **Split**, and **Memo** fields just as you did earlier in this chapter.
6. Specify the timing for the transactions in the **How Often**: list box. There are a number of different intervals, so you should have no problem finding the one that is right for you.

7. Specify the number of times that Quicken should apply this transaction in the **Number of Payments**: box. For example, a 30-year mortgage would set this value to 360.

8. Set the **Record in Register**: setting to either **Automatically enter** the transaction, or to **Prompt before enter**. The prompt option is useful for regular payments that may change between payments such as the electric bill. The payment is set up for entry, and all you need to change is the amount.

9. Set the **Record This Many Days in Advance**: option to the number of days you need between the time you want Quicken to notify you of the transaction being due, and the date that it is actually due as specified in the **Next Date**: field.

10. Click **OK** to add the transaction to the list.

11. Repeat this process for all transactions that you must pay on a regular basis.

You now have a scheduled transaction. Now look at how Quicken reminds you that the scheduled transaction is due.

1. From the **Features** menu, select **Reminders**, and then **Reminders** again from the flyout menu. The **Quicken Reminders** window tab appears.

2. Click the **Options** button to display the **Reminder Options** dialog shown in the following figure. Here you can specify the number of days that Quicken should look into the future for scheduled transactions, whether Quicken should **Show Reminders When Starting Quicken** or not, and whether Quicken should **Show Reminders From Other Files** (Quicken files, that is) or not. (Depending on your version of Quicken, your display might differ.)

QuickTip

Use the Only Once option to specify a payment that occurs one time in the future. This way you won't forget about it.

QuickTip

In the **Number of Payments**: box, setting the value to 999 makes the transaction happen every month until you specifically stop it, which is useful for utility and other recurring payments.

Voice of Experience

If you work only with a single Quicken file, which applies to most of us, you might want to clear the check box for **Other Files** to minimize the screen clutter.

Click the Quicken Reminders tab to review the Reminders List.

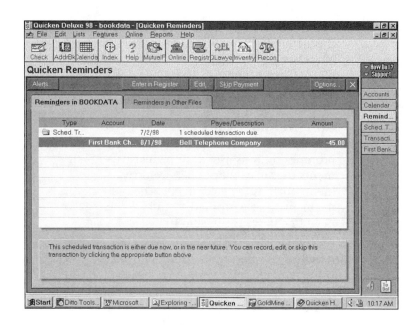

Click the Options button to set the Reminder Options.

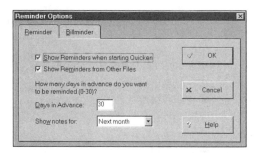

QuickTip

Exit and re-enter the **Reminders** window to see the changes take effect, if they don't happen immediately after clicking **OK**.

3. Click the **Billminder** tab to display its options. (Depending on your version of Quicken, your display options might vary.)

4. Make sure that the **Show Billminder When Starting Windows** option is checked so that you are reminded of the other checked items in this dialog box.

5. Click **OK** to apply these options to the Reminders window.

You are now set up with automatically scheduled transactions and reminders that notify you of scheduled events both when you open Windows and also when you open Quicken.

By the way, notice that you can **Edit**, **Skip**, or **Enter** (use) a scheduled transaction by clicking the proper button as displayed at the top of the Quicken **Reminders** window. These buttons allow you to manually override the automatic features, if you want. (Depending on your version of Quicken, you may see **Edit Payment**, **Skip Payment**, and **Enter in Register**.)

This automatic reminding business might occasionally feel more like nagging than support, but the good news is that you cannot ever say that you forgot your payments. Whether that is good news or not, is up to you.

The Least You Need To Know

➤ Financial management starts with accurate financial data that is entered regularly.

➤ Balancing your checkbook makes you keep your account balances under control and keeps you from writing uncovered checks.

➤ Quicken provides a number of automation features that make data entry easier.

➤ Reminders are an automatic way to keep from forgetting a bill payment.

Chapter 8

Banking Anytime—Day or Night

In This Chapter

➤ Print checks from within Quicken

➤ Learn methods for properly aligning checks with your printer to minimize wasted checks

➤ Set up Online Banking to electronically pay your bills

➤ Download account transactions electronically from your bank into your Quicken accounts

➤ Order your Quicken-compatible checks to get started

Quicken, and Intuit, recognized a great market opportunity when they automated the printing of checks from your personal computer. I have always disliked entering the same payee information in both my check register and again on the check. Quicken easily sets up your computer and printer for printing checks and does it in such a way that you should be more than satisfied with the results—it is really pretty painless.

Oh, by the way, you don't need to maintain that handwritten check register if you print all checks from the computer.

Creating Checks with Quicken

Check writing can be done one of several ways:

➤ **Conventionally** You manually write the checks into the checkbook and register, which was covered in Chapter 7, "Quickening Your Bills."

➤ **Automatically** Quicken sends the checks to your printer; you sign and mail them yourself.

➤ **Electronically** Bills are paid through an online service or in any combination of the three payment methods. With this method, no physical check is created—the transaction happens electronically.

Paying your bills using the automatic and electronic methods are the topics of this chapter. Work your way through this chapter and put the power of technology to work for you.

Ordering Your Checks

You are already familiar with the standard checks that come from your bank when you open an account. They come in various designs, but a few things are consistent with all checks. They must contain your bank's name, branch, and routing number, your checking account number at that bank, the dollar amount of the check in both numeric and written form, to whom the check was written (the "payee"), a signature line, and the check number. As long as the check contains this information, it is not only legal but can be easily processed by the banking community.

Talkin' Money

A check's payee is the person or organization to whom you are writing this check. The IRS would be the payee for a tax payment check, for example.

Quicken has specific formatting requirements that, if adhered to, enable it to print the proper check information into the proper slots on the check, meaning that you only sign and mail the check. As long as these formatting requirements are met, you can get your checks from any source.

Although you can go to a number of places to order checks, you can start most easily by ordering directly from Quicken. Intuit definitely saw this business opportunity and offers a wide assortment of designs and layouts that are guaranteed to work with Quicken. Intuit even includes a "Checks, Forms and Supplies" catalog with your copy of Quicken. You can either fill out the form that they provide you and fax it to 1-619-784-1070 or mail it to Intuit Inc., PO Box 34328, Seattle, WA 98124-9964, or call 1-800-433-8810 to start the order process if you don't have the order form.

As you cruise through the catalog, notice that Intuit also sells envelopes for the various check styles. The envelopes speed up the payment mailing process because the

destination and return address information printed on your check appears through the windows
on the envelope. No more manually addressing
envelopes! You just stamp and mail it. I really like
this capability, so I usually pop for the envelopes
either directly from Intuit or purchase them from
a local office supply store.

You can place an online check order through
Intuit by following this procedure:

1. Open the **Online** menu, point to **Quicken
   On The Web**, and then click **Intuit
   MarketPlace** in the submenu that appears.
   An Internet connection is opened and the
   Intuit MarketPlace Web site appears. Some
   versions of Quicken use an option called the
   Quicken Store. Click it and then click **Checks and Supplies**.

> **QuickTip**
>
> I have a tough time finding off-the-
> shelf double window envelopes that
> align properly with Quicken's wallet
> size checks. I have, on the other
> hand, had excellent luck finding the
> double window envelopes for the
> voucher checks.

*Ordering checks from
Intuit is easy using the
MarketPlace Web site.*

2. Follow the standard browser links contained within the site to eventually reach
   a secure site where you can order checks directly from Intuit. You can also order
   envelopes. All information that you enter into this site is security protected, so
   don't be worried.

The following are a few things to think about when ordering checks so that you do not have conflicts with your handwritten checks:

➤ Make sure that the ordered checks start with a number that is substantially different from those already in your standard checkbook.

➤ Wallet checks are a little less expensive because they come three on a page, but this also means that you generally use them in groups of three when printing them out on your laser printer. These checks also easily fit in the standard pre-addressed response envelope.

➤ If you plan to write single checks on a regular basis, I suggest that you use the voucher check. You pay a little more, but you get a lot more flexibility. These checks must usually be folded to fit in the standard response envelope.

➤ The design on the check is not so important when the only entity doing any writing on the check is the printer. You might be able to save a little money here if you opt for a basic check design, but make the check color different from your handwritten checks to make them easily distinguishable from each other.

QuickTip

An alternate source for Quicken-compatible checks is Viking Office Products at 1-800-421-1222 or fax 1-800-762-7329. I have found these checks to be a little cheaper than those obtained directly from Quicken.

Printing Your Checks

You have your Quicken-compatible checks in hand and check data entered into your Quicken checking account. The next logical step is to print the checks.

QuickTip

The checks must be set for **Print Check** in the **Num** field of the check account register so that Quicken knows that these checks are to be printed using the computer printer.

Follow these steps to set up your printer for check printing:

1. From the **File** menu, select the **Printer Setup** option.

2. From the flyout, select the **For Printing Checks** option. The Check Printer Setup dialog box appears.

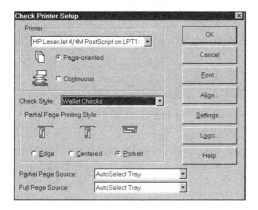

Use the Printer Setup dialog box to set options for printing checks.

3. Select the **Check Style** from the provided list that matches your style of checks. **Wallet**, **Standard**, and **Voucher** check types options are provided. Check out the Intuit MarketPlace Web site for pictures of the different check designs.

4. Select the **Printer** to be used for check printing and the feed type required for that printer, either **Page-oriented** (used by laser jet and ink jet printers) and **Continuous** (used by dot matrix or daisy wheel printers). The **Partial Page Printing** section allows you to set the mode of printing when a whole sheet is not to be fed into the printer at one time. The images display the meaning of each setting.

5. Click the **Align** button to set the printing locations for your particular check designs. The Align Checks dialog box appears.

Be sure to properly align your checks before printing.

105

6. Click the **Full Page of Checks** button to display the Fine Alignment dialog box. It contains text boxes into which you can enter the amount of offset, in 1/100th of an inch increments, for the horizontal and vertical directions. Positive numbers move the printing to the right (or up) and negative numbers move the printing to the left (or down).

7. Click the **Print Sample** button to print a sample of the alignment settings on a blank sheet of paper. This sample, after being printed, can be held up against one of your checks in front of a strong light to verify alignment.

8. Click **OK** twice to return to the Quicken screen.

You now have the printer alignment set properly for your checks. Printing your checks is a simple procedure:

1. Click the **File** menu.

2. Click the **Print Checks** option. The Select Checks To Print dialog box appears. You have the option to print **All Checks**, print only **Checks Dated Through** a specific date that you specify, or print **Select Checks** from those listed as **To Print** in the checking account. You can also specify the first check number in the series to be printed and the number of checks on the first page to be printed.

Use the Select Checks to Print dialog box to choose the checks you want to print.

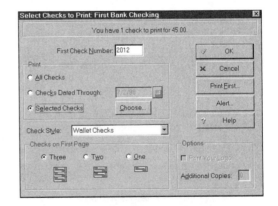

3. Set the **First Check Number** value to the number of the first blank check to be printed. Quicken inserts the default check number that it remembers from the last printing job, which may not match your check number, so always verify this number against your check numbers.

4. Set **All Checks**, **Selected Checks**, or **Checks Dated Through:** as needed.

5. Insert the blank check forms into your printer. Make sure that you verify proper check placement in your printer paper feeder as required by your printer type. Otherwise, you might print on the backside of the check instead of the front.

6. Click **OK** and your checks start to print. Quicken either prints all checks, prints those in selected date range, or presents you with a dialog that allows you to select the checks that you want to print. After the checks are printed, Quicken presents you with the Did Check(s) Print OK? dialog box.

7. In the Did Check(s) Print OK? dialog box, either click **OK,** if all checks printed properly, or type the check number where the printing goofed up into the box provided. This screen is a real time saver, because it automatically sets all checks that did not print properly back to the **To Print** status in the checking account. This allows you to reprint them without having to manually reset their check numbers. In addition, Quicken automatically voids all checks that did not print properly. So, don't skip this screen until you verify that your checks actually did print properly.

There you go! You have entered your checks, aligned for check printing, set the number for the beginning check in the series to print, and printed the checks. Now, just sign 'em and mail 'em. You can handle that without instruction, I'm sure.

Let's review some of the key points of check printing to ensure you have the best success with this great Quicken feature.

➤ Date the checks when entering your bills to ensure that Quicken knows which checks to select if you choose to print by date.

➤ Make sure that your ordered checks have a different numbering series, such as 3000+, than your handwritten checks, such as 1000+, so that they don't conflict in the check account register as two checks with the same number.

➤ Make sure that your computer checks are a different color from the handwritten checks, so that you can easily distinguish them when you receive them from the bank. (This is my own little quirk, but I like it, so I thought I'd pass it along.)

➤ Set the alignment before actually printing any checks to avoid wasting them on an improperly aligned printer.

QuickTip

You can also enter check data directly into the check register, but I prefer to use the Write Checks window to ensure that the address information is accurate for those pesky bills that do not come with a self-addressed envelope.

Paying Bills Electronically—The Big Picture

You might be one of those people who just isn't satisfied with having your checks automatically printed. "Why," you might ask yourself, "can't I just electronically receive and pay my bills from within Quicken. That, after all, saves me time and saves trees."

Once again, Intuit heard your thoughts and provided a set of online banking features that truly can enable you to bank completely paper-free.

Intuit Online Services Save Trees and Time

Well, Quicken has an answer to this request. It is provided as CheckFree, which is one of the options listed on the Online menu. By the way, CheckFree has been around since the late 1980s, according to their customer service department.

Voice Of Experience

CheckFree is not the only company in the country that provides electronic check/payment processing services. Your financial institution might also offer the same services and might even use CheckFree in the background for providing those services. At any rate, you can expect the availability of these services to increase over time as more people move to electronic accounting packages such as Quicken or Microsoft Money. Certain services are aligned with specific software packages, so if you plan to use a service other than CheckFree, you should verify that their service works with your Quicken version, or you might be causing headaches for yourself.

The following is a summary of how online payment processing works:

1. You sign up for the service, which is accomplished by calling the customer service department for your chosen financial institution. They either enroll you over the phone or send you an application form, which you fill out and return. A voided check might be needed if you are not using your home financial institution as your online payment processing service.

2. You are then provided with an **Account Number** and **Security Code** that is used to access your account. If you are using the same financial institution that handles your checking account, they probably use your existing account numbers.

3. The account from which you plan to write checks—for example, First Bank Checking—must be enabled for online payments. This is done by opening the **Accounts** window, selecting the **First Bank Checking** account, clicking the **Edit** button, and checking the **Enable Online Payment** check box (your version of Quicken might refer to it as the **Enable Online Account Access** window).

QuickTip

If you try to enable online payments without first setting up a processing company, Quicken leads you through the process of setting up your relationship with a processing company chosen from an online-provided list. As a matter of fact, this is how I found out that my bank offers online bill-payment processing. You must have Internet capability for this to work.

4. From within Quicken, you define the Online Payee List for people or companies to whom you want to write checks. The payee information includes payee name, address, account number, and phone number. Electronic payees must be specifically set up as such.

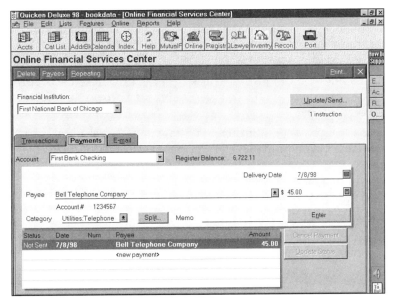

An example of an electronic online-banking payment.

5. You create the payments, designating the electronic payees as the recipients of the electronic checks, just as you would any check except the check number is replaced with a special **Send Online Payment** designation. This designation appears in the check window as a check box titled **Online Payment**, which, when checked, causes the payment to be processed by your online processor. You only have this **Send Online** option if you have set up online banking.

The CheckFree service offered as a Quicken menu option is a very cool service, but it provides only a limited service compared with a financial institution, such as your bank, that offers the same service. I checked with my bank and found out that I could have both checking and savings account information automatically downloaded from the bank and added to my Quicken accounts. My bank calls this service Online Banking, which may or may not include the electronic bill-payment service.

The following are a few things that I found out from my bank regarding online payment:

➤ Payments must be sent to the bank five days in advance of the due date to ensure timely processing and payment. For example, payments due at the payee's on the fifth should be paid from your Quicken account on the first.

➤ Some payees accept online payment directly from the bank that processes your payments. Your processor consolidates all payments due to this payee and sends a single check for the total of all payments along with a listing of all customer accounts covered by that check. This way, a single check between your processor and the payee might cover hundreds or thousands of individual payee transactions.

➤ Payments to payees who do not accept electronic payments are made by standard checks, which are mailed using the standard post office. This possibility creates the five-day lead-time.

➤ Amounts are not deducted from your account until the due date, as specified on the check. This means that you can process checks from your Quicken account for post-dated checks, a handy feature if you plan to be out of town for a few months and want your bills paid.

➤ All electronic checks are listed on a monthly bank statement just as usual, so a paper trail exists for each payment made. You can even get copies of the electronic checks.

➤ All transactions are encrypted as they travel over the Internet, making data unusable to the snooping online hacker.

➤ An Internet account is required for some online processing services, whereas others may require America Online or CompuServe. Check with the financial institution that you plan to use as your processor for additional information.

Updating Accounts Electronically

Another timesaving feature provided by Quicken and many financial institutions is the ability to download your account information directly from your bank into your Quicken accounts. This feature relieves you of the typing procedures needed to enter bank charges, ATM charges, check charges, and other account transactions that do not involve a paper withdrawal or deposit. With the rapid increase of electronic withdrawals and deposits, you'll find this feature more attractive as time goes on.

My bank wraps electronic account updating under its Online Banking service and requires that it be implemented before you can do any online bill payment. The basic procedure requires that I connect to my Online Banking account at the bank, which I must set up with my bank prior to trying to use the service from Quicken.

The entire process is operated from the Quicken Online Financial Services Center, which is activated by selecting **Online**, **Online Center**. Selecting the **Financial Institution** from the list, clicking the **Transactions** tab, and clicking **Update/Send** causes Quicken to dial your bank's online banking services (over the Internet using your ISP). Your security information is transferred and a secure link is established.

QuickCaution

I strongly recommend that you carefully reconcile your checking account information for the first few months after you start online banking and periodically after that point. I found many duplicate entries when first using these features, and it took a while before things worked as expected.

Your online bill payments are then sent to the bank, and your account information is downloaded from the bank to your Quicken accounts. You are queried about each transaction before it is added to your account to make sure that transactions are not entered more than once.

Sounds Good—How Much Does It Cost?

Prices vary from one processing company to another. Effective as of the writing of this chapter, the rates for CheckFree are $9.95 per month for up to 15 payments and $2.49 for each additional block of five payments. Use only one check of the block, and you still pay for all five.

My bank, First Chicago Bank, charges different rates based on the checking account used by the customer. In general, the charges are $9.95 for up to 20 checks and $3.50 for 10 additional. In terms of account updates, such as checking and savings accounts, you can perform 12 per month for the above fees and $1 is charged for each additional.

The Least You Need To Know

➤ Any checks can be used with Quicken's automatic check-printing features as long as they are compatible with the Quicken check-printing requirements.

➤ Electronic bill payment completely eliminates the need to write, sign, and mail checks.

➤ Intuit CheckFree is not the only bill payment service available, but it might be best for you if your financial institution does not support online banking.

➤ Checks that print incorrectly can automatically be voided and reprinted with minimal bookkeeping on your part.

➤ Your account information can be downloaded from your bank into your Quicken accounts, as long as you have online banking enabled both within Quicken and also with your financial institution.

Chapter 9

Planning for the Tax Man

In This Chapter

➤ Understand marginal tax rates and tiered tax systems

➤ Learn the basics of calculating your taxable income

➤ Set up Quicken to integrate with tax preparation packages such as TurboTax

➤ Estimate your taxes from within Quicken

➤ Integrate Quicken and TurboTax to ease tax preparation

At some point in your relationship with Quicken, you realize that most of the information needed by your tax accountant is in your Quicken file. Also, the longer you work with your data, the more familiar you become with your particular financial situation. As you learn more about the tax laws as they apply to your finances, the more likely you are to want to prepare your own taxes instead of paying a tax accountant.

Take a deep breath. This is a situation where a little knowledge can be a dangerous thing. A professional tax accountant lives and breathes the tax laws. You probably don't. Tax implications that you might completely overlook might be obvious to your tax accountant, so realize that printing numbers onto a form is only part of what you pay an accountant to do. You really pay them for knowing which forms to use, properly calculating the numbers used, and assessing the impact of taking one strategic tax direction over another.

I suggest that you become more familiar with your tax situation and try preparing a few returns on your own while actually submitting the one prepared by your tax accountant. When you feel that the two are similar enough and that you understand your tax situation, consider going it alone. This chapter defines the overall income tax reduction strategic process and defines steps you can take to prepare for automatic tax preparation.

General Tax Planning

When you have income, the federal, state, and local government expects a portion of it. The rationale behind the tax is to fund programs that are deemed for the common good of the people. These programs might include paying for the interstate system, providing a military defense, or offering welfare programs. The government doesn't have any form of income other than what it takes in through taxes, so it takes the tax collection process seriously, and so should you.

Just because there is a tax system doesn't mean that you should not take steps to minimize your tax contribution to the fund. This section covers the basic concepts behind the relationship between your annual income, deductions, taxable income, and marginal taxes.

QuickCaution

Until you become comfortable with tax terminology, methodology, and strategy, you should work through a tax professional. After you understand your particular financial situation, you might determine that your tax return is simple enough that you can prepare it yourself. Beware that going it alone might cost you valid tax deductions that could pay for the preparation services. I work out my taxes on my own and then have a professional review them before finally submitting my return.

The federal tax structure is set up as a tiered system, meaning that the marginal tax rate charged is based on your taxable income. This taxable income is determined by taking your total income and subtracting all qualifying deductions from that income to give the adjusted gross income. Standard deductions are then subtracted from the adjusted gross income to yield the taxable income.

The more you learn about the tax system, the more you respect people who prepare tax returns for a living. The tax code is incredibly complicated and always changing. In fact, a major tax reform was implemented in 1997, so make sure that any tax book you use for a reference includes the 1997 tax reform laws or you could do yourself more harm than good by using the book in question.

What Is Income?

Defining income, like everything else related to the tax system, is a complicated topic and cannot be covered in detail in only a few pages, so only a brief overview is presented.

Think of income as anything of value that you receive from a company or person. This is particularly true if you obtained this money or the items of value from performing services or as a return for investing your money.

What qualifies as a deduction is the topic of ongoing and heated debate, but there are some overall guidelines that apply to most people. They are presented in the following section.

For now, simply accept that there are deductions that, when subtracted from your income, total your adjusted gross income and ultimately your taxable income. Any income that is earned on a tax-free basis should not be included in gross income because it is free of taxes, as the name applies.

Talkin' Money

A tiered tax system is a system where the percentage taxes applied is based on the taxable income. The higher the taxable income, the higher the applicable tax percentage. The federal tax system has 15%, 28%, 31%, 36%, and 39.6% tiers that are invoked at different taxable income levels based on the taxpayer's status.

The marginal tax rate is the percentage tax rate applied to a particular tax tier. For example, for single persons with a taxable income between $24,650 and $59,750 the tax rate is 28%.

The gross income is the total of all income for a given tax year. This includes salary, bonus, interest, dividend, royalties, rents, and other income items.

The adjusted gross income is the income level calculated by subtracting the deductions from the income. This is the gross income adjusted by certain deductions.

The standard deduction is a standard amount of money that is deducted from the adjusted gross income to total the taxable income upon which tax is calculated.

A tax credit is the amount subtracted from the tax owed as opposed to a deduction that is subtracted from income. Credits give you a dollar less tax for the amount of credit, where deductions reduce taxes based on your marginal tax rate. Tax credits are usually more valuable than tax deductions.

What Is a Deduction?

A tax deduction is something that is subtracted from the gross income or the adjusted gross income. A certain set of deductions, when subtracted from the gross income, yield the adjusted gross income. And the marginal tax rate is applied to this adjusted gross income.

A lot of jargon is contained in that preceding paragraph, and if you understood it, move on. If not, read the preceding section and the preceding paragraph again until it makes sense; otherwise, tax planning won't make any sense.

The important concept to grasp at this point is that the lower your adjusted gross income, the lower the taxes you are required to pay. Adjusted gross income, and ultimately taxable income, is lowered by lowering the gross income, increasing deductions, or both.

There are literally thousands of valid tax deductions, and you should get a detailed tax preparation guide if you plan to stand a fighting chance against the tax code. My favorite guide is the *J.K. Lasser's Your Income Tax* preparation book and series. I have had excellent luck in finding my needed information in this guidebook and learned a lot about tax preparation along the way.

Your deductions fall into two basic categories:

➤ Those items that are subtracted from gross income to give the adjusted gross income

➤ The standard deductions that are subtracted from adjusted gross income to give the taxable income

The following items, along with others, are subtracted from gross income to provide adjusted gross income:

➤ IRA and retirement plan contributions

➤ Rent and royalty expenses

➤ Moving expenses

After the adjusted gross income is determined, you deduct the standard deductions or itemized deductions, as applicable, to arrive at the taxable income.

The standard deduction is available to you if you do not itemize your deductions. You would itemize deductions if the amount allows you to take a larger deduction than the standard deduction. The standard deductions vary from $3,450 for a married person filing separately, to $4,150 for a single tax payer, to $6,900 for a married couple filing jointly or qualified widow(er).

Itemized deductions are claimed for items such as mortgage interest, property taxes, charitable donations, medical expenses, and other items shown on Schedule A of Form 1040. Tracking all these items to get a valid number for your itemized deductions is the point of personal accounting systems in general, and Quicken in particular.

Notice that reaching a $4,150 itemized deduction level is not very difficult if you own a house, because your mortgage interest and property taxes are included. Heck, your property taxes alone might push you over the itemized limit. After you break the itemized deduction threshold, you want to deduct everything legally possible. This is when accurate Quicken records really help to not only easily obtain valid category totals, but also to validate your submitted expenses should your return be audited by the IRS.

Voice of Experience

I know people who plan their financial lives around not paying taxes. They may enjoy the game, but they often don't seem to enjoy their lives. Paying a dollar for something you don't want just to avoid 30 cents in taxes doesn't make much sense to me. I would rather have the leftover 70 cents than something I don't want.

I had an old-time, crusty sort of accountant named George fill me in on the reality of taxes. He said, "Paying taxes is a good thing in that you only pay taxes if you make money. Try not making enough money to pay taxes and see how much you enjoy your life. So, you worry about making the money and I'll worry about keeping as much of it out of Uncle Sam's pocket as is legally possible. Okay?" George's advice made sense to me then, and it makes more sense to me now. Plan your financial life so that you enjoy it to the fullest while accumulating adequate wealth to provide for retirement, and take advantage of every tax advantage you can along the way. That is your short course on tax planning.

Planning Accounts for Tax Preparation

You know what they say about death and taxes, so I won't go into that here. But, because you know that taxes are going to come around in April of each year, it makes sense to plan for them when creating your accounting tracking system.

Putting tax-related items into their own categories means that the yearly totals can be easily pulled from the accounting records and inserted into the proper location on the tax return.

Listed in Table 9.1 are the major items that you must track to ensure simpler tax return preparation. Instead of frantically looking for receipts and figures, you simply look in your accounting records and grab the number.

Table 9.1   Primary Tax Categories

Salary and bonus income

Interest income

Dividend income

Royalty income

Typical Expense Categories

Mortgage interest payments

Second home interest payments

Refinancing expenses

Automobile registration fees

Medical expenses

Charitable cash and item donations

Tax payments of all kinds, except sales tax

Property tax payments

Any number of other expense items that may be listed on the various tax forms

Tracking these items is particularly important if you have an inconsistent income, such as a salesperson who is paid on commission. Your income may fluctuate a lot over the year. If you have a good estimate of your tax deductions, you can accurately judge the amount of money to take out of your check to cover income taxes.

The Overall Tax Structure

I have talked a lot about income, deductions, and taxes. Now take a moment and review the tax rate schedules for single and married filing jointly couples in Table 9.2.

Table 9.2   Tax Rates for Single and Married Couples Filing Jointly

Over	Under	Tax Due
Single Taxable Income Thresholds		
$ 0	$ 24,649	15% of income
$ 24,650	$ 59,749	$3,967.50 + 28% amount over $24,650
$ 59,750	$124,649	$13,525.50 + 31% amount over $59,750
$124,650	$271,049	$33,644.50 + 36% amount over $124,650
$271,050+		$86,348.50 + 39.6% amount over $271,050
Married Filing Jointly Taxable Income Thresholds		
$ 0	$ 41,199	15% of income
$ 41,200	$ 99,599	$6,180.00 + 28% amount over $41,200
$ 99,600	$151,750	$22,532.00 + 31% amount over $99,600
$151,750	$271,050	$38,698.50 + 36% amount over $151,750
$271,050+		$81,646.50 + 39.6% amount over $271,050

There are other tax tables for different situations, but these tables give you a general idea of how tax payments are calculated. Figure your taxable income, calculate the taxes due, and pay, pay, pay. And this is just the federal taxes. You might also have to pay state income tax, which basically uses the same information that you provide to the IRS and applies a state-specific tax to that income reported.

For example, in Illinois, the state tax is 3% of income. So, the formula for your total income tax bite if you are single and making $50,000 in Illinois would be: Federal tax = $ 3,967 + .28 × (50,000 – 24,650) = $11,065. State tax is 3% of $50,000 = $1,500. So your total estimated taxes are $12,565—about one-quarter of your income!

Notice that reducing our taxable income by $1,000 would decrease your tax bill by 31% of $1,000, or $310. Decreasing it by $10,000 decreases your tax bill by $3,100. Can you start to see why tracking valid tax deductions can really add up to tax savings? This is where Quicken enters because it enables you to easily track your expenses during the year, so tax preparation becomes a much simpler process.

Take it from me. Looking for deductions in a pile of receipts is no fun and generally not very effective.

Looking for Deductions

Quicken Deluxe (the Tax Deduction Finder is not part of Quicken Basic) helps you find deductions that may apply to your tax situation through its **Tax Deduction Finder**, which is accessed by clicking **Features**, **Taxes**, **Tax Deduction Finder**. Some Quicken versions do not contain this feature, so check your Help utility to see whether your particular Quicken version has this feature.

Use Quicken's Tax Deduction Finder to help find possible tax deductions.

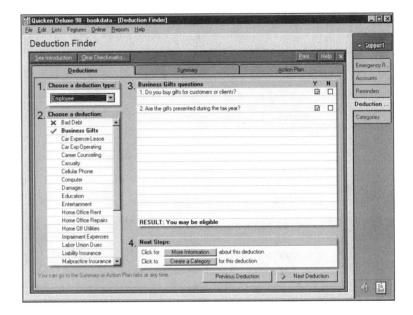

Quicken leads you through a series of questions that, after they are answered, inform Quicken of your eligibility for specific deductions. It is a time consuming process that often becomes tedious, but following the indicated steps might save you thousands of dollars in unnecessary tax payments. Spend an hour and save thousands. That sounds like a good tradeoff to me.

1. Open the **Tax Deduction Finder** by clicking **Features**, **Taxes**, **Tax Deduction Finder**. (Depending on the version of Quicken you use, you might see an **Introduction to the Deduction Finder** dialog box. Read it and click OK.)

2. Choose an option from the **Choose a deduction type** list (area 1). For example, choose **Employee**. You could also select **Homeowner**, **Investor**, **Individual**, **Medical**, and **Self-Employed** if they apply to your situation.

3. Select one of the items displayed under the **Choose a deduction:** section of the screen. The displayed selection items vary with the **Deduction Type** selected in step 2.

4. Answer the questions displayed in **section 3** of the screen. These questions change with the item selected in step 3. Simply answer **Y** (yes) or **N** (no) to the presented questions by clicking the proper answer that applies to you.

5. After all questions are answered, check out the **Result** section of the screen (located at the bottom of section 3) to obtain Quicken's assessment of your eligibility for this particular deduction.

6. Click the **More Information** button in section 4 for additional information regarding this deduction. It includes applicability and restrictions.

7. Click the **Create a Category** button in section 4 to have Quicken automatically create a category for tracking this particular set of deductions.

8. Click the **Next Deduction** button at the bottom of the screen to move through the available deduction list provided by Quicken in section 2 of this screen.

9. Click the **Summary** tab to review the number of questions that you have answered and how many deductions you are eligible for.

10. Click the **Action Plan** tab to see a detailed action plan related to implementing your tax deductions. Click the **Print** button to print this plan for later review.

You may find that none of these deductions apply to your financial and tax situation, but wouldn't it be great to find some that do? Taking the time today to work through this wizard might save you tax payments for years into the future.

QuickTip

Many tax items relate to estate planning. It is a good idea to understand the impact of estate planning on your taxes and vice versa. Read Chapter 23, "You Can't Take It with You, So Plan Your Estate Now," for additional information on tax planning that minimizes estate taxes.

Quicken's Relationship to TurboTax

Intuit saw another solid market connection between computerized accounting and tax preparation. Quite often, people enter all of this information into their accounting system and run summary reports around tax time. These reports are then taken to a tax professional who interprets the data, puts the proper numbers into the proper tax form locations, prints out the forms, and bills you several hundred dollars.

Intuit designed TurboTax as separate application that presents an alternative to using a tax professional to prepare your taxes. You can enter your data directly into TurboTax and allow it to guide you through form completion, or you can integrate

Quicken and TurboTax so that the Quicken data automatically transfers to the proper TurboTax form locations.

Setting Category Properties for Tax Integration

It is now time to look at the tax aspects of Quicken accounts and categories. Tax relationships are defined in the properties section of accounts and categories, which is accessed by displaying the **Account** or **Category** window, right clicking the item in question, and selecting **Edit**. After the **Edit...** dialog appears for the item, click the **Tax...** button to access tax-specific information pertaining to this item. A similar dialog box is presented when setting tax preferences for a category.

Use Quicken to set up tax preferences for your categories.

You can edit each account separately by following the prior procedure, but you'll find it tedious and time consuming. Plus, if you are like me, you'll want to see everything summarized in a single spot. Once again, the Intuit people picked up on this preference and added a solution.

Select **Features**, **Taxes**, **Set Up for Taxes** to display the **Tax Link Assistant** application, which is part of Quicken.

The Tax Link Assistant helps you relate Quicken categories to tax form fields.

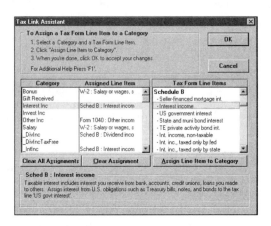

The left column (**Category**) of this dialog box presents the various Quicken categories included with your particular setup. The middle column (**Assigned Line Item**) indicates the IRS tax form and field with which this category is to be associated for tax purposes. The right column (**Tax Form Line Items**) displays a listing of the various IRS tax forms and fields.

QuickCaution

Notice that many of the default Quicken categories are already correlated to specific IRS forms and fields. Make sure that these category correlations work for your setup and that you are disbursing your transactions to the proper categories. Otherwise, the Quicken tax preparation information is misrepresented.

To correlate a category to an IRS form and field follow these simple steps:

1. Open the **Tax Link Assistant**.
2. Select a **Category** from the left column.
3. Select a **tax form** and **line item** from the right column.
4. Click **Assign Line Item To Category** and notice that this form line item now appears in the center column next to the category name.

QuickTip

When you select a form and line item from the right column, a description of the tax item is displayed at the bottom of the dialog box. These are often informative to read, and you are encouraged to keep your eye on this box while assigning categories to tax forms.

Getting a Rough Estimate of Your Tax Bill

Assume that you have diligently tracked all your major income and expense items and that you plan to use a tax professional when tax time arrives. You really don't need to correlate categories with tax forms because you never plan to use this information. But, you still want to estimate your tax bill before the end of the year so that you can take proper steps to minimize its financial impact.

Intuit saw this need and provided a great tool that is simple to use yet very effective in estimating your taxes. The tool is found under **Features**, **Taxes**, **Tax Planner** and is called the **Quicken Tax Planner**. (This tool is not included with Quicken Basic.)

Use the Quicken Tax Planner to estimate your taxes.

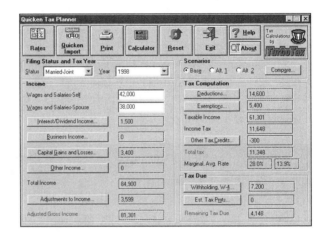

You must know some basic income and expense information to use this tool to its best advantage, but don't let that stop you from at least taking a look at it.

This planner is pretty self explanatory, so I won't go into detail about its use other than to say that clicking the **Quicken Import Iconbar** button imports your Quicken data into the planner if you have already set up the category-to-IRS forms correlation. Entering the data, including the amounts you pay in taxes, provides the Tax Planner with enough information to estimate your end-of-year tax bill. I like this tool and think you will, too.

Two other Quicken features are included that you might find helpful when verifying your tax situation. The two reports, titled **Tax Summary** and **Tax Schedule**, and are both found in the **Reports**, **Taxes** menu option (your version of Quicken might store this option in **Reports**, **Home**). Only tax related items are included in these two reports. The other Quicken reports usually print all transactions, whether tax-related or not.

The **Tax Summary** report provides a listing of all tax-related transactions that have occurred during the defined tax period, which defaults to the calendar year. Click the **Customize** button to define your desired report layout. This is an excellent, quick way to estimate your taxable income based on your actual historic data. In addition, this report provides your accountant with tax category totals along with enough detail to assess the validity of the deduction. Use this report during the year to gather the information needed to manually enter accurate information into the **Tax Planner**. See whether you have paid enough taxes and run it before going to see your accountant.

The **Tax Schedule** report prints transactions as they relate to specific IRS Schedules such as the A, B, C, and so forth.

By the way, I also take a copy of the **Transaction Report** for the calendar year with all accounts marked, all categories marked, and subtotaled by **Payee**, as displayed under the Customize button. This report is accessed under **Reports**, **Banking**, **Transaction**. This lists all transactions for the year and provides a great reference when talking with your accountant.

QuickTip

After you have your Quicken categories and accounts properly related to their respective tax forms and fields, your accounting data should work with TurboTax or any other standard tax preparation software package that is Quicken compatible.

The Least You Need To Know

➤ Taxes are a way of life. You can't avoid them if you make any money, which you want to do. You can only minimize your tax expense through proper planning.

➤ Decreasing income (not desirable), increasing expenses (sometimes scary), spending in tax-deferred areas (preferred approach), or a combination of the three are possible tax reduction strategies.

➤ Quicken provides a number of tools that enable you to predict your tax liability for the calendar year on a future projected basis.

➤ Tracking your expenses with an automated accounting software package, such as Quicken, enables you take maximum advantage of available tax deductions.

➤ Relating the Quicken categories and accounts to the proper IRS forms and fields enables you to quickly create tax returns.

➤ It is always a good idea to have a tax professional around for answers to those complicated tax questions, which inevitably come up as your portfolio grows and becomes more complicated.

Part 3

Give Yourself Some Credit

It's tough to live today without credit of some kind. It may be a mortgage, a car loan, or a credit card, but credit is part of modern life. Just as driving lessons are important to safe driving, credit lessons are important for safe use of credit. The use of credit can either add to the quality of your life or put you into financial ruin. Read this part and learn the rules for making credit a lifelong friend.

Whisper
Whisper

Chapter 10

Lend Me Your Ear...

In This Chapter

➤ Learning the right reasons to borrow

➤ Cautions about being a lender

➤ Respecting loan interest payments

➤ Understanding loan jargon

➤ Techniques for paying off loans sooner than expected

➤ Automating loan tracking with Quicken

If you've ever looked at your mortgage loan documentation, you've had sticker shock. Homeowners gag the first time they see the amount of interest that they pay over the 30-year life of their mortgage loan. It hardly seems worthwhile until you consider the personal and financial benefits associated with owning your own home.

Even though you are shocked, it doesn't mean that you are powerless in how you deal with these loans. You have a number of options available to you that help ease this interest payment burden, and these options are available not only when choosing the loan, but also after it is issued.

The short time that you spend with this chapter might save you thousands of dollars. Interested? Read on.

A Time to Lend and a Time to Borrow

I was taught from early in my life that I should "neither a borrower nor a lender be." This maxim may have made sense as a strict personal finance mandate back when credit was not an all-pervasive part of daily life; however, it is difficult to live life today without borrowing money in some form. The following are some typical reasons why people borrow money:

➤ Loans to cover the mortgage on a home

➤ Loans to help pay for a car

➤ Credit cards to minimize the need to carry cash

➤ Retail finance loans that enable you to more easily afford big ticket items such as furniture or an appliance

➤ Student loans needed to pay for tuition because a student's income is minimal and expenses are high

➤ Loans to cover the building costs associated with that new addition to your home

Most people I know could not afford to buy their home without a mortgage note. If you insist on paying for everything with cash, then you may never own a home or your first purchase might happen much later in your life than for your peers.

Each time you borrow money someone acts as the lender. Whether it is $20 for lunch, or $150,000 for a home, the lender goes through a process of determining whether he or she will get repaid. As you get older and your financial position improves, you might be in a position where lending money to someone is something that you are not only capable of doing, but really want to do. The personal impact of making the lending decision is clearly as important as making a borrowing decision. This is particularly true as the dollar amounts involved get large.

The following are a few valid reasons for borrowing money:

➤ The item being purchased is so expensive that there is no possible way of buying it without a loan. For example, a house or a car that you as a family agree should be purchased.

➤ When buying the item with cash would deplete your cash reserves below your comfort level. Borrowing the money and paying it back over time enables you to buy the item and retain your cash reserves.

➤ When charging the item provides additional benefits not provided with cash, such as renting a car on a major credit card. The card often provides auto insurance when used as collateral for the rental agreement. Cash provides none of these benefits.

➤ When unexpected situations occur that require large sums of money in a short period of time, such as for medical or legal emergencies. I recommend keeping a line of credit on hand to help through emergency situations such as these so that last minute borrowing isn't a personally humiliating and expensive experience.

➤ You might also hear people talk about leveraging their money when purchasing assets such as real estate. Using the house example, this means that they only invest an initial $30,000 but receive the appreciation on the full $150,000 that they purchased with the $30,000. It is not quite this simple because you also have to make the mortgage payments, but you see the overall concept.

Borrowing money because it is more convenient than paying cash can get you into real trouble. Continued use of unnecessary borrowing can very well get you into a financial hole that you can't dig out of. Know anybody like that? I bet you do.

It is important to keep in mind that you and the lender are typically thinking about very different things when working out a loan agreement. Whereas you are thinking about all the things you can do with the loan money, the lender is wondering: Can you repay the loan, will you repay the loan even if you can, and what recourse is available if you don't repay the loan? So, if you've ever felt as if you were speaking a different language than that of your lender, think about the transaction from his or her side of the desk and it might help your discussions.

Lenders make money by lending money out to people and obtaining interest income from the loan. Assume that the lender has access to money and pays 5% annual interest for the use of that money. When the lender loans it to you at 8% annual interest rate, he is overall making 3% interest income on the money (8% revenue – 5% cost = 3% income). Whereas most companies sell products or services, lenders sell money. They have a cost associated with producing the money and obtain revenues in the form of interest income from the sale of that money as a loan.

Assume that you have $100,000 in your savings account that, at the time of this writing, is making 3% annual return. Also assume that you plan to borrow $20,000 for a car, and that the loan costs you 11%. Taking out the loan to pay for the car, instead of simply paying for it with cash, costs you 8% interest expense per year. By choosing to keep the $20,000 in savings and not spend it on the car, you are saying, "I am willing to pay 11% for a $20,000 loan and keep my $20,000 in the savings account where it earns 3%." You pay 11% and get back 3%, or lose 8% in the transaction.

In financial terms, your choice has an opportunity cost of 8% associated with it because it is costing you 8% per year. This is not necessarily bad because you might have a personal reason for keeping the $20,000 in savings that has nothing to do with financial management. But, if you are taking out the loan to be a slick financial manager, you should seriously consider skipping the loan and paying cash for the car.

Voice of Experience

There are also times when you make money by borrowing money even when you have enough cash to purchase the item without a loan. For example, many mutual funds today pay 15% or higher returns, where a typical loan costs between 7% and 12%. Leaving the money in the mutual fund at 15% and taking out a loan at 9% to pay for the item means that you make 15% – 9% = 6% on your money.

This strategy looks fine and dandy while the market is at 15% or higher, but what happens if the mutual fund market goes to 8% and you have all these 9% loans out there. Oops! Now you are in a losing situation. If your mutual fund money is tied up for a longer period of time such that you incur penalties for early withdrawal, then you could have to make some pretty painful financial decisions.

Don't borrow yourself into a position that you can't get out of if the markets drop off. Stocks pay a higher return because of their higher risk. Temper your lending/investment strategy with the knowledge that the market could turn sour for reasons completely outside of your control.

How Loans Get Paid Off

There is a saying among boat owners that the best two days in their lives are the day they buy their boat and the day they sell it. I think the same is true for loans. You are happy when the loan is approved and you finally receive the check. You are even happier when you receive the loan payoff notification after making your last payment.

With that stated, assume that any loan you get has some interest applied to it. A typical home loan, at the time of this writing, is running at around 7%. This means that the bank charges 7% interest annually on the outstanding loan amount, called the outstanding principal. If the amount is compounded annually, the bank computes the interest charges once a year and bills you the proper amount.

Looking at a $5,000 loan that is paid off over seven years at $1,000 per year principal payment plus interest, you can get a better idea of what happens with the principal and interest over the life of a loan (see Table 10.1).

Table 10.1 A Simple Amortization Schedule Example

Year	Starting Principal	Interest Due	Principal Payment	Ending Balance
0 (first day of loan)	$5,000	$0	$0	$5,000
1	$5,000	$ 350	$1,000	$4,000
2	$4,000	$ 280	$1,000	$3,000
3	$3,000	$ 210	$1,000	$2,000
4	$2,000	$ 140	$1,000	$1,000
5	$1,000	$ 70	$1,000	$1,000

Notice a few important things about the amortization schedule shown in Table 10.1:

➤ There is no interest due in year zero because the money has not been held for any length of time.

➤ The interest due each year decreases along with the principal, and the interest payment is made in addition to the principal payment.

➤ The principal balance decreases each year by $1,000 when the principal payment is made. Eventually, the ending balance is $0 at the end of the five-year term.

➤ If the total outstanding loan amount of $5,000 had been repaid at the end of year 1, the only interest payment due would be the $350 due at the end of year 1. The others would not be due because the loaned money was not held into those additional years.

➤ The total of principal and interest changes with each year because the amount of interest due changes with each year even though the principal payment remains the same.

The example shown in Table 10.1 is a loan-amortization schedule. The payback of the loan is divided into, or amortized, over a number of smaller payments.

This general combination of principal and interest is typical of any loan obtained through any standard, commercial, or consumer lending institution. The principal amount, interest rate, duration of the loan, number of payments, and final payoff amounts vary, but all loans are based on the same basic financial concepts.

Typical Loan Terms and Their Meaning

Financial people often talk as if they learned to talk in the "dazed and confused" school of interpersonal skills. The jargon can be pretty overwhelming until you get some basic terms under your belt.

This section introduces you to basic loan philosophy, explains some loan jargon, and provides a framework for you to understand your legal commitments when taking out a loan.

Most loans have an interest amount that is charged to you for the use of the loaned money. The interest rate is tied to the amount of risk perceived by the lender. Risk from a lender's perspective means the possibility that the lender never sees the loan repaid, even if the best possible circumstances occur. They look for the worst even when things look great. That is lender psychology 101.

Talkin' Money

Risk, as viewed from the lender's perspective, is the likelihood that the loan will not be repaid as outlined in the loan agreement.

The interest rate defines the amount you must pay each year for the right to use the lender's money. It is usually expressed as a percentage of the loan amount, such as 8% per year.

A loan is given for a specified length of time, which is then divided into a number of payment periods. For example, a 5-year loan requiring payments once a year would have 5 periods, where a 5-year loan requiring 12 payments per year would have 60 periods.

The principal is the amount of the loaned money that is still owed by you to the lender. It starts out as the original loan amount and decreases over the life of the loan.

The interest payment is the amount of each periodic payment that is used to pay the interest due on the loan. This payment amount decreases over the life of a loan.

A secured loan is one that uses some asset as security for the loaned money. If you default on the loan payment, the lender sells the asset assigned as security to recover any money it might have lost on your loan default.

Homes traditionally have an excellent history of retaining their value, so home loans are generally offered at lower interest rates than a used car or boat. If the lender is stuck having to sell the asset that secures the loan, the lender wants to make sure that the asset can be sold at a price high enough to recover the loaned money. By the way, don't take this personally, but personal guarantee loans have the highest interest rates attached to them. Why? Well, think about it. You are getting the money simply because the bank thinks you, and your credit rating, are worth the risk. Your home, car, or other assets that can be sold if you default do not secure it. In addition, if you declare bankruptcy, the personal guarantee note becomes worth about the same as a bubble gum wrapper. Higher Risk = Higher Interest Rate. Get it?

The number of payment periods defines the frequency with which payments are made and how interest is calculated on the loan. For example, a loan with payments made annually for five years has $1 \times 5 = 5$ periods. A loan with payments made monthly over five years has $12 \times 5 = 60$ periods.

The interest rate charged on the loan is usually based on an annual time frame, but the interest payment calculations themselves may be based on a smaller portion of the year such as daily, weekly, monthly, quarterly, semi-annually, and so forth. This may seem like a small detail, but the timing of the periods can make a huge difference on the amount of interest you pay over the life of a loan.

Interest rates are usually fixed over the life of the loan at a set percentage, such as 8%. Some common loans allow for changes in the interest rate over the life of the loan. These are called variable rate or adjustable rate loans. Variable rate loans generally start out at several percentage points below their fixed rate alternatives, which makes them an attractive loan for people on a low income who want to qualify for a larger loan amount.

The variable loan base rate is usually tied to some common financial entity, such as the government treasury bill, or T-bill. The interest rate charged to you is this base rate plus some percentage, such as 3%. So, if the T-bill is at 4.5% today and the lender charges a 3% additional fee, then the interest rate to you, today, is 4.5% + 3% = 7.5%. This might be good, for today. What about next year? What if the T-bill goes up to 6%? Your interest rate now becomes 6% + 3% = 9%. Now that is not so good because a fixed interest rate could still be at 8%. What if the T-bill goes up another 2% the year after that? You get the picture.

Variable rate mortgages can also go down if the rate on the T-bill goes down. So, these notes can work either for or against you. But remember, no borrower ever complains when the rate goes down, but they can really sweat if the rate goes up.

Most variable rate loans have maximum amounts that they can increase in a single year and a ceiling, or cap, over which the interest rate cannot climb during the life of the loan. If your lender tries to sell you a loan without annual and lifetime caps, I suggest you look elsewhere. Typical annual and lifetime caps that I have seen are 2% and 6%, respectively.

Does this make a variable rate loan bad? Not at all, just be aware of what you are getting yourself in to. A great rate today doesn't mean a great rate next year or five years from now.

Another loan animal you might come across is the "negative amortization loan," which is a loan to treat like a salesperson selling ice to Eskimos.

Talkin' Money

A variable interest rate loan has an interest rate that can change over the life of the loan.

A fixed interest rate loan is one that has an interest rate that stays the same over the life of the loan.

A negative amortization loan has a periodic payment amount due that is lower than the amount needed to pay the principal and interest due on the note. The result is that the principal actually grows larger with each payment until the negative amortization period ends with either decreased interest rates or higher payments.

A loan cap specifies the maximum increase allowed for this particular loan during the period of time specified.

Talkin' Money

A balloon payment is any additional amount paid on a loan. Making an additional payment every six months would be a balloon payment, as well as using that surprise inheritance to make a $10,000 payment against your mortgage note.

This loan generally has a very low monthly payment rate at first because you are not paying enough on the loan to cover both the interest payment and the amount due on the principal. As a result, you make your payments and the principal amount actually increases with every payment. You are basically taking out a loan against your existing loan to pay off your existing loan. This is definitely not an option you want to pursue for a long term residence, but it is one you might like if you plan to purchase a piece of property, hold it for a few years, and sell for a gain due to sweat equity or other types of appreciation. You have minimal cash outlay, and you did not hold the property long enough to make any substantial dent in the principal owed, anyway.

Most loans allow you to make balloon payments, which are large payments made over and above those due as part of the standard amortization schedule. Assume that you got $500 from a friend and wanted to put it against the loan. Simply paying the $500 and allocating it to principal payment decreases the outstanding principal amount by $500 from that day forward. This means that the amount of interest due on the next payment is less because the outstanding principal on which the interest was calculated was less.

You might have to explicitly specify to your lender that the extra money in your payment is to go toward paying down the principle balance and not toward offsetting future payments, which is what they normally assume.

This also means that the same payment made next month goes toward more quickly paying off the principal because the total payment amount is the same and the interest amount is lower. The total payment amount minus the interest payment equals the amount applied to principal, which is larger because interest due was lowered as a result of the $500 balloon payment. So, the question now becomes, "Are balloon payments generally good?" My answer to this is a complete "yes," unless you must

QuickTip

Balloon payments are only useful on loans that do not include a prepayment penalty. Make sure that your loan does not penalize you for paying it off earlier than expected. I suggest you never sign a loan agreement that includes a prepayment penalty clause.

have the balloon cash for another purpose or perversely like paying more interest expense.

You might also come across loans that require "interest only" payments. These loans require that you only pay the interest accrued on the principal to keep the loan current. Some people forget that the borrowed principal must also be paid back at some point. Don't get fooled by the interest only payments when borrowing a loan of $5,000 over five years, like the example in Table 10.1. At some point you must come up with the $5,000 that you borrowed in the first place. Obtain a few of these interest only loans for any substantial amount of principal and you might never get yourself out of debt because nothing will ever be left over to apply toward principal.

A Close Look at Loan Interest

As mentioned earlier, interest accrues over a period of time and is paid with your loan payment. In Table 10.1, you saw that the annual payment changed due to the changes in accrued interest.

Having a loan payment that changes every month would be a pain to keep track of and would hinder effective budgeting. An alternate approach, and the one generally used, is to keep the payment amount the same over the life of the loan and simply adjust the amount of the payment that goes to principal and the amount that goes to interest.

QuickTip

A table listing the division of principal and interest over the life of a loan, for a constant payment amount, is called a loan amortization table. The division is dependent upon the interest rate, the loan amount, the total number of periods of the loan, and the specific period in which the payment is made. Standard tables are easily obtained at any book store, or simply buy yourself a solar-powered financial calculator while standing in the checkout line at Kmart. In addition to the tools provided by Quicken, you can easily create an amortization table using a spreadsheet program, such as Lotus 1-2-3 or Microsoft Excel. Simple amortization tables can also be easily generated using utilities freely available on the Internet.

See Table 10.2 for a breakdown of the principal and interest payment based on a $120,000 loan at 8% over 30 years.

Table 10.2   Abbreviated Principal and Interest Breakdowns over the Life of a Standard $120,000 Home Mortgage Note at 8% in Multiple-Year Increments

Year Ending	Payment	Principal	Interest	Ending Balance
Starting Balance	*$120,000*			
1 (First Pmt.)	$880.52	$ 86.62	$793.89	$119,919
5	$880.52	$119.16	$761.36	$114,084
10	$880.52	$177.54	$702.98	$105,270
15	$880.52	$264.50	$616.02	$ 92,138
20	$880.52	$394.07	$486.45	$ 72,574
25	$880.52	$587.10	$293.42	$ 43,426
30	$880.52	$874.67	$ 5.85	$ 0

The following are a few characteristics associated with the type of loan outlined in Table 10.2 that apply no matter the reason for the loan and its specific terms:

➤ Payments made early in the loan's life are primarily interest payments with only a little of the payment going to paying down the principal. Notice that in Table

10.2 the loan principal is reduced only a small amount in the first five years of the loan.

➤ As the loan approaches the last third of its life, the payments shift to being primarily principal and a little interest. The principal is drastically reduced in the final five years of the loan.

➤ The ratio of interest and principal payment changes with each payment.

➤ If a balloon payment is made along the way, the outstanding principal is reduced, but the payment amount stays the same. This means that each payment pays less interest expense, leaving more of the payment for paying down the principal.

➤ Most tables assume that the payment is made at the end of the loan period (for example, at the end of the month.) Loans can also be amortized assuming that the payment is made at the beginning of the period. The payment amounts and specific amortization information change based on the beginning or ending payment assumption.

➤ The total amount of interest you pay on a standard 30-year mortgage note is several times the amount of money you borrowed in the first place. For example, the loan amortized in Table 10.2 requires that you pay almost $197,000 in interest alone over the 30 years. Ouch! Think about this; it is real important. You borrowed $120,000 and paid $197,000 in interest over the 30 years for the right to use that money. No wonder lenders are so anxious to give you money.

➤ Decreasing interest payments is a good thing, even though interest payments are tax deductible, because every dollar spent on interest only gives you back around 30 cents in deductions.

Accelerating Payment Schedules

All of this loan, interest, principal, and time frame stuff might start to jumble together at this point. Understanding this section can save you a ton of money over the life of a loan, so let me reinforce a few basic loan concepts:

➤ You pay interest on the outstanding principal amount over a specified period of time.

➤ The more frequently you make payments of the same amount, the shorter the money holding interval and the faster your loan gets paid off.

➤ Decreasing the principal balance in any way early on in a loan's life saves substantially over the life of the loan.

➤ Most loans keep the periodic payment the same and simply adjust the principal/interest allocations from that payment.

➤ The lower the interest rate, the less interest expense you pay.

Take a look at this discussion associated with making more frequent payments, and use it as a benchmark for your understanding of the relationship between principal and interest payments over a loan's life.

Take your monthly mortgage payment, and divide it in to two equal halves. Pay the first half in the middle of the month and pay the second half at the end of the month. It is hard to believe, but this simple change in how you pay your mortgage decreases a 30-year note's term to 23 years and decreases the amount of interest paid by over 25%. Why? Because you are paying the same amount of money over the course of the month, but use the principal loan money for only half of the prior full month period. Because you are making principal payments more frequently, you are using the money for less time and amortizing the loan more quickly. This is pretty interesting (no pun intended). It is also easy to implement if your lender allows you the option of automatic payment withdrawal. Who cares whether the computers withdraw once or twice from your account during the month (provided that the money to make the payments is there when the computers decide to make the withdrawal)? The total payment amount is the same, but the benefits to you definitely offset any interest loss you may incur by not having that money in your checking account for the extra two weeks.

Think about this scenario, too. Assume that you have an extra $10,000 that you applied to your mortgage loan in year 5 of its life. This pays off your loan in just under 25 years instead of 30, and saves you around 30% of the interest that you would have paid without the $10,000 balloon payment. Even little balloon payments made along the way, especially in the early years of a loan, can make a big difference in the amount of interest paid.

Another great way to pay off a loan earlier is to pay a little more each month than is required by the lender. Make sure that your lender knows that the additional payment amount is to be applied to the outstanding principal amount, and not toward future payments. For example, paying $1,080 on your example $120,000 loan instead of the required $880 cuts the interest payments in half over the life of the loan and pays off the loan in a little over 15 years, instead of the original 30-year term.

A natural question at this point is, "Why not just get a 15-year mortgage in the first place?" Good question, but think about these things for a moment. You might not be able to qualify, through the lender, for the higher 15-year payment but can qualify for the lower 30-year payment. Using my recommended approach, you can always go back to making the lower 30-year payments if you hit hard times, where having a 15-year loan means that you have to make those payments or be in default. Period. You might pay a little higher interest rate for the 30-year loan instead of 15-year note, but I believe the added flexibility makes it worth it, especially if you can exercise the self discipline to increase the payments and amortize the loan more quickly.

Tracking Loans with Quicken

Keeping track of the proper split between principal and interest for a given loan payment is a routine and often cumbersome task. It is not really difficult after you have the loan's amortization table created. To create an amortization table, follow these steps:

1. Select the proper installment payment number from the amortization table that applies to the loan payment being entered.

2. Write a check to the payee for the amount of the payment. For example, the year 5 payment in the prior table would require writing a check to the payee for $880.52.

3. Enter the amount of the payment that goes to paying principal as a split that decreases the outstanding loan amount in the loan's liability account. For example, the year 5 payment in Table 10.2 would split $119.16 to the loan liability account.

4. Enter the portion of the payment that applies to the interest due as a split expense to the proper loan interest expense category. For example, the year 5 payment in Table 10.2 would split $761.36 off to the loan interest category.

5. Check your work by adding $119.16 + $761.36 = $880.52.

Quicken makes the completion of these bookkeeping entries a snap by not only creating the amortization table for you, but also by creating a special transaction that automatically enters the proper principal and interest payments for the loan, and installment, in question. Follow these steps to create a car loan and its associated automatic transactions:

1. Rest your cursor over the **Home and Car** icon at the bottom of the Quicken main screen.

2. Click the **Set Up or Track A Loan** option.

3. If the **Loan Setup Wizard** does not appear, click the **New** icon in the upper-left corner of the window to start the wizard.

4. Click **Next** to start the setup process.

5. Select **Borrow Money** to indicate a loan where you are getting money from someone else. Click **Next**.

6. Quicken asks for information regarding the account where it is to store the liability information. This can be either a **New Account** (entered in the text box) or an **Existing Account** if already created prior to invoking the wizard. Type Chevy Loan into the **New Account** text box as shown in the figure, and then click **Next**.

Use the New Account text box to create a new loan tracking (liability) account.

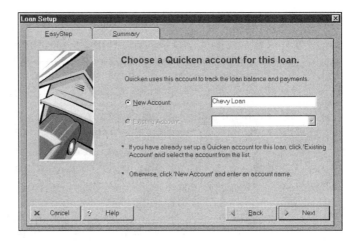

7. The next dialog asks whether payments have already been made on this loan. Click **Yes** if payments have already been made and **No** if it is a new loan. Click **Next**.

QuickTip

Quicken calculates the proper outstanding principal on the loan and creates the proper entries to ensure that the proper loan balance is displayed. It does not, however, calculate the interest paid on the loan in this calendar year. For this reason, you are better served by starting your loans from the first payment, if possible. Otherwise, let Quicken calculate the loan balance as of the end of the last tax year and enter the payments that take place in this year to ensure proper accounting of interest expenses.

8. Enter the loan **Opening** (origination) **Date** and the amount of the **Original Balance** (loan amount) in the spaces provided. Click **Next**.

9. Click **Yes** if there is a balloon payment at the end. Otherwise, leave the default at **No**. Check your loan documentation to determine whether you have a balloon due, or not. Click **Next**.

10. Enter the number of years for the loan, such as 5 years in the **Original Length** text box. Click **Next**.

11. Select the proper period between payments. Most desired timings are contained under the **Standard Period** listing, but you can enter a custom period by clicking **Other Period** and entering the number of payments desired per year. Click **Next**.

12. Set the **Compounding Period** for the loan, which is generally the same as the period between payments. Check your loan documentation, or contact your lender if you have questions. Click **Next**.

13. Answer the next questions regarding whether you know the principal balance due on the loan as of the last statement. If this is a new loan, the amount is the original loan amount on the date of origination. If this is a loan on which

payments have been made, then check your latest statement and prepare to enter the amount if you click **Yes** on this screen. Otherwise, click **No**. Click **Next**.

14. Enter the **Date** of **Next Payment** when asked and click **Next**.

15. Answer **Yes**, click **Next**, and enter the payment amount, if you know it. Otherwise, select **No** and click **Next**.

16. Type the Interest Rate (for example, 9.5%) into the text box provided and click **Next**.

17. Verify the Summary Information, such as that shown in the figure, by clicking **Next** through the screens. Modify any information that is not correct. Click **Done** when finished.

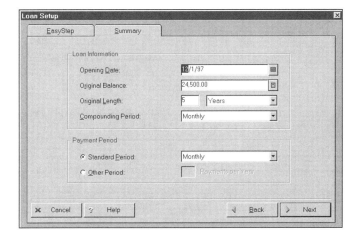

This is a partial summary of the loan setup information.

18. Quicken notifies you that it will calculate the currently outstanding principal balance and required payment and allows you to review the information. Accept the defaults until you get to the **Set Up Loan Payment** screen. This screen sets up the automated transaction information.

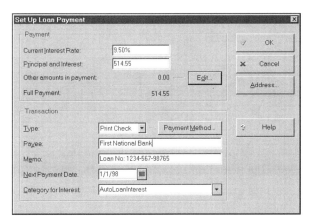

Use this screen to set up the automated payment information.

143

19. Select a payment **Type** (for example, Print Check), **Payee**, **Memo** information such as the loan number, the **Next Payment Date**, and **Category for Interest** for tracking of interest expenses. You can also enter the address of the payee from this dialog by clicking the **Address** icon and entering the proper information. This option only applies when printing checks is selected. Click **OK** to finish the process.

This might seem like a lot of work to set up a loan account, but think of it as laying the groundwork for easy, accurate bookkeeping entries later. Every time a payment is made, Quicken automatically updates the principal and interest payments for the loan in question and ensures that your personal financial statements are accurate.

You can always review the loan information by resting your cursor over **Home and Car** icon, selecting the **Set Up** or **Track A Loan** options, and choosing the loan to be reviewed.

The loan's amortization schedule is included on the **Payment Schedule** tab, as shown in the figure.

> **QuickTip**
>
> You can use the Home and Car icons, Set Up, or Track a Loan options to set up any type of loan. It is not restricted to home or car loans. Just make sure that you select the proper accounts and interest tracking expense categories and all will be fine.

You can display the amortization schedule for your loan by choosing the correct loan from the Payment Schedule tab in Quicken.

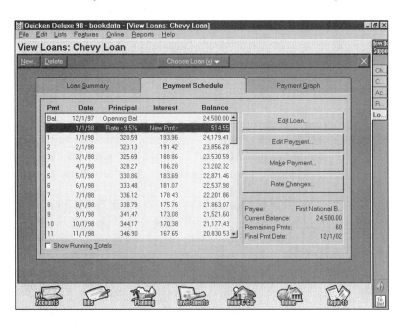

This procedure covered the creation of a car loan; the same procedure can be followed for any other type of loan, including personal and home mortgage loans.

If you are comfortable with accounting principles, you can also set up a loan as a new liability account using the **Create A New Account** option displayed on the **My Accounts** icon. The wizard steps are almost identical.

The Least You Need to Know

➤ Interest rates and risk relate directly insofar as higher risks almost always come with higher interest rates.

➤ Whenever you have a borrower, you almost always have a lender, and each are looking at the transaction from different viewpoints. The lender might want more interest for taking on higher-risk clients.

➤ Utilizing a fully amortizing constant payment loan. The ratio of principal and interest that is paid off with each payment changes over the life of a loan.

➤ Paying a little more early in the life of a loan saves a lot of money over the life of the loan.

➤ Quicken enables you to automatically track your loan payments while distributing the principal and interest payments properly.

Chapter 11

Keeping Your Credit Cards at Bay

In This Chapter

➤ Learn the proper use of credit cards

➤ Use the Quicken Debt Reduction Planner to become debt free

➤ Reduce interest payments and monthly credit card payments while getting a tax deduction, all in one step

➤ Establish a healthy relationship with your credit capabilities

➤ Review your credit report for accuracy

Remember the joy you had when you qualified for your first credit card? My first card was with Sears in Chicago. I had heard that you should first establish credit with a single chain, and then you could move up to the Visa, MasterCard, and American Express levels. This approach worked for me, and I still recall the thrill that I got when charging on my Sears card. I really felt like I had arrived.

Well, I kept arriving, and arriving, and arriving until I had arrived myself into a several thousand dollar account balance, which was a lot of money for a college student in the 1970s. I had the good sense to realize that the card was a means to an end, not an end in itself. I was lucky in that I caught it early. Others I have known got themselves deeply into debt and had a difficult, painful time getting their debts down to manageable levels again.

In this chapter, I show you how to decide where credit cards fit in your life and how to use them without jeopardizing your financial well being.

Credit Cards—Financial Friends or Foes?

Credit cards truly have a place in modern life. There is a strong possibility that we may not even carry cash in the near future. I know people who carry $10 on them for emergency purposes and pay for everything else with a prepaid pass, credit card, or ATM card. These people could not function efficiently without the use of credit cards.

Talk to anyone who travels on business a great deal, and you find someone singing the praises of credit cards. Renting a car, buying airline tickets, paying for hotels, and charging business meals are all much easier with a credit card. Even if your company provides cash advances, you must still complete the expense report including receipts for expenses when you return. Why carry thousands of dollars in cash or travelers checks, when you could simply charge the expenses on a credit card, submit the expense reports, receive reimbursement from your company and repay the cards when the bills become due? Charge cards have their place.

The following are some reasons to carry credit cards:

➤ Credit cards minimize the need to carry cash.

➤ You receive a cash float, where you charge the item during the month, and do not actually have to pay the bill until 2–4 weeks later. You get to keep your money for a few weeks longer than if you pay cash.

➤ Emergencies can be covered by a credit card, where you probably don't carry enough cash to cover anything but the most minor incidents.

➤ Credit cards tell others that a separate organization such as Sears, Visa, or American Express has checked out your credit and said it was good enough to trust you with a credit card.

➤ Try renting a video without a credit card. This could require a deposit and a great deal of detailed personal information where the credit card handles the transaction in a single step.

➤ People who travel a lot find that their life is much simpler with credit cards. This is important when you travel a lot because traveling on a schedule is complicated enough.

➤ Credit card companies offer incremental services such as car rental insurance, lost card insurance, buyer protection insurance, and discount programs that you don't get when you pay cash.

Voice of Experience

A few years ago I had all my identification, credit cards, tickets, and travelers checks stolen on the Ramblas in Barcelona, Spain. I dropped my guard for a moment: These thieves were professionals, and I was stuck. The police department in Barcelona was moderately helpful and allowed me a phone call, so I called American Express in Spain, who immediately transferred me to England, to someone who spoke English. He understood my situation in that the police did not want me using their phone, asked me for the name of the restaurant across the street and told me to go there and have a cup of coffee. I did just that.

A few minutes after sitting down, I was paged in the restaurant and, to my surprise, found the American Express representative on the other end of the phone. "I knew that you couldn't talk in the police station and thought that this would be better for both of us," he said. My other credit card companies left me high-and-dry, but American Express came through with new checks, canceled and reissued tickets, addresses for reissuing of my passport and other important items. When traveling internationally, I never leave home without it. This is an absolutely true story, and useful for reinforcing the intangible benefits associated with credit card ownership.

Credit cards are a part of contemporary life, just like cars, TV, and the Internet. At some point you need to define your relationship with them, and the sooner you define the good and dangerous parts of credit cards as they pertain to your life, the better off you are.

Tracking Credit Card Transactions

Quicken can help you understand your relationship with credit cards and how they are used. It is one thing to charge as needed, pay the minimum payments, and then get another card when the credit runs out on the first one. This is the road to credit ruin.

It is another to enter all your credit charges on a monthly basis, track where the money was spent, and issue a check for the entire amount so that you always maintain a zero balance. This is the path to effective and safe credit card use.

If you track your credit card expenses with Quicken, as outlined in this chapter, you get a handle on your credit card situation and start taking the proper steps to get it under control.

The following are the steps involved with tracking credit card usage with Quicken.

1. Create an account for each of your credit cards. This is accomplished by resting the cursor over the **My Accounts** icon, selecting the **Create A New Account** option, and then following the wizard steps involved in creating a **Credit Card** account. Remember that this is a liability account because everything that you charge becomes a credit card debt that you must repay. In some versions of Quicken, you want to open the **Accounts** window by pressing Ctrl+A and clicking **New** to launch the wizard.

2. Use the credit card to charge your purchases, just as you always do.

3. After your credit card statement arrives, enter the transactions into the credit card account you created in step 1. This is done by opening the **Accounts** list, selecting the **Credit Cards** tab, and double clicking the desired credit card account. Transactions are entered just as with a checking account, except you are entering transactions into your credit card account, instead. Make sure that you enter the finance charges, late charges, and other charges associated with owning a credit card. Some versions of Quicken have no **Credit Cards** tab. Credit card accounts are included in the **Accounts** list, which includes all accounts.

4. Make credit card payments by writing a check just as you would any bill, except the **Category** becomes the **Credit Card** account you created in step 1. Pay the total remaining credit card balance to avoid future finance charges or at least the minimum required payment by the due date. Naturally, the more you can pay, the better off you are. Writing the check against a liability category decreases an asset account and decreases a liability account. If you think about it, this is just what you want to do.

That is all there is to tracking credit card transactions. By using the categories and splits as you do when writing checks, you obtain detailed tracking of your credit card expenses. In addition, entering all this information makes you evaluate your credit card spending habits, which I believe is a good thing. This practice becomes even more important when you have more credit cards. Refer to the chapters in Part 2, "Getting It into the Computer," for details regarding the actual entry of Quicken data.

I know people with more than $30,000 in revolving credit, who make in the $50,000 per year salary range. Fifty thousand dollars in salary is certainly adequate for daily living, but it dwarfs pretty quickly when you start to look at $30,000 in credit card debt at interest rates that run 18% or higher. To make it even worse, the credit card finance charges are non-tax deductible interest expenses. Ouch!

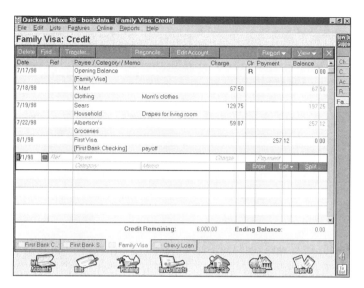

Open Quicken's Account lists, and choose an account to see your credit card account purchases and payment transactions.

Voice of Experience

It is real easy to get into credit card trouble, and you are better off knowing it before it happens because it can be a pretty deep hole after you are in it. I have a friend who came by the house one day to show me his new notebook computer. It was a great machine and I was impressed. When I asked him what he paid for it, he said that it was free. He had charged it.

Although the notebook system was noteworthy, his comment is what really got my attention. This person ran his own business and was a very bright individual, yet he thought that using his charge card was "free" money. He got himself deeper into debt, and he eventually had to work diligently for several years to get himself, and his family, back onto a solid financial footing. By the way, he pays cash for a lot of his purchases because he doesn't trust himself with the credit cards. Like Harry Callahan from the "Dirty Harry" movies says, "A man's got to know his limitations."

Don't think that it can't happen to you. It can and probably will if you are not careful from the beginning.

151

Picking the Right Credit Card

How many credit card applications did you receive in the mail this week? I seem to get 10 or more a week. Somebody has a lot of money, and they sure want me to spend it for them...but at 15%–22% interest rates. No way.

Picking a credit card is a little like picking a roommate in that you may live with this card's conditions for a long time. Understanding your particular situation is important to finding the right card.

If your credit is spotty, then you might have to go with a secured card where you put $500 or more into account, and charge against it. You get the convenience of a credit card, up to the deposited limit, and get a chance to re-establish your credit. These cards typically have high interest rates and should be a card of last resort.

If you have decent credit, then you should qualify for a card that has either no annual fee and a higher interest rate or a card that has an annual fee but a lower interest rate. Which is better? Depends on whether you repay the balance in full each month.

Suppose that you carry a $1,000 balance on your card and the card charges an 18% interest rate, but no annual fee. You pay $180 per year in finance charges on this card ($1,000 × 18%). If you were to go with a card that had a $25 annual fee and a 13% interest rate, then you would pay a total of $130 interest + $25 annual fee = $155. This is $25 lower than the $180 you paid with the no annual fee card.

If your credit is good, you should be able to qualify for a no annual fee, low interest rate card. Once again, make sure that you pay the balance off every month or you could be looking at substantial accrued finance charges.

Quicken's Billminder is a great way to ensure that your bills get paid on time. Take a look at Chapter 8, "Banking Anytime—Day or Night," for additional information about Quicken's other bill payment automation features.

Voice of Experience

I recently signed up for a credit card that allows me to earn frequent flyer miles on my charged items. The card's annual fee is $50, and it has an 18% interest rate, but I figured that I would pay it off every month and earn a free ticket or two for my trouble. That would easily offset the annual fee.

Well, I got busy and missed the last payment. I not only do not get the mileage credit because my payment was late, but I also got charged 18% interest on my purchases. Ouch! Every program has its catches, and you want to handle things properly or you can pay higher fees and not gain the benefits that prompted you to want the card in the first place. You can be sure that this card is the first one I pay every month.

Checking Your Credit Rating

American law entitles the accused person to face his accuser. This applies almost anywhere, except with credit. I have been denied credit in the past, when my credit rating was excellent, because of mistakes on my credit report. I may not even know the people who dinged my credit rating, but it is now my job to respond to their claims or have my credit rating tarnished.

Can you correct inaccurate credit reporting information? Sure. But, don't expect it to happen overnight or simply because you have a nice smile. My experience is that it takes paperwork and diligence to get it corrected.

QuickCaution

I recently saw a special television news report about a woman—we'll call her Kimberly—whose credit rating was destroyed by someone she did not even know. A person intercepted the credit card applications that arrived in Kimberly's mailbox and responded on Kimberly's behalf, using a different address and phone number. This fraudulent procedure was done with a number of cards. The imposter then took the cards and charged to her heart's content, then did not pay the bills.

Naturally, when the creditors wanted payment they went after Kimberly. She did not even know that these cards existed, but she still had to take responsibility for the cards. Frequent credit checks keep you from ending up in Kimberly's position, and may be worth the expense.

The upshot of all this is that it is a good idea to review your credit report every year or two, simply to ensure its accuracy. You cannot get a free credit report from any of the reporting agencies unless you sign up for one of their credit tracking services.

Federal law entitles you annually to one free credit report if you meet the following criteria:

➤ You receive public assistance.

➤ You believe that fraudulent activities have caused inaccuracies in your credit report.

➤ You are unemployed and looking for employment in the next 60 days.

➤ You have been denied credit because of the information contained in your report. (This entitles you to a free report from the agency that provided the credit report in question.)

➤ In addition to federal law, state law entitles residents of New Jersey, Vermont, Colorado, Maryland, and Massachusetts to one credit report per year. You folks in Georgia are entitled to two reports per year.

QuickTip

One great way to learn more about credit reporting is to visit Experian's Web site (formerly TRW) at `http://www.experian.com`.

Quicken offers a free credit reporting service, which is really an enticement to enroll in one of several credit reporting services.

Use Quicken's free Credit Reporting Service Programs and Alliances to get free credit reporting.

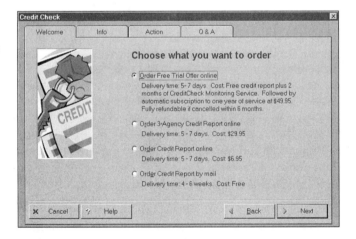

You access the Quicken credit reporting features by resting the cursor over the **Planning** icon, and then selecting the **Order A Free Credit Report** option (this is called the **Order My Credit Report** option in some versions of Quicken). A wizard starts that leads you through the various reporting service options, as displayed in the figure.

Your credit report has information that is divided into several different categories. These categories include your credit history, who has reviewed your credit history, special information that you gave the credit agency, and any identification information specifically related to you. The report also contains special notes explaining the information on the report.

Spend some time with the report, or even better, spend some time with your lender and the report. This way you learn how the information is used by a lender and what needs to be done to ensure that your credit is perceived as favorably as possible.

Closing and Consolidating Accounts

Do you have charge cards or accounts that you really don't need, but you want to keep around for any "rainy day" times that might come along? When you applied for credit, did they say that you had too much credit extended for your income level, but all your credit balances are at zero? Confusing? Sure, until you look at the amount of available credit you have instead of what is actually used.

The available credit is the amount that you can charge, should you get a wild streak and buy like there is no tomorrow. The lenders may look at the total amount of credit you have available in your name, and decide that you really don't need the additional credit you are requesting of them. Or they may ask you to close certain credit accounts to free up some of your credit to accommodate the loan you are requesting.

I suggest that you take a hard look at the credit you currently have available to you and what you are currently using. Verify the interest rates and annual fees on each of the accounts, along with their total credit limits, and decide which card is right for you. If you find that the card with the most favorable credit terms, such as annual fee and interest rate, has too low of a credit limit, you might simply call the card issuer and ask for an increase. Explain that you intend to cancel your other cards and want to standardize on theirs. You should get a favorable response if your payment history on that card is also favorable.

Some cards provide very low interest debt consolidation credit where you get a 6% interest rate for a time frame of say six months for any debt transferred to the new credit card. This is a great way to consolidate your other cards into a single card and drop your interest rate from a higher rate of 18% to around 6%. After consolidated, the trick is to cancel the old cards that now have a zero balance and stick with the new card alone. In addition, make a concentrated effort to pay down the balance on this new card while the interest rate is low, because after the interest rate goes back to its 18% norm, you will have a much harder time paying down the balances.

A home equity loan is a great way to consolidate your credit cards debts, decrease your interest rate, decrease your required payments, and get a tax deduction in the process.

Assume that you have several credit cards with a total used credit of $15,000, and the average interest rate is 18%. This equates to $2,700 a year in interest expense payments, or $225 per month, just to keep the cards current. This doesn't include any principal payments on the outstanding balance.

Assume now that you took out a $15,000 home equity loan at 11%, amortized over 15 years, and paid off your credit cards with the $15,000. Your required monthly payments on the home equity drop to $170, and the loan is paid off over 15 years. You could increase your payments to $300 per month and pay off the loan in a little more than five years. There is no way you could do this with a credit card. Oh, by the way, the interest payments you make on your home equity loan are tax deductible because it is interest paid on your home mortgage. This also takes a little of the sting out the payments.

Naturally, the best option is to not get deeply into debt in the first place. But if you find yourself neck deep in high interest loans, you really should look at consolidating the loans into a single loan of a much lower interest rate and paying it off as quickly as possible.

If you don't have the option of a debt consolidation loan, I suggest you pay off your highest interest rate cards first and work your way down the list until all are paid off. Don't then turn around and charge them up to the limit again. Cancel the high interest cards and get yourself down to the one or two cards that work for you.

When Is Cash Better than Credit?

We sometimes lose contact with the underlying money that is exchanged with our checks and credit card transactions. If you don't believe me, try this little exercise. The next time you owe someone some money, say $500, pay them in $100 bills instead of by check. Watch the way their eyes light up when you count out five $100 bills. No way they would react that enthusiastically to a check.

If you find yourself out of control with your use of credit, I suggest that you stop using your credit cards and pay for everything in cash. Two things happen with this approach. First, you have first-hand knowledge of how your cash is spent because you are doing it yourself, in person. Second, you do not get deeper in credit debt and you certainly are not able to spend beyond your means to pay because your spending stops after you run out of cash.

It is sometimes good to fast from eating for a day to really appreciate the food we eat; perhaps the same is true of credit. Perhaps we don't appreciate our credit until it is taken away. I suggest that you put yourself on a credit fast as an attempt to get your credit relationship back on track.

If you don't like carrying cash, use your debit card because it automatically draws the purchased amount from your checking account. This approach also keeps you from spending past your available cash limit, but it doesn't provide the visceral shift that handling cash provides.

Using the Quicken Debt Reduction Planner to Owe Less

Check out the following list to determine whether you are already in credit trouble:

➤ Do you only make the minimum monthly payment on your charge cards or other loans?

➤ Do you regularly use money from one credit account to pay off another?

➤ Do you routinely receive overdue notices or collection calls from your creditors?

➤ Do you worry about losing your job because the loss of your job would immediately put you into serious financial trouble?

➤ Are your credit accounts at their limits?

➤ Are you looking for another credit card application in the mail so that you can continue buying because your current cards are at the maximum limit and there isn't enough money left over every month to buy the desired items?

➤ Do your friends or family members not want to lend you money because they know you can't pay it back?

If you answered yes to any or all these questions, you really should take a hard look at your credit-handling habits and start seriously looking at steps that will get you back into financial health.

Quicken provides a handy tool that enables you to evaluate your current debt situation and devise a strategy for getting yourself out of debt. This tool is the Quicken Debt Reduction Planner, and it is accessed by resting the cursor over the **Planning** icon and selecting the **Create A Debt Reduction Plan** option. You must have the Quicken CD in your CD-ROM drive, or this option does not function.

Following are the basic steps presented by the wizard:

1. The **Debt Reduction Wizard** leads you through an analysis of your current debts and ranks them from highest interest rate to lowest interest rate and suggests that you repay the higher interest notes first.

2. It then asks you for the amount of money that you are willing to withdraw from your investment and savings account to reduce the debt.

3. You are then walked through an analysis of your current expenses and asked to evaluate budget areas where reduction would be in order.

4. Finally, Quicken presents you with a summary of your debt reduction plan as shown in the figure. The plan can be printed out. The actions that you specified while completing the wizard are presented. It is now up to you to follow the recommendations.

The debt reduction planner works most effectively if you already have expense information entered in to accounts and categories. Otherwise, you are simply making guesses based on minimal historical data. I suggest that you spend some time entering data from the last few months, and preferably from the beginning of the current tax year. This way your yearly data is current and any historical information has greater validity.

The Debt Reduction Planner creates a plan based on your debts that helps you get back on the road to financial health.

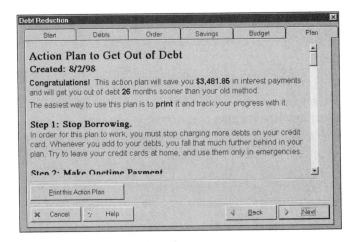

No matter what approach you take, make sure that you start getting out of debt today. Not taking the required steps today when you see there might be a problem may quickly get you into a hole that you cannot get out of without serious lifestyle changes or loss of your credit reputation.

There is an old saying that states, "The best way to get out of a hole is to stop digging." Taking control of your credit today is the best way to stop digging so that you can get out of the hole before it is too late.

The Least You Need to Know

➤ A credit card can be a friend or an enemy depending on how you use it.

➤ Protecting your credit is critical in today's heavily credit-oriented society.

➤ Debt consolidation home equity loans reduce interest payments, decrease monthly payments, and provide a tax deduction.

➤ Pay off your higher interest credit accounts first and work your way down to the lowest interest rate account.

➤ The Quicken Debt Reduction Planner helps to get a handle on your debts and create a plan for becoming debt free.

Chapter 12

There's No Place Like Home

In This Chapter

➤ The financial benefits of home ownership

➤ Taxes and home ownership

➤ Tips for buying your first home

➤ Properly using home equity loans

➤ Understanding escrow accounts

Buying your first home is a big deal and probably the wisest personal financial move you make. Other types of investments fall in and out of favor, but home ownership remains both a solid investment and is personally rewarding. This chapter looks at the various financial aspects of home ownership, including whether it is right for you in the first place and strategies for buying your first home.

Purchasing a home is probably your most important personal financial goal. Deciding when to buy that home or how to pull off it's purchase are not trivial topics and deserve a dedicated investigation. For this reason, this chapter concentrates on the various aspects of purchasing a house and minimizes the Quicken coverage associated with home ownership.

Your Home Is a Great Investment

Owning a home is part of the American dream. For most people, buying a home and buying a car are the two largest purchases they will make in a lifetime.

You can probably picture three bedrooms, a kitchen, and two baths. Now, I want you to picture the best investment you can find.

Real estate usually increases in value every year, although there have been times and locations where this has not been true. Average appreciation values vary by the location of the property and the overall state of the economy, but in general, real estate appreciates around 3–5% per year. What does that mean to you? Think of it this way. If your home has a value this year of $100,000, it is worth $103,000 next year if 3% appreciation is applicable. Oh, by the way, it also appreciates 3% again next year, giving you compounded appreciation over the years that you own your home.

Talkin' Money

Appreciation is the increase in value that an asset sees over a period of time. Most of us really appreciate when that happens.

The benefits don't stop there. There are also substantial tax benefits associated with owning your own home. Interest paid on mortgage for a first and second home is tax deductible. Property tax payments are tax deductible. Closing points paid when purchasing your home are usually deductible because they are treated as prepaid mortgage interest, making them tax deductible.

The following is a brief summary of the major financial benefits associated with home ownership:

➤ Annual appreciation.

➤ Mortgage interest deduction.

➤ Property tax deduction.

➤ Qualify for itemized deductions on tax returns.

➤ You are perceived more stable by the financial community and others, meaning it is easier for you to secure loans.

You would expect that everyone would own a home if the benefits are so great, yet many opt for renting or leasing instead of owning. The following are a few reasons that people choose not to buy their residence:

➤ You must sell or rent your residence if you decide to relocate. This may take time, and it may also cost you money if your home has not appreciated enough in value to offset the selling costs, such as realtor commissions.

➤ You can quite often lease a residence for less monthly expenditure than paying the mortgage, taxes, insurance, and maintenance on a home you own.

➤ Banks usually require a 10–20% down payment on the home, which means that to buy a $150,000 house you must come up with $15,000 to $30,000 in cash before you can buy. This is a lot of money, especially for young people starting out with a new career and family.

➤ Houses require maintenance, whereas rentals only require that you call the landlord who inherits the problem.

➤ If your career requires that you relocate on a regular basis, you might find your-self selling your home so frequently that the cost of selling offsets any apprecia-tion gain, making the ease of renting very attractive.

Leasing Versus Buying

You probably expect a book on personal finance to look at the financial aspects of buying a home compared to leasing or renting. And, sure enough, here it is. The pre-vious section looked at the personal aspects of renting compared to buying. Now walk yourself through the financial aspects of buying versus leasing. To do this, use the fol-lowing example. Of course, your situation will be different, so feel free to substitute your own information for the following to help you with your decision.

➤ Assume that you plan to live in a $150,000 house in an area that appreciates by 3% per year.

➤ Property taxes on the home are $3,600 per year.

➤ Your down payment on the home was 20% ($30,000).

➤ The $120,000 balance ($150,000 – $30,000 = $120,000) was financed at 8% annual interest rate for 30 years.

➤ You are in a 28% tax bracket.

➤ Leasing (or renting) a comparable house would cost you $1,100 per month.

Take a look at Table 12.1 to see how the numbers work out over a three-year period. The numbers I've used here are derived using the following criteria:

➤ Appreciation is calculated by taking $150,000 and multiplying it by .03 ($150,000 × .03 = $4,500), adding those two together ($150,000 + $4,500 = $154,500) to come up with the ending year appreciation value and repeating the process for all three years. So year two calculations are $154,500 × .03 = $4,635, which added to $154,500 + $4,635 = $159,135. And so forth for each following year.

➤ Payments are calculated using standard payment tables (also called amortization tables), assuming that all of the payment is deductible (which is not exactly accurate, but close enough for our purposes here), and then adding the $3,600 in property taxes. (See Chapter 10, "Lend Me Your Ear...," for additional infor-mation about loan amortization procedures and calculating loan payments, or check out the **Quicken Loan Planner** that is accessed from the **Features** menu, **Planning**, **Financial Planners**, **Loans** selection. This tool calculates loan payments and prints amortization schedules.)

➤ Tax benefits are calculated as 0.28 times (28%) the total of interest payments, which is an approximation of your tax deductions received annually from own-ing your house. Know that this is a valid approximation during the first 1/3 of the loan term because most of your payment goes to interest. The last 2/3 really require accurate interest calculations.

Table 12.1   Simplified Owning Versus Leasing Analysis

Item	Year 1	Year 2	Year 3	Total
Appreciation	$ 4,500	$ 4,635	$4,774	$ 13,909
Home Payments	$-14,166	$-14,166	$-14,166	$-42,498
Tax Benefits	$ 3,967	$ 3,967	$ 3,967	$ 11,900
Net Cost	$-5,699	$-5,564	$-5,425	$-16,688
Leasing Expense	$-13,200	$-13,200	$-13,200	$-39,600
Net Savings with Owning Compared to Leasing:				$ 22,912

I took a few liberties with the home analysis side of things by not considering utilities, insurance, real estate commissions when you sell (usually 6%), and other incidentals that always mount up when you own your residence. But, those incidentals would have to add up to a lot to offset the almost $23,000 in benefits associated with owning your own home. Plus, when you own you don't have to worry about putting holes in the walls to mount your pictures or having to move in a few years because the landlord is selling out from under you. In my opinion, owning your residence, whether a condo, town home, or a house, is a good financial and personal decision.

My intention here was to show, by the numbers, the tremendous benefits associated with home ownership and skip the intangible aspects that come from owning your own home. Even if you take compounded annual appreciation out of the equation, it still makes sense to own instead of lease unless your lifestyle matches the criteria set out in the last section (your job requires frequent relocation, for example). The tax deductions alone are worth almost $12,000.

Buying Your First Home

There is a saying in business that seems to hold true across the board. "The first one is always the toughest." This is absolutely true with respect to buying your own home. I bought my first home in California in the early 1980s. I remember real estate brokers literally laughing in my face when I told them that I wanted to buy, especially when they saw my yearly income. I couldn't even get them to show me property because I had no money for a down payment and not enough income to qualify for a loan on a shack in the mountains. I got incredibly discouraged and angry, but I never gave up. I wanted to own a house. Period. And I was going to make that happen. Period.

I finally found a guy who was willing to take a chance on me and sold it to me "by owner," which means that he carried the mortgage note. No real estate agents were involved in the deal. He made a solid profit off of the deal, and I was lucky to have found him. I might also have made my own luck because I had previously looked at literally hundreds of houses before finding the deal that worked for me.

Voice of Experience

The benefits of home ownership increase the longer you own your home. Just as interest income on an account accumulates over the years, so does real estate appreciation. It is difficult to see any major appreciation increases in only three years, but over 20 years you can see substantial gains. In addition, the mortgage principal balance (the amount you borrowed to purchase your home) decreases every year, whereas your property increases in value, which increases the amount you get to keep when you do sell.

You get to live in the home you want. You're not disrupted by moving every few years. Your house payments remain the same instead of increasing annually like rental payments are known to do, and you get the tax benefits. If you do not own your home, you should have a hard talk with yourself and commit to buying something if your lifestyle can support it. I have never regretted home ownership.

Owning that home became a passion for me, and I acquired my first financial breathing room when I sold it eight years later.

It was an okay house in an okay neighborhood that I got for 3% down and high monthly payments. I rented out rooms to college students to make ends meet, and I even brought in a partner to help financially when inflation drove interest rates up to 17%. I was going to hold onto that house. And it worked for me.

That was my first house. Yours doesn't have to be so traumatic if you follow a few rules.

QuickTip

No matter how you buy your house, always be smart enough to have an attorney review the paperwork before signing anything. The fee—which could be a few hundred dollars—is money well spent because you learn exactly how far you are crawling out on a legal limb.

➤ Start saving for your down payment today. If you can't save the money on your own, start looking for people to loan you the down payment money in exchange for a portion of the home proceeds when sold or to give it to you simply because they are good people, such as family members. Needless to say, they probably want their money back when you sell the house.

165

Talkin' Money

Sweat equity is the amount of appreciation derived directly from working on the property either yourself or through the management of others to do the work. Do it yourself to make the most sweat equity and, almost always, lose your evenings and weekends at the same time.

Equity is the difference between the market value of an asset, such as your house, and what you owe on that asset. Subtract the value of your home loans from the market value of your house to get an estimate of the current equity. The equity is always an estimate until the asset is actually sold and selling expenses are deducted.

Restoring a house generally involves rebuilding the house so that it looks like it did when first built, with the exception of more contemporary kitchen and bathrooms.

➤ Don't shoot for a great house in a great neighborhood as your first house. You generally build up to that after you have owned a few houses.

➤ Consider a condominium or town home as your first home. The property values are less, which makes the purchase price less. Make sure that you check out the homeowner fees associated with your condominium complex.

➤ Take on the worst house in the best neighborhood so that you get a lower initial purchase price (because nobody else wants it) and build equity faster as you remodel, or restore, the house. Doing this work yourself builds "sweat equity" in the property.

➤ Make friends with a good realtor who is sympathetic to your cause and let this person know how willing you are to buy your first house. Most people like to help out people who are responsible and motivated, and real estate people are the same. They also have a profit motive in that they make money when you buy the house, and when you sell it because you will probably use them to sell your home when you decide to move up. Make sure that this realtor doesn't lock you into an agreement that requires that you use them, even if you find an unlisted home on your own, such as a "for sale by owner" house.

➤ Let your banker know what you are up to. If you don't have a banker, find one and get to know him or her personally. The lender might have special loan programs that "normal" people don't know about but bankers do. It can't hurt, and it sure can help if your banker is on your side.

➤ Check out those parts of town that have special building incentives allocated for them. This often means that the banks, and even the government, have special real estate loan programs set up just for people like you who want to build or remodel in these special areas. Check with your local government and real estate associations to learn about deals in your area.

➤ Look for a more financially secure partner to cosign the loan. This gives you the credibility needed to get your first loan and home. The gains from this home will probably give you enough to go the next one on your own. You also have a track record when you apply for your second home. Remember, the first is always the hardest.

➤ Do what I did. Buy a house and rent out every square inch of it that you don't need for yourself. As your financial situation improves, take over more of the house for yourself. Eventually, you have the whole place to yourself.

➤ Move in under a lease-option arrangement where you have reserved the home for yourself and are officially still making lease payments. The interesting part is that a portion of the lease payments can be applied to the purchase price should you decide to buy. The percentages are negotiated between you and the seller.

➤ Don't forget that everything is negotiable. My first house included my pickup truck as part of the down payment collateral.

➤ Investigate the various zero-down real estate purchase programs. The financial arrangements required to make these deals work are creative, and they generally require that you have a sale-by-owner

QuickCaution

Your realtor might be buddy–buddy with you, and that is her job. But always remember that the seller pays his or her commissions as part of the 6% selling commissions. The selling broker gets 3% and the buyer's broker (your broker) gets the other 3%. They get paid from their 3%, which they only get if you buy the house. Ever felt like a meal ticket? Your broker has a duty to inform you of this arrangement, but some are less complete in this duty than others.

situation. However, I know people who have bought houses for zero money down because the seller had enough equity in the house, and was motivated enough, to negotiate the deal in the buyer's best interest. Look hard enough and you find these deals.

➤ Check out the various government funding programs such as FHA and your VA benefits, if applicable. Don't assume that you don't qualify. You just might, and with a 3% down payment instead of 20%. Some programs even allow for a zero down payment. It doesn't get much lower than that. By the way, the paperwork hassles are substantial with these loans, but what else would you expect from the government?

➤ If you are really adventurous, you might consider moving to a depressed area of the country that you believe will rebound within the next few years. Buy your home there: once again the worst house in the best neighborhood. At this point you are buying when the market is low, which minimizes your financial outlay up front. When the area rebounds you should make enough off of the appreciation to compensate for your relocation troubles. Do this a few times, and you could easily build up a substantial nest egg.

➤ Ask your real estate agent (who is now your best friend) for mortgage broker recommendations, and talk to them directly. Often, they prequalify you for a loan of a maximum amount. In this way, you know the price range in which you should be searching, and when the right deal comes along you have the funding ready to go. This makes you a stronger buying candidate and helps you negotiate a lower purchase price.

➤ Know that there is an special loan type called a "low-doc" loan that does not require the strict financial verification of a conventional loan, but does require a larger down payment that is usually 25% or higher. These low-doc loans are a great option if you are self employed or have a questionable income, yet have cash on hand that can be applied to the down payment. If you cannot make the monthly payments, they still eventually declare the loan in default and repossess the home, putting some or all your down payment in jeopardy.

Voice of Experience

There are three critical things to consider with a real estate purchase: location, location, and location. Get the picture? Location is critical when buying real estate if you plan to get the maximum appreciation in the shortest amount of time. My wife says that I have a golden rabbit's foot when it comes to real estate. I haven't got the heart to tell her that the rabbit's foot is simply a lot of looking in the best neighborhoods for the worst house, buying with owner financing, fixing it up, and selling it after more than five years.

I enjoy doing the remodeling work and every nail increases the value of the house. Don't overlook the stress associated with working on your own house, but if you can pull it off, the equity builds up faster and you are able to buy your dream house earlier than you think.

One other word of advice, if you decide to take the remodel-it-yourself-while-living-in-it approach, fix the foundation and roof first, and then finish your bedroom and bathroom completely before taking on the rest of the house. You must have somewhere you can go to get away from the dust, and I never liked sleeping in plaster dust. It breaks your heart to finish an interior room just to see the walls crack from a creeping foundation or streaked walls from a leaky roof.

No matter what happens, don't lose track of your goal to buy a house. If it is important to you, it happens and people appear in your life to help you in your quest.

Owning your residence is the best financial decision you can make, and it is personally rewarding. I lived in a house for eight years, and then I moved into an apartment. It just never felt like home to me, even after three years of living there. I then bought a house, owner financed, and knew right away that this was the right thing for me.

Please understand that I am not saying that this is the only way to go, but it has surely worked for others and me. Treat it like a game and you have more fun, are less frustrated, and are more successful. Success in any game requires that you learn the rules, find a good coach, hone your skills, and don't let the setbacks knock you out of the game. Millions of people win the first time buyer game every year, and so can you.

Tracking Mortgages

Congratulations on the purchase of your new home. The boxes are unpacked and the pictures are finally on the walls. Life is great, and then comes the first mortgage installment bill. Life is still great, but you might be confused by some of the things associated with the bill. Don't worry, though, it's all easy to understand, and with Quicken, you learn to track your payments in a snap.

The bill asks for payment on the mortgage for the month after you lived in the house, as opposed to your rent check that was always due at the beginning of the month. This makes sense if you consider the mortgage payment a bill for the use of the money required to purchase the house. Assume that the lender gives you a $120,000 loan so that you can buy your house and charges you 8% per year interest over a 30-year period. The monthly payment on this loan is $880.52. This amount does not include the insurance and property tax payments that are also required. The total of all required payments is called principal, interest, taxes, and insurance (PITI).

Talkin' Money

PITI stands for principal, interest, taxes, and insurance and reflects the total minimum payment required to financially maintain your home payments.

The mortgage bill is not due until the end of the month because no interest is due on money until you have held it for a period of time. The lender bills you interest at the end of the month because you have had the use of the money for the month, and you have agreed to pay that month's accrued interest on a monthly basis. There is also a small amount of the payment applied to the principle amount that you still owe on the loan. This amount of principal payment is small during the first 7–10 years of a 30-year loan, but it quickly increases in size as you pay down the loan. The payment amount always stays the same. Only the ratio of principal and interest changes as applies to the payment. (Refer to Chapter 10 for a detailed discussion about loan amortization.)

Don't forget that your final monthly payment not only includes the mortgage principal and interest, but also property taxes, insurance, and any other costs related to your home's escrow account. These charges can be substantial, so make sure that you verify them in advance to avoid unwelcome surprises.

Your monthly mortgage payment requires that these bookkeeping entries be made (using the same example I started earlier). Of course you want to substitute your own numbers.

➤ The payment amount is deducted from checking (for example, $880.52).

➤ The interest amount is applied to the Mortgage Interest expense account (for example, $800.00), which increases the Mortgage Interest expense category balance by $800.

➤ The balance (principal minus interest, or $880.52 – $800 = $80.52, in this example) is applied to the Home Mortgage Loan liability account, decreasing it by the amount of principal paid.

The amount of principal and interest paid every month varies even though the payment amount stays the same. These two amounts are important because the interest payment is tax deductible, and the principal payment decreases the amount you owe, which increases your equity, which also increases your net worth. Unless these amounts are automatically calculated for you, an amortization table must be created so that the monthly entered amounts are accurate. Luckily, Quicken includes a loan tracking feature that automatically calculates the proper loan amortization amounts for the loan and month in question and applies these amounts when the payment is made. (Refer to Chapter 10 for a detailed discussion of entering loan amortization information.)

Property Taxes

This should come as no surprise. The government always wants its cut and it certainly has its hand out when it comes to property taxes. These taxes are used to pay for all types of things, including school funding, junior college funding, road maintenance, and local and county government funding, along with other miscellaneous items that apply to your local area. The amount of property tax can vary widely between counties and states and are worth considering before you buy. California property taxes were low in the 1980s (around 1% of appraised value), where taxes in Texas and Illinois sat at around 3%. On a house appraised at $150,000, this is the difference between $1,500 and $4,500 per year in property tax payments.

Appraised value is the key item to consider. When you buy a house, you set the appraised value because you were willing to pay that amount for the house. The tax districts generally increase that amount every year as their way of estimating the appreciation on your property and, by the way, also increasing their tax income. You can contest your home's tax district appraised value if you think that it is too high. Contact your local taxing authority to determine the proper procedure to follow.

Also, check into possible exemptions such as those that might apply to senior citizens, veterans of foreign wars, homestead, and other types that might apply to your locality. Be forewarned, however, that building additions increases the value of your home. If a contractor performs the work, the increased appraisal amount generally is the amount paid to the contractor. If you do the work yourself, your appraisal amount is more open to negotiation, and generally lower.

This also applies to building your house as opposed to buying one already built. When you buy a house, you set the market value. When you build a house, you pay for materials and labor, which is far less than the amount a contractor would charge for the same house. If you do some of the labor yourself, you save money not only on the construction cost but also on the appraised value. This decreases your taxes every year from that point forward, which can result in real savings over a 10–30 year period.

Property taxes must be paid each year. Depending on your mortgage lender, you can either pay them on your own or pay them through an escrow account that is maintained by your lender. By the way, homeowners insurance is also generally paid out of escrow because lenders want to ensure that their collateral, your house, is properly insured in case something such as a fire burns it to the ground. Some lenders charge premiums if you do not put tax and insurance money in escrow, because of the increased risk of leaving it all up to you.

QuickTip

Appraised and assessed values can mean different things under different circumstances. For example, the tax assessor sets an assessed or appraised value for your home that is used for levying taxes. Your lender wants an appraised value that reflects the current market value for your home. The two appraisals generally have different values and may even change from one appraiser to another. As always, ask more questions and have fewer surprises.

Talkin' Money

Escrow accounts are financial accounts maintained by your financial institution. You pay money into this account on a monthly basis so that the amount of money in this account grows over time. When required, the financial institution pays property taxes and other required charges from this account. The financial institution is said to be holding that money in escrow for you until the payments are due. These are non-interest bearing accounts. Sorry.

Escrow accounts are valuable in that the monthly amount you pay stays the same. Otherwise, you must make sure that you have adequate money on hand to pay the property taxes when they become due at the beginning of next year. Coming up with a few hundred dollars is generally not a problem, but coming up with several thousand dollars can often be an interesting exercise in creativity.

Taxes and Loan Interest Deductions

There is a little good news buried in all these interest and property tax payments. They are tax deductible. This means that you deduct the total mortgage interest and property taxes paid over the course of the year from your overall income.

Assume that your income for the year is $55,000 and you paid $14,000 in interest and property tax payments. This means that your taxable income drops to $55,000 – $14,000 = $41,000. From this $41,000 you take out other tax deductions further decreasing your taxable income. Right off the top, you have decreased your taxes by 28% (0.28) of $14,000, or 0.28 × $14,000 = $3,920. That takes a little of the sting out of paying all this interest and property taxes.

QuickCaution

Beware of 125% loans. They are based on the lender's, and your, expectation that your property will increase in value over the life of the loan. We are currently in a boom economy, and people can't imagine the economy slowing down. If the slow down happens, your house could lose value, and you might find yourself owing $125,000 on a house that has only an $80,000 market value. Don't believe it can't happen? Talk to someone who owned property in Texas during the early to mid-1980s.

Equity Loans

Equity is the difference between your home's market value and what you owe. For example, assume that the house you bought for $150,000, on which you owe $120,000, is now worth $175,000. You now have $55,000 in equity on your house. Over time, your loan amount decreases and your home value increases, which increases your equity.

Tapping this equity can be a great way to pay for college, vacations, credit card debt, and various other items. Remember that interest paid on credit cards or personal loans is not tax deductible, where home mortgage interest is tax deductible.

You can take out an equity loan on your home for anywhere between 50% of the equity, up to 125% of the value of your house. These loans are secured by your home. If the loan goes into default for nonpayment, you could lose your home even if you keep making payments on your original, or first position, loan. Beware. These equity loans are a popular lender marketing item, but they carry a substantial downside should you not handle them properly.

On the other hand, equity loans can be a great way for you to use your built-up home appreciation. (See Chapter 11, "Keeping Your Credit Cards at Bay," for more information on using your home's equity for credit card debt consolidation.)

Line of Credit Accounts

Another handy financial tool is the line of credit account secured by your home's equity. This account is like a checking account in that you write checks from it, but the check is actually secured by your home's equity. The lender pays the check amount and instantly creates a loan for the check amount that is applied to your line of credit account. You then make loan principal and interest payments on this account, just as you would any loan. Some lenders allow interest only payments and spread out the payoff over a seven year period. The interest on this loan should still be tax deductible because it is secured by your home and is treated as mortgage interest.

The interest on these line of credit accounts usually runs a few percentage points over your standard mortgage loan interest rate, but it also runs well below that of most credit cards or retail organization loans. For these reasons, many people keep an equity secured line of credit account on hand just in case they ever need it.

The Least You Need to Know

➤ Your home is your best financial investment.

➤ Mortgage interest and property taxes are both tax deductible. Homeowner insurance payments are not deductible.

➤ Owning a home is almost always a better investment than renting or leasing.

➤ Buying your first home might be a challenge, but with creativity and commitment it can be done.

➤ Equity loans are a great financial convenience, but you can still get yourself in financial trouble if you don't manage them properly.

Chapter 13

Make It a Dream Home

In This Chapter

➤ Tapping your home's worth through a home equity loan

➤ Refinancing your mortgage can save you big money

➤ Selling your home and keeping $500,000

➤ Setting up your Quicken accounts to track real estate

Expanding Your Home with Home Improvement Loans

When you want to replace the flowers in the front yard, you can probably charge that amount on a charge card and pay it off in no time. When you want to add a second floor to your house, you have a completely different animal.

You are not the only person who wants to keep the same address, but have more living space. Affording the $15,000 to $100,000 or more that it takes to add the extra space is usually beyond our checkbook's capability. This doesn't mean that the dream must go unfulfilled. It means only that you have more paperwork to complete before you get to see it become reality.

Home improvement loans, sometimes called "multi-payout construction loans," have been around for a long time. They are designed to allow you to take out a loan on your house, usually in second position behind the first mortgage loan you already hold. These are like a home equity loan except with one important and special difference. Equity loans are not earmarked for a specific purpose, whereas a home improvement loan is earmarked for the specific improvements you have in mind, and that were approved by your lender.

For example, suppose that you want to add another 900 square feet to your house in the form of a larger master bedroom suite, master bath, and a loft/den area. Also assume that you plan to contract the work through a licensed contractor who says the work will cost $45,000.

QuickTip

A standard equity secured line of credit is typically used when you want to add onto your house and need a loan to pay for it. Notice that you already have this line of credit based on your home's current equity. Multi-payout construction loans are for situations when the current equity in the house cannot support the loan amount needed to fund the construction.

The sequence for obtaining the loan and using the money looks something like this, and may vary with your lender:

1. Determine the scope of work for the project, down to the most minuscule details.

2. The contractor provides you with a proposal for completing the work.

3. Present the scope of work (what you plan to do) to your financial institution. This includes building blueprints and contractor sworn statements.

4. The lender evaluates your building objectives, your credit, and whether your house, in your neighborhood, can support this much of an addition without pricing itself completely out of the market.

5. The lender evaluates your chosen contractor and your credit.

6. After approved, you define interim payment terms so that checks can be issued to the contractor by a third party, such as a lending institution, to keep the work moving forward. Checks are probably issued in your name *and* the name of the contractor. This way, neither you nor the contractor can individually make off with any of the money.

7. When the work is completed, you contact the lending institution and have it issue checks that you then endorse over to the contractor.

8. No final checks are issued until the work is inspected by the lending institution's approved representative. It wants to make sure that the money was spent to do the designated work, and that it was done satisfactorily. After all, the institution is paying for it and assuming that it is at least as valuable as what it paid. This final check is really in your best interest, although it may feel like overkill if things are done properly by the contractor.

9. Move into your new bedroom and begin enjoying the new hot tub or spa that you naturally included with the design. By the way, did you put the white wine cooler near the hot tub? After all, it is your design.

The lender begins charging you interest on the loan at the moment that money is issued against the loan. As the loan amount increases, the required payments also increases.

Does this sound like a lot of hassle? Well, it is not a trivial amount of work, but look at it from the lenders' perspective. You are using their money and securing it with your house and the contractor's work. The safeguards also help you from getting involved with the wrong contractor, because your lender might very well know this contractor and whether he does very good or very poor work. Remember, the lenders do this every day. You do it once in a decade, or even less often.

There is an excellent chance that the lending institution wants to have an appraisal or a survey performed on your property if the addition affects the existing boundaries of the house. These cost money that comes out of your pocket. By the way, all these steps add time to the process.

QuickTip

Typical home improvement loans are issued at a few percentage points over the standard home mortgage interest rate, and are issued with a shorter amortization period, such as five years, although some automatically roll over into a standard 30-year mortgage loan when the construction period is completed. A home equity loan might have a typical amortization period of 15 years, but at a similar interest rate.

The decision to fund your loan is not made in a vacuum. The lender has specific ratios, or percentages, that your house and loan must meet to be approved. Ask your lender about the approval process, and he can probably tell you. In this way, you might want to scale back or expand the scope of construction work to keep your work in compliance with the bank's ratios. Otherwise, you must either fight the lender's loan committee for approval of the higher loan amount or change the plans anyway after you are turned down. Which one do you think it will be? That's right, change the plans unless you absolutely must have them just like they are. In that case, ask the lender what must be done financially to obtain the approval. Your lender will probably just tell you what to do. Remember that the lender approves loan deals all day and knows how to get things done quickly.

Don't let this process scare you away from obtaining home improvement loans. They have their place and can be used to your advantage as long as you know what to expect.

Refinancing

How many times in the last month have you been called by someone wanting you to change your long distance carrier, order another charge card, or refinance your house? Plenty, I'm sure.

There is a reason for the glut of telemarketing sales pitches for refinancing. Interest rates, at the time of this writing, are the lowest they have been in decades. If you got your original home financing in the late 1980s or early 1990s, you might have a 10% or higher interest rate on your home loan. Refinancing that loan at 7.5% could save you a bundle.

For example, assume that your $120,000 loan was financed at 10.5% over 30 years. Your monthly principal and interest payments are $1,097.69. The same loan amortized at 7.5% would cost you $839.06 per month. That is a savings of $258.63 per month, or a savings of almost 24%. That amount of savings makes a sizable dent in a new car payment, or it simply puts $3,103 more dollars into savings every year.

This argument is pretty strong for refinancing, which is why you are getting all the phone calls. The following are a few additional considerations that could affect your decision to refinance your current mortgage:

➤ Refinancing the loan may cost you 1–3% of the loan amount, along with document preparation and recording fees that can also run over $1,500. So, the minimum that this loan might cost you through a standard financial institution is $2,700. Divide $2,700 by $258.63, and you find that in 10 months you have saved enough money in monthly payments to pay off the refinancing fees. After that, the savings go straight into your pocket. This is called the break-even point for the refinance charges.

➤ If you have been paying on your loan for 15 years of a 30-year term, you are finally to the point that you are actually paying down the principal in sizable amounts. Starting all over from the beginning of a 30-year loan means that you start making mostly interest payments for 15 years before you are amortizing your principal amount at the same rate you are today. Which is better? You might find that refinancing at a lower interest rate lowers your required monthly payment but may cost you more interest payment expense over the life of the newer 30-year loan than paying for only 15 more years on your current, higher interest, higher payment loan. On the other hand, if you need to lower your monthly payments for personal reasons, refinancing is an excellent way to go.

➤ You might be planning to move in a few months, and refinancing is just not worth the cost or hassle.

➤ Your credit rating might not be adequate to qualify you for the refinance loan, even though the monthly payment is less than you already pay. Irrational? Sure seems that way to me, but this is just the way it is. Bankers! Go figure!

➤ You might consider increasing the amount of your loan when you refinance instead of taking out an equity loan on top of your first mortgage. The first mortgage rate is always lower than an equity loan rate, and the paperwork must only be completed once instead of twice.

➤ If you buy a house and finance it with less than 20% down payment, the lender is probably going to require that you take out Private Mortgage Insurance (PMI) that covers the mortgage payment should you go into default.

➤ Suppose you had a $120,000 loan that you had paid on for five years out of 30 at 10.5%. You still have 25 years to pay on the note. Suppose also that you chose to refinance the loan at 7.5% for 30 years but kept making payments on the loan just like you did on your old 10.5% note. Instead of paying off the old loan in 25 years, you now pay off the new loan in a little more than 15 years! That is a huge interest savings of: $1,097.69 per month (the mortgage payment at 10.5%) × 12 months × 10 years (the number of years saved) = $131,000! Now, if that doesn't get your attention, nothing will!

This last example may seem too good to be true, but it is true! By simply refinancing from 10.5% to 7.5%, and keeping your mortgage payment the same as it was with the old note, our example saved more than $130,000 in interest and paid off the loan sooner.

Voice of Experience

There are mortgage brokerage companies out there that can refinance your loan for free! Sound too good to be true? Maybe, but the offer might just be on the level. The brokerage house makes its money not only on the loan points and up-front fees, but also on the commissions paid to it by the lender who actually ends up funding the note. These commissions are called service release premiums within the industry.

The brokerage house rarely finances its own loans, but instead sells the loans to another financial institution, which is probably a bank. The lender pays the broker-age house a commission on the sale, which it can afford to do because of the interest income it makes off of the loan over the next thirty years.

When the brokerage house drops its up front fees to close the refinance deal with you, it is making up the lost up-front fees on the increased sales volume that it sees from having lower consumer cost. The brokerage pays its own bills from the lender's commission payments. Don't be afraid to negotiate the fees if you are a strong credit customer, because there is money to be saved if you just ask.

When is it time to refinance? The following are a few rules to get you started:

➤ Only refinance if you save money overall on the refinance.

➤ Only refinance for the amount of money that you realistically need to pay off the first mortgage and consolidate some of your other debts.

➤ If it takes you more than 18 months to recover the cost of refinancing with your reduced monthly payments, the interest rate reduction is not large enough, and you should wait.

➤ As a general rule of thumb, if you are within the first five years of your loan and can save 2% on your interest rate, you should probably look at refinancing. This is particularly true if you can find a lender that charges no up-front fees or points.

Sell It and Keep the Gain!

The recent 1997 tax law changes passed by Congress opened a great financial door for consumers who are also homeowners. You can now sell your principal residence once every two years and pocket the gain from the sale without paying any income tax on the gain. That's right. Keep the gain without paying income tax on it. The following are some of the requirements to qualify for this tax benefit:

➤ The sold home must have been your principal residence for two of the last five years. The years need not be consecutive, but there must be two of them.

➤ It must have been sold after May 7, 1997.

➤ Only the first $250,000 of gain is exempted for a single person, or a married person filing separately. This means you can pocket up to $250,000 profit on the sale of your home without paying taxes.

➤ Only the first $500,000 is exempted for a married couple filing jointly.

As with any major financial activity with tax consequences, verify your situation with a tax professional. This new law, however, opens the door for you to pocket some of the equity built up in your home and do something with it other than invest in another home of equal or greater value, which was the last tax rule on home sales until you were 55 or older. (Refer to the "Taxpayer Relief Act of 1997, Section 312: Exemption from Tax for Gain on Sale of Principal Residence," for more information.)

What Have You Got to Gain?

I talked a lot about gain in the last section, but I never really defined what it means from an IRS standpoint.

Use the following procedure to get a rough estimate of your gain on a piece of property:

1. First, you must determine the total sale amount for the residence you just sold.

2. You must then calculate your basis (base cost) for the property that you just sold. The explanation for calculating your base cost follows. The cost of selling your current residence is added into the basis of the property.

3. You then subtract the total from step 2 from the sale amount determined from step 1. This gives you a solid estimate of the gain.

QuickCaution

This procedure is potentially complicated, so please use this example as a rough starting point, and verify your calculations with your tax professional.

As a more detailed example, assume that you just sold a residence that you originally bought five years ago.

The process starts with determining the actual realized sale price of the property that you just sold—for example, $305,000. This amount is taken directly from the sales documents drawn up as part of the sale process.

Follow these steps to calculate the basis of the residence that you bought five years ago:

1. Start with the net purchase price of the house when you first bought it five years ago. (For this example, I use $135,000 as the purchase price.)

2. Determine the value of any major improvements such as an addition or major renovation of the building. (For example, $45,000 for adding 900 square feet.) This number is added to the amount in step 1.

3. Total any depreciation that might have been applied to the property. If it was used as a rental at any time since you have owned the property, you might have taken a depreciation deduction. (For example, $7,500 in depreciation for renting out several of the rooms.) This number is subtracted from the amount in step 1.

4. Determine the total cost of selling your current residence and add this to the net purchase price from step 1. This amount is generally the 6% real estate commission fees plus whatever other fees you might have incurred that are specifically related to selling the house. (For example, $305,000 × .06 = $18,300.)

5. Perform the required math to calculate the basis of the property. (For example, $135,000 (net purchase price) + $45,000 (improvements value) − $7,500 (depreciation deductions) + $18,300 (real estate commissions on sale) = $190,800.)

Calculate the gain realized on the sale of your residence by subtracting the basis from the total realized sale price. For example, $305,000 (realized sale price) − $190,800 (basis of sold property) = $114,200 is the net gain on sale. This amount is under the $250,000 ceiling for a single taxpayer, so no tax is paid on the gain assuming it was sold on or after May 7, 1997.

Selling and Buying Another Home

Assume that you sell a home that qualifies as your principal residence and is covered under the 1997 Tax Relief Act exemption. This means that you can take as much or as little of your house sale gain as you choose and apply it to the purchase of another residence. It is strictly a matter of personal financial preference, and taxes need not enter into the decision.

Now assume that you sell your home within two years of moving into it. Under these circumstances, you do not qualify for the exemption and are not entitled to the full $250,000/$500,000 exemption, but you may still be entitled to a portion of it, depending upon your specific circumstances. As always, these rules have so many restrictions and alternate interpretations, and the dollars involved can be so large that it is worth it to seek the advice of a tax professional. A few hundred dollars spent for credible advice might save you thousands in tax payments.

If you sell your house and realize a gain of more than the $250,000/$500,000 exemption limit, and then buy a house of equal to or greater value, you owe tax on the amount of gain realized over the exemption limit that applies to you.

Using Quicken to Track Home Sale Items

A common theme permeates this entire topic: You must keep records on the components that comprise the basis of your prior home, the selling costs associated with the sale of that home, and the costs associated with the purchase of your new home. This is where Quicken makes life easier. Although you need to keep paper copies of these records for IRS purposes, you can easily keep track of the numbers in Quicken by creating the appropriate dedicated accounts and categories and making the required bookkeeping entries.

Most of your bookkeeping entries involve disbursing checking or credit card transaction amounts into the proper expense categories. As long as the accounts and categories already exist, this is a simple task.

The following are some recommendations regarding Quicken accounts and categories that should get you started with effective bookkeeping records:

➤ **Asset Account for Prior Residence**   You not only set the beginning balance of this account at the house's initial purchase price, but you also place all items that increase the basis of the home into this account.

➤ **Depreciation Expense Account for Prior Residence**   Used if you plan to rent out a portion and take the depreciation expense deduction.

➤ **Maintenance Expense Account for Prior Residence**   Tracks all expenses that are typically not deductible unless you rent out the property.

➤ **Property Tax Expense Account for Prior Residence**   Tracks tax deductible property tax expenses.

➤ **Asset Account for New Residence** You not only set the beginning balance of this account at the house's initial purchase price, but you also place all items that increase the basis of the home into this account.

➤ **Depreciation Expense Account for New Residence**   Records all depreciation expenses you may take against your new residence should you rent it out during your period of ownership.

➤ **Maintenance Expense Account for New Residence**

➤ **Property Tax Expense Account for New Residence**   These are absolutely tax deductible and should be tracked.

QuickCaution

I recommend that you place your house sale/purchase documents in a secure place such as a fireproof safe in your home or, even better, in a safe deposit box at your bank. Why? Simply stated, these documents can have profound tax implications if lost, and they are time consuming to replace. Place them somewhere safe, where you don't need to worry about them, and where you know they will be when you need them.

Voice of Experience

When tracking maintenance on two separate houses, I like to create the maintenance, depreciation, and property tax categories as subcategories under their respective main categories. For example, if tracking two houses (one on Ogden Avenue and the other on Norwalk Street), I first create a category called Home Maint and then create a subcategory called Ogden Maint for the Odgen Avenue house and Norwalk Maint for the house on Norwalk Street. This way, the two maintenance categories get subdivided when reporting, but all home maintenance is totaled under a single category.

This Quicken account setup assumes that you pay your property taxes and insurance directly and don't use an escrow account. Escrow accounts require another asset account named something like Ogden Escrow, for the Ogden Avenue house. You make payments into this escrow account when you write your mortgage check. This is simply done by adding another split line item to the mortgage memorized transaction. The escrow account is like a cash reserve account; when the lender pays taxes and insurance from escrow, you simply decrease the amount in the escrow account and increase the property tax and insurance expense accounts.

The Least You Need to Know

➤ Gain is tax free on the sale of your principal residence up $250,000 for a single person and $500,000 for a married couple filing jointly.

➤ Accurate paper and accounting records are needed to fully take advantage of the taxable exempt gain rules.

➤ Refinancing a higher interest mortgage loan for a lower interest loan can save more than a hundred thousand dollars over the life of the loan.

➤ Tracking real estate transactions with Quicken categories/subcategories is easy and informative.

Chapter 14

Cars, Cars, and More Cars

In This Chapter

➤ Decide whether a new or used car is right for you

➤ Determine the overall cost of a car purchase

➤ Compare leasing to buying when getting a car

➤ Learn how to avoid being "upside down" on a car loan

➤ Enter the vehicle expense tracking data into Quicken

It is difficult to function in American life without a vehicle, unless you live in a city with excellent public transportation, such as New York or Chicago. Even in these cities, a lot of people still own cars simply because they make life easier.

Buying a home and a vehicle such as a car or truck are the two largest purchases most people make in their lives, but few people really work to decrease the cost of vehicle ownership. This chapter looks at the costs associated with owning a vehicle and how Quicken can be used to track these costs. The chapter uses the car terminology, but applies to the purchase of any vehicle including a truck, van, minivan, or sport utility.

The Car Purchases—New Versus Used

Have you ever owned a new car and had to trade it in within two years of the purchase date? Did it cost you money to pay off the loan so that you could sell the car? If not, you were lucky. It has happened to me and to others I know. They purchased a car and financed it over 48 months and then had to sell after two years.

The shock came when they learned how much the dealer was willing to give in trade for their car and how much principal had actually been repaid on their loan. Almost always, the car had devalued faster than the decrease in principal, and they had to add money to that offered by the dealer to sell their earlier car.

I have a saying, and a belief, that the value of a new car decreases by thousands of dollars the second you drive it off of the dealer's lot. Don't believe it is true? Ask a dealer what he will give you for the car you are about to purchase if you were offering it in trade after having driven it for only a month. After you learn this simple rule about cars, your financial relationship with them will always be on a firmer footing.

Cars are a money drain. They never (except for collectable cars) increase in value. They always decrease in value. Period. You can only minimize the amount that the car costs you per year. You cannot save money by owning a car unless car ownership saves you money in alternate transportation costs.

So, if cars cost you money, why own one? My opinion is that they provide freedom with respect to time in that you don't have to travel around the public transportation schedules, convenience in that you can take more stuff with you when you travel, security in that you don't need to take public transportation during low traffic hours, flexibility in that you can live in town and work in another with minimal inconvenience, and personal reward in that you can travel to an unfamiliar location and still feel like a little of your home travels with you.

Why buy used instead of new? This is a simple answer, in my book. Buy a car with 8,000–12,000 miles on it that is more than 1 year old, and you save the initial loss associated with driving the car off of the lot. This can save thousands of dollars on the purchase price of the car and still provide you with reliable transportation.

Some people view their cars as a status symbol and are willing to pay what it takes to have their new toy. I know people who dislike driving a car that is more than 12 months old, and buy a new car every year. That is what they like to do, and they pay the price for their habit. Leasing is a viable alternative to buying for these people because financial management does not drive their car purchase and use.

Others view a car as a tool that gets them from here to there and want the most reliable tool for the least amount of money. In case you haven't figured it out yet, this is the category that I fall into. I have driven more than one car over 100,000 miles, and I still felt like I got ripped off when I sold it.

Voice of Experience

My last car was a Chrysler Le Baron GTS that I bought new in 1985 and sold in 1994 as an $800 trade-in on another used car. It had 114,000 miles on it and looked pretty rough, so I thought that was a good price. Plus, I was just ready for a new car.

A few days after selling it, I got a call from a local used car dealer who said that he had a customer who wanted to buy the car and wanted to know how often the oil was changed. I answered and asked what they were selling the car for. The dealer answered $2,800! I almost fell out of my chair.

The following are a few recommendations if you decide to take the plunge on a used car instead of buying new:

➤ Know that you are buying the car at your own risk, unless you buy it from a dealer who provides some type of warranty.

➤ Remember that you don't know anything about this car's history unless it was owned by somebody you know or you have access to the maintenance records.

➤ Make sure that you take it for a long enough test drive that you get a comfortable feeling about the car. Check reverse, forward, the brakes, steering, radio, A/C, heat, and so on until you feel as if you have been paranoid. It will save surprises later.

➤ Above all, don't be rushed into making a snap decision. If you feel pressured, I suggest walking away from the deal. The car should sell itself.

➤ Have a mechanic check out the car for you. Ask your local garage, service station, or friend who knows cars to check it out for you if you don't have the background yourself. There are companies, such as LemonBusters (`http://www.lemonbusters.com`), who specialize in used car inspections for a nominal fee—when compared to the cost of a new engine or transmission. Get an estimate of the cost of repairs to bring the car up to a safe, reliable standard. This helps in negotiating a fair purchase price.

➤ Check the odometer reading and the condition of the car. If the odometer reads 35,000 and the car is trashed, it probably means 135,000 or more. Walk away.

➤ Check the title for important sounding terms such as "reconditioned," which means that the car was once considered a total loss by an insurance company.

➤ Check out the car's price by looking it up in the N.A.D.A. used car price book, which is available at any bookstore or library. In fact, you can check out the national average purchase price for the car online at http://www.edmunds.com or get your trade-in price by viewing the Kelley Bluebook information at http://www.kbb.com.

Everyone likes driving around in a new car. It is truly one of life's pleasures, but you pay for the privilege. If money is tight and you like to turn over your cars every 3–4 years, which is the national average, then I suggest you look at a used car with low mileage. You pay less for the car, you pay it off sooner, and you probably get your 3–4 years of use before having any major mechanical troubles as long as you perform the required routine maintenance.

Buying a New Car for Long-Term Ownership

Nobody wants his or her car to break down on a freeway at 2 a.m. A new car minimizes the likelihood of this happening because it should be more mechanically sound than a used one. A new car can almost be thought of as insurance against this happening. But, just like insurance, a new car has a price tag associated with its ownership.

Take a look at Table 14.1 to see the truncated amortization schedule associated with a new car paid off over a 5-year period, with a 60-month term, and at an 9% interest rate. Assume that the car cost $22,000 and that you put no money down.

Table 14.1 Amortizing a Five-Year Car Note

Year	Balance	% Remaining
0	$22,000	100%
1	$18,668	85%
2	$14,708	67%
3	$10,375	47%
4	$ 5,637	26%
5	$ 0	0%
Interest Paid: $5,401		

For the previous example, I used an actual 1997 model car with a retail price of around $22,000 from a major manufacturer. I then looked at its financial situation should you sell it in 1998. The loan balance is $18,668, as shown in Table 14.1, whereas its market value is $14,335, and its trade-in value is $11,900 as obtained from the Edmund's Web site. This is called being "upside down" on a car loan.

The loan principal had decreased by around $3,400, but the car had decreased in value either $8,365 or $10,800 depending upon whether you sold it yourself at retail or traded it in for a new car.

Talkin' Money

An upside-down loan is when the amount still owed on the loan is greater than the value of the item purchased with the loaned money.

The following is a financial summary of what happened to this car in its first year of existence if you sold it at retail:

➤ You made loan payments of $5,480 over the 12 months.

➤ The car cost $22,000 when first purchased in 1997.

➤ The car sells at $14,335 in 1998. This is $8,365 less than its original cost to you.

➤ You must give the lender who holds the loan on the car $18,668 – $14,335 = $4,333 to pay off the loan difference between what you sold the car for and the amount of loan principal still outstanding.

➤ The total cost to you of having this car for a year is $5,480 (payments) + $4,333 (loan payoff) = $9,813, or $818 per month, over 12 months.

➤ Assuming that you need a car, you have to turn around and repeat this process again for your next car.

You can see that turning over your car on a yearly basis becomes an expensive hobby.

Holding your car for a longer period of time, on the other hand, makes buying a new car look financially more reasonable. Assume that you put the average 12,000 miles per year on your car and that your car remains reliable up to 84,000 miles. Your car can be reliable for up to seven years (84000/12,000) and still have some resale value at the end of the seven years. For example, the same car model from year 1991 is priced at $5,495 market value and $3,790 trade-in. The following is a summary of the financial analysis associated with holding your car for seven years and then selling it at market value:

➤ The car is sold for $5,495 at the end of the seven years.

➤ You made $27,360 in car payments over the 60 months of the loan.

➤ Your net expense for the car is $27,360 (payments) – $5,495 (resale price) = $21,865. The car holding period is 84 months (7 years), so your cost per month for holding the car is $260 per month.

This analysis does not include maintenance costs and other items that inevitably occur over the life of a car, but these incidental expenses would have to be large to offset the savings. Should you hold the car for an even longer period of time, the monthly cost becomes even smaller.

Holding a new car for seven years or more drops the monthly cost of ownership to the point you might actually be able to talk yourself into buying a more expensive, more reliable car that can run for 150,000 miles or more. Amortizing the cost of a $35,000 car over a 13-year period might drop the monthly expense down to where you can have a high quality driving experience and not pay high premium prices.

Lease to Drive More Car for Less Money

If you are the type of person who holds a car for less than two years, and have traditionally bought and sold your cars, you should now be shaking your head in agreement with the prior two sections. You know how expensive this rapid turnover is and know that it can cost you tens of thousands of dollars when repeated over a number of cars, but you still might want that new car feeling around you year after year. I have good news. Leasing was designed just for you.

When you lease a car, you never really own it. You basically rent the car for a few years from a leasing agent and then give it back. You don't create equity, pay off a loan, or actually own anything by the time you give back the car and terminate the lease.

Leasing is attractive to those people who continually want to drive a new car, because the overall payments during the leasing period are generally lower than the cost of buying and selling the same car over the same period.

The lease payment is based on the following components:

➤ **Capitalized cost**   The purchase price that you agreed to pay for the car.

➤ **Residual value**   The value of the car at the end of the lease period (which is the agreed upon estimated market value of the car at the end of the lease).

➤ **Capitalized cost reduction**   The down payment you make when you sign the lease.

➤ **Money factor**   The interest you pay for borrowing the money. This value varies with the company, and you should clearly understand how it is calculated before signing the lease.

The money factor varies. It can be calculated as the periodic interest rate divided by 24, independently of the length of the lease period. It is sometimes reached by dividing the prevailing interest rate by the number of months in the lease. Or the money factor might be any arbitrary calculation determined by the leasing company.

Talkin' Money

Term depreciation is the amount that the item being leased decreases in value over the duration of the lease. It is calculated by subtracting the residual value from the capitalized cost less the capitalized cost reduction.

Lease rate is a nebulous term that means different things to different lenders, and probably is not the same as the annual percentage rate used for a conventional loan. Verify the leasing company's lease rate calculations to know the interest charges you pay and how they are calculated.

The lease arrangement does not require that you pay for the entire car, assuming that the car is expected to retain some residual value at lease termination. Amortizing less capital cost generally means that the monthly lease payment is lower, but remember that the lease period is also shorter, which generally increases the payment.

Make sure that you consider the following items when negotiating your lease:

➤ Negotiate the lowest possible purchase price for the car.

➤ Negotiate the highest possible residual value for the car. Check out the *Automotive Lease Guide* for industry standard residual value estimates.

➤ Negotiate the highest possible annual mileage allowance for the lease term. You have to pay a per-mile charge for each additional mile over the annual allowance and this can run into a lot of money.

➤ Get your credit pre-approved before you go see the dealer, because this makes you a much stronger buyer and increases your negotiating position.

➤ Make sure that you only lease for the term of the manufacturer warranty to avoid responsibility for any major repairs.

➤ Look for a subvented lease deal, which is a lease that is subsidized by the manufacturer. This often provides you with a higher residual value, lower money factor, and more favorable terms because the manufacturer is subsidizing the financial arrangement.

➤ Only sign a closed end lease where the lease termination fees are minimal as long as the car is in reasonable condition and the mileage is not excessive. You should know from the beginning what lease-end charges could be assessed. If you cannot get this, don't sign the lease.

➤ Only sign a lease that irrevocably defines the residual value of the car, or you could find yourself paying the difference between the assumed residual value and the fair market value of the car when your lease period ends. Ouch!

➤ Consider adding gap insurance to your lease to protect you from getting stuck with a lease payoff amount if the car is stolen during your lease period. It shouldn't cost more than a few hundred dollars, and it might be included in the lease rate.

➤ Try not to make a down payment (capital cost reduction, remember?) because this increases the cost of getting into the lease, and it defeats the low cost purpose of leasing.

➤ Verify your costs if you terminate the lease early, just so you know what you are signing.

➤ Verify the minimum insurance required by the lease agreement before you sign, and factor that into your financial estimates.

Your choices do not stop here when dealing with a leased automobile. Assume that you really liked this car and did not put the miles on it that you expected, so the car is still in good condition. After you reach the end of your lease agreement, you can choose from several options in determining your best approach to closing out the lease:

➤ You can give the car back to the lessor, who is really the owner of the car, and walk home—unless you bought another car or like taking public transportation.

➤ You can purchase the leased vehicle for the residual value stated in your lease agreement. This could be a viable option if the car has not decreased in value as much as expected and remains in good condition. Make sure that you arrange your financing in advance of the termination date if you want to exercise this option.

➤ You can extend the lease period, usually at the same monthly payment level.

➤ Trade the previously leased vehicle in for a new vehicle covered under a new lease agreement.

➤ Take out a new lease agreement on your previously leased car, essentially to creating a used car lease.

Take a look at the following section to review the details associated with leasing or buying the same $22,000 car you reviewed in the preceding section.

Voice of Experience

Make sure that you let your lessor know in writing that you plan to terminate the lease at the end of the agreed upon period. I missed their notice—it was on the statement in 6 point type—and did not notify the lessor in writing. Instead, I called them at the end of my lease agreement and told them that I planned to pay the residual value. At that time, I was notified that my lease had extended automatically for a year at the same payment level and that I was now obligated to pay another year in lease payments and the agreed upon residual amount.

I went ballistic and then went to see my attorney, who informed me that I had little legal ground to stand on because the agreement I signed stated this as the proper procedure, even though it was unconscionable. A lot of pushing and many threats of lawsuits later, we worked out an arrangement that was fair to all parties. I really was lucky under the circumstances.

Make sure that you comply with the termination clause required actions completely or you could be caught like I was.

Leasing and Buying Compared

You should expect by this point in the book to get a specific financial example that compares leasing to buying for the same car. Here it is.

The example assumes that you intend to lease the same $22,000 car you looked at purchasing in the previous section. Table 14.2 lists the financial analysis associated with leasing this car for a three-year period.

Table 14.2   Calculating Lease Payments and Costs

Lease Variable	Amount	Calculation
Capitalized Cost	$22,000	Negotiated Price
Residual Value	$12,100	55% of Purchase price
Term Depreciation	$9,900	$22,000 – $12,100
Monthly Depreciation	$275	$9,900 / 36 = $275
Money Factor	0.0033	.08 / 24 or 8% / 24
Monthly Interest	$112.53	($22,000 + $12,100) × .0033
Total Monthly Payment	$387.53	$275 + $112.53 = $387.53
36 Month Total	$13,951.08	$387.53 × 36 = $13,951.08

Sales tax and other charges such as dealer prep, destination charge, acquisition fee, security deposit, and so on must be added to the analysis to get a completely accurate picture.

The analysis in Table 14.1 shows a total expense of $27,401 over a five year period, where the leasing analysis in Table 14.2 shows a total expense of $13,951.08 over three years, or $4,650 per year. At the end of those three years, assume that you exercise one of the options outlined in the earlier section. If you choose to get another car of similar value that has a similar monthly lease payment, you repeat the process and end up with a five year cost of ownership equal to $23,251 ($13,951 + $4,650 + $4,650). This is less than the total cost of ownership outlined in Table 14.1, but you still don't own anything with a lease where the car can then be resold to recover some of its cost. If you compare the two options over a longer period of time than 2–3 years, buying almost always represents the more economical option.

QuickTip

Multiplying the money factor by 2400 provides a rough estimate of the interest rate applied to the lease. In addition, lessors are not required to reveal the lease factor as part of the negotiations. You can get a rough estimate by first calculating the monthly depreciation, subtracting that amount from the monthly lease payment, dividing that number by the sum of the capitalized cost plus the residual value, and multiplying that result by 2400. Does this sound complicated? I think so, and it just gives you a taste of the complexity associated with lease financing.

Tracking Automobile Costs with Quicken

The standard Quicken installation includes several categories related to automobile ownership. They can be viewed by selecting the **Lists** menu, and then selecting the **Category/Transfers** option, or simply by pressing **Alt+C**. Click the **Expense Categories** tab to display only expense-related items. (In some versions of Quicken, you need to click **Options** and choose **Display Expense Categories** from the menu that pops up.)

The following are the default automobile-related expense categories provided by Quicken:

➤ **Auto main category** Used as a central heading under which other expenses can be grouped.

➤ **Fuel subcategory** Used for tracking gas expenses.

➤ **Insurance subcategory** Used for tracking vehicle insurance expenses.

➤ **Service subcategory** Used for tracking service and maintenance expenses, such as oil changes, brake repair, and other service items.

Neither the vehicle loan liability account nor the auto loan interest expense category are automatically created with the default installation. You also need to add an account to track the automobile asset itself because it is not automatically provided. Also, this category structure does not easily allow you to break out expenses associated with multiple vehicle households. There is also no account for tracking vehicle registration expenses, which is a tax deductible item. I suggest you add the following categories and accounts to your Quicken setup:

➤ Create an asset account for the purchased vehicle and set its starting balance at the vehicle's initial purchase price. This is done by resting your cursor over the **My Accounts** icon, selecting the **Create** a **New Account** option and following the steps to create a new asset account with a name representative of your vehicle, such as **Camaro 96**. (Some versions of Quicken require you to press Ctrl+A and click the **New** button on the button bar.)

➤ Repeat the above steps until you have created an asset account for each of your vehicles.

➤ Rename the default **Auto** main category to something indicative of the expenses being tracked, such as **Camaro 96 Exp**. This is done by right clicking the **Auto** category listing, selecting **Edit** from the list, and then changing the **Name** and **Description** to something that make sense to you.

➤ Create a new category for each additional vehicle, and then create the insurance, fuel, and insurance subcategories needed for tracking this vehicle's expenses.

➤ Create a subcategory for tracking vehicle registration under each of the vehicle main categories.

➤ Create a liability account for tracking your vehicle loans. This is done by resting the cursor over the **Home and Car** icon, selecting the **Set Up or Track a Loan** option, clicking the **New** button, and following the instructions. This wizard leads you through creating both the liability account and the interest expense tracking account.

➤ Set up a new expense main category called **AutoLoanInterest**, and then create subcategories under this main category for tracking the interest associated with each of your vehicle loans.

QuickTip

You can always change the relationship between your main and subcategories at a later date if you so desire. The most important thing is to have a category created somewhere that separately tracks your expenses at the desired level of detail.

The preceding category creation recommendations enable you to track expenses by vehicle, such as Camaro 96. This enables you to track all expenses related to that particular vehicle, which is the way I prefer to track my expenses.

You could also set up the categories so that the overall fuel expenses are tracked, and subcategories track fuel for each of the vehicles. Create Fuel as a main category, and create a separate fuel subcategory for each of the vehicles.

This way you track and total the main category expense item, such as Fuel, and separately monitor fuel expenses for each of the vehicles as a subcategory under Fuel.

After these categories and accounts are created, select the proper category or account when disbursing the funds from the checking, credit card, or cash accounts. Use the splits and automated transactions to speed up the bookkeeping process.

The Least You Need to Know

➤ Buy a car that you plan to keep for more than five years.

➤ Lease a car if you plan to turn it over every two years.

➤ You really need to keep a car for at least three years to avoid being upside down on a car note.

➤ Tracking vehicle expenses is a simple task with Quicken, and special categories are automatically created.

➤ If you want to track expenses related to multiple vehicles, you have to create new categories and asset and liability accounts.

Part 4

Getting Better Mileage with Smarter Choices

Nobody ever expects the worst to happen to them, but life is often full of surprises. Sometimes those surprises are a booming stock market and huge investment returns. Sometimes the surprise is a 12% downturn in the Dow. Sometimes the surprise is an unwelcome theft, fire, accident, or medical emergency.

This part covers strategies for dealing with future uncertainties in your life. Insurance covers you if something unfortunate happens. Your investments take advantage of the future benefits of money markets and company stocks. Work your way through this part to make sure that you have the proper financial safety nets in place to deal with whatever the future holds.

Chapter 15

Cover Your Personal Assets

In This Chapter

➤ Decide between term and other forms of life insurance

➤ Determine your required level of life insurance coverage

➤ Decide whether disability insurance is right for you

➤ Use Quicken to compare insurance costs

➤ Set up Quicken accounts to properly track insurance items

Paying insurance premiums often feels similar to washing money down the drain, until you need to collect on the policy. Then you are really glad you had the foresight to get the insurance.

It is difficult to imagine a well-rounded financial picture that does not include some combination of life, disability, and health insurance coverage. This chapter introduces you to several forms of insurance and outlines methods for you to use in determining the right insurance type and coverage level for your situation. We also discuss how you can use Quicken to compare insurance costs and to track insurance items.

Life Insurance Issues

It is time to face the fact that nobody gets out of this game of life alive. At some point in your life, you die. You won't much care what happens after you die, but those you leave behind have to deal with your absence. (In this case, we'll assume that this person is your spouse.)

A number of financial things have to be dealt with after somebody passes away. The following are just a few of the things that need to be considered if you are married and want to be prepared for the worst:

➤ Funeral expenses that can run between $4,000 and $10,000 depending on what you have in mind (or what your spouse wanted).

➤ Emergency expenses associated with the funeral, such as last minute travel arrangements for family members living in other cities.

➤ Paying off the mortgage with life insurance or other inheritance (if that is a financially wise thing to do).

➤ Estate taxes, which vary based on the value of your estate and the mix of assets.

➤ Transition costs for those people left behind to cope with your not being there. Believe it or not, some people miss you, and it may take them some time to get over your loss. They may not feel much like working, so the financial cushion gives them some breathing room. Spouse education or retraining expenses would fall into this category.

➤ How will your family support itself without you, if you are the primary money-maker, or if your contribution is keeping the daily household running.

➤ Paying for child care if you are the one taking care of the kids.

➤ Paying for home nursing if you are someone taking care of another person requiring medical support (possibly a parent with ailing health or a sick child).

QuickTip

Check with your company, Social Security, and any other related organizations, such as the Veteran's Administration (VA), to see whether they have programs that help defray the funeral costs based on the deceased's specific circumstances. For example, the VA pays the funeral expenses for anyone who dies in a VA hospital. They also pay for a headstone, under specific circumstances.

Are you starting to get the picture? You contribute in ways that are invisible while you are around but highly visible when you are not around to do them. Your death alone causes hardships on those left behind, and it is the gracious thing to at least provide enough money for your funeral expenses.

Most people plan for retirement and really don't start planning for their death until the grim reaper is at their door or do not plan for their death at all. What a mess this causes. (Chapter 23, "You Can't Take It with You, So Plan Your Estate Now," deals with the intricacies of estate planning.)

Making sure that your family is financially secure is a critical part of financial planning. I have seen people pass away knowing that those left behind are financially protected. I have also known people who approach their mortality unsure about the financial condition of the ones left behind. The pending feeling of desperation that appears in those with concerns is enough to make you start planning for your death today.

You can offer your loved ones little emotional support after you pass away, but you can plan for their financial support by taking concrete steps today.

It is not necessary that you have life insurance, but it is probably a part of your estate plan unless you have amassed enough of a nest egg that your loved ones can live comfortably without the life insurance.

Life insurance is used as gap insurance, because it provides the money needed to cover the gap between the amount of money needed for your loved ones to live in a financially secure way and the amount of money provided by your estate without the life insurance. Without the gap insurance money, financial hardship could result.

QuickTip

Gap insurance is the amount of life insurance coverage needed to cover the difference between your survivors' monthly expenses and the amount of money that can be drawn out of your estate.

If your estate is large enough to comfortably provide for those left behind, you might not need life insurance. If not, life insurance should be one of your top priority financial planning items. Depending upon the size of your estate, the entire amount of life insurance benefit provided by the policy might pass to your heirs on a tax-free basis.

Life insurance comes in different flavors: term and cash life. Each category has its own variations, but the overall goal of the insurance is always the same—to ensure that you have enough coverage to handle your final expenses and gap insurance.

How Much Is Enough?

You hear all kinds of estimates regarding the minimum amount of life insurance you should carry. Some people say that two times your annual salary is enough. Others say 10 times your annual salary is the right number. I say that the amount needed to cover your gap income needs is enough. This amount varies with each individual set of circumstances and is often presented as a multiple of your annual income.

QuickTip

In general, you probably need anywhere between 2 and 10 times your annual salary in life insurance. Perform the detailed analysis to get a solid idea of where your requirements lie.

Calculating that gap income insurance is not a trivial matter. To do it properly requires some time and detailed analysis on your part. Luckily, Quicken makes this process much simpler than trying to do it from scratch because you should already have your financial data in the system.

This data provides you with a historical record of your expenses and income. From this you can calculate your gap insurance needs.

Remember from the earlier section that the gap insurance is there to cover the difference between what is provided by your nest egg and what is needed to cover your funeral expenses and also to support those left behind. This amount of money varies based on your situation:

➤ If you are young and single, with no children and minimal financial obligations, you may just need enough to cover your funeral expenses, estate administration fees, and leave a few extra dollars for your family.

➤ If you are young and single but financially support a sick parent, you have to leave enough to cover your parent's medical maintenance expenses for whatever you estimate that parent's surviving years may be.

➤ If you are the sole working parent of a household, you need to leave enough to cover the period of time your surviving spouse will take to get over your loss, retrain and actually find a job, and if needed, a little extra to cover the difference between your spouse's expected income level and the one you leave behind.

➤ If you are one of two working parents in your household, the situation is not as critical, but you still should allow enough money for your spouse to get over your loss and make up for your portion of the income that is needed to cover family expenses.

Are you getting the picture? There is no definite multiplier rule that is right for you. Think about your requirements as being divided into three basic areas:

➤ Short-term expenses directly related to your passing away

➤ Intermediate major expenses, such as taxes, educating your spouse for new employment, education expenses for your children, or even paying off the mortgage

➤ Longer term continuing expenses, such as making the car payments, mortgage payments, food, utilities, and so on

Take a look at Table 15.1 to figure the amount that is right for you.

The table shows that the short-term and intermediate-term items can be treated almost as lump sum financial requirements because they are needed within 12 months of your passing. The continuing expenses recur on a monthly basis for an extended period of time and maybe for the remaining life of your spouse or other loved one.

Table 15.1   Estimating the Overall Financial Requirements of Those Left Behind After You Pass Away

Short-Term Immediate Expenses

Funeral expenses

Medical expenses related to your passing

Last minute expenses related to your passing

The various miscellaneous expenses that always accompany the loss of a loved one (This might even include a vacation fund or a psychological counseling fund for the surviving family members.)

Total: $_____

Intermediate Expenses

Federal state and local taxes that were already due when you passed away, or those that are expected due from your passing

Tuition or retraining expenses related to spouse retraining

Tuition expenses for children already in school who depended on your income to pay their way

Paying of the mortgage or car note to provide the surviving spouse with a little more breathing room

Total: $_____

Annual Continuing Expenses

Utilities

Food

Car and mortgage payments (if not already paid off with intermediate expenses)

Insurance

Household maintenance

Timeshare and/or second home maintenance expenses

Retirement planning for surviving spouse

Clothing

Federal, state, and local taxes

Recreation (yes, they take vacations after you are gone)

All the other daily living expenses incurred by active family life

Monthly Total: $_____

Annual Total: $_____ for _____ number of years

There is some good news in the continuing expenses category because you can allow the power of compounded interest to work for you in helping to pay these expenses. The short and intermediate term expenses must be covered in full from the point where you die. Take a look at Table 15.2 to determine how you pay these expenses.

Table 15.2   Paying Your Survivor's Expenses

1. Overall net worth. $_____

2. Amount of liquid assets. $_____

3. Six months of living expenses. $_____

4. Sum of short and intermediate expenses. $_____

5. Subtract the sum of line 3 + 4 from line 2. This is the amount of pension, Social Security, and other insurance coverage needed to cover the short and intermediate expenses, assuming no taxes are taken from the insurance. Factor tax expenses in accordingly, if applicable. $_____

6. Total the after-tax monthly income expected from spouse salary, your recurring survivor income. $_____

7. Total the after-tax monthly income expected from existing investments. $_____

8. Total the continuing monthly expenses from Table 15.1. $_____

9. Subtract line 8 from total of lines 6 + 7. This is the net (after tax) amount of monthly income required to cover your income loss to the family. $_____

10. Multiply the number from line 9 by 12 to determine the annual gap insurance income required. $_____

11. Determine a reasonable annual portfolio return rate.   _____%

12. Divide the number from line 10 by the fractional equivalent of the return rate used in line 11. For example, assume line 9 = $25,200 and the annual return rate is 8%, then the division would be $25,200 / .08 = $315,000.

13. Add the number from line 12 to the number found in line 5 to get the total estimated insurance you should have. $_____

The amount you calculate for line 13 of table 15.2 represents the minimum amount of insurance you must have to allow your survivors to live in a comparable style to that lived while you were still around. If you are performing the calculation to cover the loss of a spouse that takes care of the household, you should increase the expenses as needed to cover the increased cost of daycare or other domestic help.

Your insurance needs vary with the income expected from investments, expense level, and personal desires such as paying off the mortgage. Also, do the best you can to estimate the taxes associated with the estimated incomes and try to estimate on the high side, because your survivors would rather that you had more insurance instead of less.

Your need for life insurance might decrease as you get older because your investment income should increase and your mortgage should be closer to being paid off. In addition, your children are probably through school and your overall expenses are probably lower.

Medical expenses increase as you get older, but this can be handled with the proper insurance coverage and really should not be included in this analysis as anything other than an insurance expense to be paid.

Avoid optimizing too much and putting your heirs in a difficult position. If you make the assumption that your surviving spouse will only live for 15 years after your death, and he/she doesn't join you for 25 years, your spouse could be left with minimal income if you optimized an annuity for only a 15-year period. It is always better to have extra money than not enough, so I encourage you to err on the side of having a little left over.

> **QuickCaution**
>
> Beware of the Social Security blackout ages and how they affect income streams. The surviving parent stops receiving child payments when the child reaches 16. The child stops receiving payments when he/she reaches 18. Payments to the spouse do not pick up until he/she reaches 60. It is difficult to anticipate all possible changes, but these you can predict and accommodate.

Insurance Strictly for the Big "Adios"

Life insurance can be purchased to provide a specific amount of coverage for a specific period of time. This is called term coverage because the policy is applicable for a specified term, or period of time. Term insurance policies are usually issued for 1-, 5-, 10-, and 20-year time periods. The premium paid during the period of the insurance term remains the same throughout the life of the policy. Every time you renew the policy, which results from happily having outlived the policy, you can expect your premiums to increase because you are now older and a higher life insurance risk. Try to get term insurance in your 60s, and you understand the benefits associated with buying insurance earlier in your life. The premiums are usually staggering and probably not worth it.

Be clear on one thing regarding term life insurance. The only way you ever collect money from a term policy is to die, which means you never see a nickel from a term policy, but your surviving family members would.

Term life insurance coverage is designed to provide a death benefit only and does not provide any investment benefits associated with cash value policies. (See the next section for cash value policy coverage.) The major benefit with term insurance is that it is inexpensive when compared to cash value policies. Most investors who go with term policies do so for the lower premium. They then invest the premium difference between the term and cash value policies at a higher rate than that offered by the life insurance company.

Some people go with term insurance because they believe that their investments pay off substantially enough so that they do not need life insurance after the term runs out.

Insurance as an Investment

The theory behind cash value policies is this: You are going to be putting your money into a life insurance account anyway, simply to get your required life insurance coverage. Why not put that money into an account that earns you some interest and actually increases in value over the years? In other words, your monthly life insurance premium payments actually build up some cash value over the years. How that cash value accumulates and what you can do with it depends on the type of policy chosen. Keep in mind that you must cash in the policy to receive the cash value. If you keep the policy until you die, your heirs will only receive the face value of the policy.

➤ Whole life policies, also called straight life, are policies where you pay a set premium over the term of the policy, assumed to be your lifetime. The premiums are higher than term because this policy also provides you with a tax-deferred investment on the premiums paid. You still get your life insurance benefit coverage, but you also make tax deferred interest on your investment. This policy builds up to a cash value, usually at the rate of 4–10% per year. You can borrow money from the cash value if you choose, or use the cash value to pay your premiums in the form of an annuity or single payment negotiated with your insurance company.

➤ Universal life policies are cash value policies, but the premium payment schedules are more flexible. You can also vary the amount of coverage provided as your situation changes. These accounts typically invest your cash value into higher-yield instruments such as money markets. This means that your returns vary with the market, as opposed to the whole life policy that is a guaranteed return. You still maintain your specified life insurance coverage unless you stop making premium payments. Some people like these policies for the detailed reporting, which breaks out how your premium is spent with respect to insurance coverage, savings, and administrative costs.

➤ Variable life insurance is also a cash value plan, but it allows you more flexibility on where your cash value is invested as long as it is offered by the insurance company. The death benefit may vary over the life of the policy but never drops below the amount you originally contracted for.

When you take out life insurance, you establish a lifelong partnership with your insurance carrier. Check them out financially before moving in with them. Use the Quicken features or check with your state's board of insurance for details about their financial condition.

Think about life insurance in the following way. It is always basically term insurance, with the term ending when you die. You are simply trying to find the best financial way to pay for that coverage. Cash value policies differ from term in that you get flat premiums over the life of the policy and can even set it up so that the account premiums are paid out of the account itself. When term insurance ends, it ends. Period. It is like a lease on a car because when it is over, you have nothing to show for it, unless you died. That is a tough way to get a return on investment and one you can only use once in your life.

Insuring Your Kids

Is it a good idea to insure your children? Once again, it depends on your particular circumstances. There is something to be said for taking out a cash value policy for your children when they are young, because you get death benefit coverage, which hopefully will not be used, and also build up a cash value for your children to use when they are older if they cash in the policy. You also lock in a premium that is very low given the young age at which the policy started. If they have some type of health complication later, they are guaranteed this life insurance policy. If they ever need money, they might be able to tap some of the cash value built up in their account.

And if the worst happens to your children, you have some financial cushion to get you over the grieving period associated with the loss of a child. That financial breathing room could be greatly appreciated depending on how the family deals with the child's death.

Buying Life Insurance

You can buy life insurance from all kinds of companies and in all types of ways. The most common way is through an insurance agent. The agent usually provides guidance on the insurance types and levels best suited for your situation, and that advice may be worth going through an agent. Use your agent to verify your numbers and to make recommendations on things that you might have overlooked. Better to find these things out now instead of when your family tries to collect. This agent makes a living off of commissions, so expect that insurance purchased through an agent may cost you a little more.

QuickCaution

Independent of how you obtain the benefit level you choose, make sure that you get the best possible coverage from the best possible company for your situation.

Some insurance providers allow you to purchase directly from them and not incur the commissions associated with working through an agent. Don't save a little money on the premium to get your insurance from a financially unreliable company. This is a short-sighted strategy that can cost you big time when your family really needs the death benefit money.

Group insurance obtained through your employer is probably the most economical and reliable way to obtain your insurance. If you are self-employed, look for organizations that offer umbrella group policies, such as professional organizations.

Disability Insurance Issues

If you are like most of us, you think that a disability happens to other people, not to you. Unfortunately, you have a higher risk of becoming disabled than you may think, and being disabled can put your financial well being in serious jeopardy.

At the risk of sounding really callous, let me put it to you this way. After you die, you don't cost your family anything on a monthly basis. If you are disabled to the point that you cannot work, you are not earning any money, which decreases the household's income, and you probably require more special care and treatment services every month as a result of the disability. Household expenses increase, and household income decreases. This can be a serious combination if not properly planned for. Your family definitely prefers that you are around instead of gone, but you should take precautionary steps to minimize the negative impact of your disability.

Your employer probably has some type of disability coverage as part of your benefits packages. This coverage might start with simple sick time off and lead to short-term disability that kicks in after a few weeks and goes up a to a few months. Needless to say, this is appreciated, but not very helpful if you are in your 30s and can never work again.

Social Security provides some Social Security benefits, which are dependent upon your income level and the length of time that you paid into Social Security before becoming disabled. The following are a few things to consider with regards to Social Security disability benefits:

➤ You are dealing with the government, which is never an easy situation.

➤ You pay taxes on Social Security benefits if your adjusted gross income exceeds $34,000 for a single person and $44,000 for a couple filing jointly.

➤ You must be completely disabled from performing any job at all, not just the one you had when you became disabled.

➤ You must be disabled for at least five months with expectations of being disabled for at least a year before you qualify.

➤ Any income you receive from other government programs reduces your Social Security benefits.

➤ Even if you get the most out of Social Security as is humanly possible, you probably won't make enough money to enable you to live anywhere near the lifestyle that you had before becoming disabled.

Disability insurance is designed to fit in where Social Security leaves off. It is designed to provide you with a specific percentage of your predisability income if you become disabled for an extended period of time. The higher the monthly coverage amount, the more the insurance costs. It is typically pretty expensive compared to other types of insurance.

The premiums are dependent upon several factors including the danger associated with your job, the level of desired coverage, your age, medical history, and general health. Insurance companies are very conservative when providing long-term disability coverage. Why? Well, think about it this way. Assume that you need $48,000 per year in disability income coverage, and you are 40 years old when disabled. The insurance company is obligated to paying you $4,000 per month for the rest of your life, which could be more than 35 years. That equates to $1,680,000 in payments, when not adjusted for inflation.

QuickTip

Long-term disability insurance payments derived from policies where you made the premium payments are federal, state, and local tax exempt. Make sure that you insure yourself for a monthly disability benefit that is equal to your actual required expenses, not the pretax income you had before your disability occurred.

They are banking on your staying healthy and never collecting on the policy, which is good news for everyone.

Voice of Experience

You might occasionally hear about partially disabled people living the good life off of their disability, and I'm sure that there are people out there who abuse the insurance companies. But, I have a friend who injured his back to the point that he just cannot work and lives off of his disability. He is in constant pain and only functional for part of the day. His disability happened when he was in his 30s, and several surgeries have not improved his prospects. There is no doubt in my mind that he would trade his disability for a job any day of the week.

Medical Insurance Overview

Have you ever had to deal with the American health care system? If so, I am sorry for you. If not, I am happy for you so far and sorry for you when it inevitably happens. Medical care today seems to be one part medicine and nine parts economics. Even hospitals deserve to make a living, but more than one family has had a lifelong savings strategy stripped from them in a matter of weeks or months due to an unexpected illness that was not covered by insurance.

Going without major medical insurance coverage is playing with financial fire. It is one thing to tough it out through a cold or the flu without medical insurance; such an incident might cost you a few hundred dollars. It is another to work through something serious such as an automobile accident or cancer without insurance. You might spend the rest of your life paying for a few weeks in intensive care.

I'm not going to cover health insurance in great detail at this point, other than to encourage you to at least get coverage for major medical incidents. (Chapter 17, "An Apple a Day Won't Keep the Doctor Away," takes a detailed look at medical insurance coverage. Make sure that you review this important information, especially if you are approaching retirement or have a parent who is.)

Mortgage Payment Insurance

Things can get pretty bad, but still be okay if you have a place to sleep and call home. When things turn bad and you also lose you home, it can be devastating. For this reason, many people consider mortgage disability insurance that covers your mortgage payment for you should you not be able to make the payment.

This type of insurance is usually available from your lender, and may even be required by your lender under certain circumstances. If you have the financial reserves to cover payments for a while and enough equity in your home that you can sell it quickly if things get rough, you might not need this insurance. But, if you run things a little tight on the financial side, you might consider talking with your lender about this type of insurance.

Talkin' Money

Credit disability insurance covers your credit card payments if you become disabled and unable to make the payments. It is usually offered by the credit card companies, but at an expensive rate.

Be aware that this type of insurance can be expensive and unnecessary, if you have planned your long-term disability coverage properly. Don't pay twice for the same coverage, and you probably find that disability insurance is less expensive than mortgage disability insurance.

Using Quicken Financial Services to Review Insurance Coverage

Once again, the folks at Intuit didn't miss the opportunity to help you with your insurance research. In fact, Quicken provides a special feature called the InsureMarket that provides you with online insurance quotes for auto, homeowners, disability, and other types of insurance.

Information from most of the big name companies in insurance, such as Allstate, State Farm, AIG, Travelers, MetLife, and others, is available using Quicken and your Internet connection. Access InsureMarket by simply placing your cursor over the **Home & Car** icon and selecting

QuickTip

You must have an Internet connection to get detailed information using Quicken's InsureMarket.

Research Insurance Rates. Follow the browser links from that point forward to let Quicken do the walking for you. This feature is handy and simple to use. It is also a great place to acquire the phone numbers for the various carriers should you want to call them directly.

Tracking Insurance Transactions

Insurance-related transactions are pretty simple, because payments you make are treated as expense items and money you receive is treated as income. The only decisions come in separating the categories along taxable/nontaxable lines.

The only exception to this rule is a cash value account that is a combination of expense and asset accounts.

➤ Track life insurance expense payments that you make in an expense account. You might consider creating a main category called **Life Insurance** and then creating subcategories for each person covered by the life insurance and for each account on which coverage is paid.

➤ Track disability insurance premium payments that you make under a separate account, because you may need to prove to the IRS that you made the payments to avoid paying taxes on any income you receive due to a disability.

➤ Cash value accounts have two parts: an expense category and an asset account that tracks the accumulated cash value. When you make a premium payment into a cash value life insurance account, distribute the proper payment percentages between expense and asset increase.

211

➤ Create separate income accounts for the various insurance-related incomes that you receive during the year because each may be taxed in a different way. For example, create a single income account for disability insurance income, another for life insurance received from a parent, and another life insurance income account for disbursements received from an uncle.

➤ All other insurance premium payments and income can be tracked as you desire.

I am a firm believer in more detailed account creation because this saves you from having to manually break out expenses and income at a later date. If you lump all your automobile insurance payments into a single expense category and later want to know the amount spent on your teenager's car insurance, you have to manually total the payments. If you had created a separate insurance account for your teenager and another for the rest of the family, the category totals would instantly give you the total.

The Least You Need to Know

➤ Life insurance is an integral part of any personal financial-planning procedure.

➤ Life insurance is not generally set up for you to use. It is mostly set up for those left behind after you depart.

➤ Long-term disability insurance is a good idea if your lost income would place your financial household in jeopardy.

➤ Quicken enables you to electronically compare insurance rates from major companies, as long as you have an Internet connection.

Chapter 16

Don't Prove Murphy Right: Protect Your Home and Car

In This Chapter

➤ Determine the right auto coverage categories and coverage levels

➤ Protect yourself from drivers without insurance

➤ Pick the right car for you and your insurance premiums

➤ Define the proper homeowners insurance coverage categories and coverage levels

➤ Use Quicken to automate your insurance research and tracking needs

---

Most of us don't live our lives expecting the worst to happen. But sometimes it does, and often it happens to your home or while you are driving your car. Insurance is rarely used, but when it is needed, you are happy that you took the time to get the right coverage from the right company. Take a look through this chapter and make sure that you understand your auto and homeowners insurance coverage and verify that you are covered for the proper dollar amounts. Spending a few minutes here might help you from spending more money on premiums than you need to spend and might save you from a tragic financial situation should the worst happen to you or a family member.

Automobile Insurance Overview

Driving a car without auto insurance is similar to diving into a swimming pool without checking the water depth. You might survive the first few dives into the first few pools, but at some point, you're going to get hurt.

Driving in any major metropolitan area is often a frightening experience, and it is difficult to drive each day and not see an accident of some type. The American College Dictionary defines an accident as "an undesirable or unfortunate happening: casualty: mishap." Insurance is there to protect you, your family, your car, and any other involved parties in the unfortunate event of an automobile accident.

The jargon associated with automobile insurance can make it appear complicated, but it is actually pretty simple to understand. Work your way through this section to get a handle on the coverage you actually pay for when you get vehicle insurance.

QuickCaution

Auto insurance covers the car, not you. If you are driving a car owned by someone else and that person does not have insurance, you must have a special clause in your policy that covers you when driving a car other than your own. If someone else is driving your car, they are covered because your policy covers your car—provided, of course, that you have insurance yourself. Verify your specific coverage with your insurance provider and don't assume any coverage levels for vehicles belonging to your employer. Check it out with your employer.

Automobile insurance coverage falls into the following few basic categories:

➤ Insuring yourself and others in your car

➤ Insuring others from your actions

➤ Insuring both your property and other people's property

The rest is in the details.

Talkin' Money

No-fault insurance does not require that a driver be found at fault before claims are paid. Both drivers file a claim and their respective insurance companies immediately provide financial assistance to their respective insured driver. The other party's insurance company then contacts the insurance company associated with the driver who caused the accident. The two companies work out payments to each other. If you caused the accident, you should expect your premiums to increase.

Fault insurance requires that a driver be found at fault before claims are paid. This drives up litigation costs, extends the time between the occurrence of the accident and the receipt of payments by the drivers, and decreases the dollar amount actually received by the drivers because a big chunk of it goes to the lawyers. If you caused the accident, you should expect your premiums to increase.

Insuring Yourself and Others in Your Car

Of primary concern to anyone in an accident is the health of those involved in the accident. Medical payments (med pay) insurance provides typical health care coverage of up to $5,000 per person in your car, which would make the maximum for an accident with two people $10,000. You can vary this amount if want to, but you might have a state-imposed minimum coverage level. The cost of this insurance might be reduced if your insurance carrier provides an in-network physician discount, just as seen with HMO and PPO medical plans. (See Chapter 17, "An Apple a Day Won't Keep the Doctor Away," for additional information on health and medical insurance plans.)

Medical expenses from several major categories are covered in the medical payments section of your auto insurance coverage, including the following:

➤ Doctor and hospital expenses arising from an accident when you are driving

➤ You or your family member's medical expenses arising from riding as a passenger in another car that has an accident

➤ Funeral expenses arising from an automobile accident, which I sincerely hope you don't need

➤ Expenses arising from being hit by a car while walking as a pedestrian

➤ The other passengers in the insured car are covered under this section, which may be a big deal if those people do not have their own insurance

Needless to say, $5,000 won't completely cover the medical expenses that arise from a serious accident, so you want to have other medical insurance coverage. But med pay does cover funeral expenses, which might be useful if the worst happens. This usually doesn't cost very much, so I recommend that you add between $5,000 and $10,000 to your coverage, if it is not already required in your state. Have a long talk with your agent about the specific level of coverage provided by your policy. It is best to know before something happens, not after.

Personal injury protection (PIP) insurance coverage is used as a supplement to medical payment coverage. PIP provides extra coverage for lost wages, additional medical coverage, and additional services required as a result of the accident. For example, assume that an injured person from your accident must pay someone to do their grocery shopping. The fee for this grocery shopping service would be covered under the PIP coverage section of your policy.

Uninsured and underinsured motorist is used to cover you and your occupants if the other person in your accident does not have insurance or inadequate coverage for the accident involved. The other driver's bodily injury insurance covers you for these expenses. If that person is not insured and you don't have uninsured/underinsured motorist coverage, you could be in a bad situation from no action of your own. Even worse, this person may have nothing of value if you win a lawsuit against him or her.

There are people out there who refuse to buy car insurance for a variety of reasons, not the least of which is that it costs a lot of money. Having this extra coverage on your policy is not that expensive, and it adds the protection you need if this unfortunate situation happen to you. I suggest $100,000/$300,000 coverage. The top number ($100,000) indicates the maximum coverage per person and the bottom number ($300,000) represents the maximum coverage per accident.

Covering Others for Your Own Actions

Suppose that you lose control of your car, hit another car, and injure someone in that other car. If it is determined that you were negligent in your driving, you could be held responsible for the other car's passengers' recovery expenses. Your auto insurance policy has a "bodily injury" coverage section, also called "liability," designed to cover the accident-specific expenses associated with the following:

➤ Medical treatment

➤ Lost wages

➤ Legal judgments that award pain and suffering payments to this person

➤ Loss of income to this person's family should the injured person die

Most states have a minimum liability coverage that is required by law to register your vehicle or to get it inspected. If you are stopped for a moving violation in these states, the police usually asks for proof of insurance, which is a card provided by your insurance carrier that verifies that you have at least the minimum level of insurance coverage required by your state. The minimum is really the "bare minimum" and you should almost always carry more insurance than the minimum required by your state law. Once again, check with your agent about common coverage levels and what is right for your situation.

You can see that the cost of the accident could run into substantial amounts of money if the other person is seriously injured or die. The coverage is divided into two numbers, such as 25/50. The top number represents the maximum amount of coverage provided per individual, and the bottom number represents the maximum total coverage per accident for all individuals. So, 25/50 covers two people at $25,000 maximum each or three people for lesser individual amounts that total a maximum of $50,000. It is common to have $100,000/$300,000 bodily injury coverage and some people prefer to have $250,000/$500,000 limits as added protection.

Covering the Car and Other Property

After the dust settles on a car accident and the passenger conditions are verified, all eyes turn to the cars to assess the level of damage sustained. The collision insurance section of your policy is designed to get your car repaired or reimburse you for the car's book value after industry depreciation is applied, if it is not repairable.

It costs you your agreed-upon deductible amount, but you should either end up with a repaired car or enough money to buy another of comparable value. In reality, you rarely get enough money from an insurance settlement to buy a new car. Sorry. It almost always winds up costing you something in cash and a lot of time.

Talkin' Money

A car is assumed totaled by the insurance company when it determines that it costs more to fix the car than the car is worth. In this case, the insurance company pays you the car's value and often leaves you with the car if you so desire.

The deductible is the amount that the insurance deducts from the agreed-upon settlement amount. In essence, you pay the deductible out of the insurance settlement check.

Your "collision" premiums are based on where you live, the value of your car, and the amount of your deductible. If your deductible is low, say $50, the premiums are higher because the insurance company is exposing itself to more dollar risk. If your deductible is high, say $1,000, the premiums are lower because the financial risk to the insurance company is lower. I suggest that you start out a new car with a low deductible of around $250, and move it up as the car ages, because the value of the car also decreases. At some point, it seems hardly worth it to carry collision at all, and many people drop their collision coverage on an older car that is only worth a $1,000 or so.

What if something happens to your car while nobody is driving it? What if it is parked on the street and is stolen or vandalized? What if a tree limb breaks and lands on your new car? Ouch!

After you are done crying, check out the "comprehensive" insurance coverage section of your policy. It covers you for those times when your car is damaged but not as the result of a driving accident with another car. Typical claim events that involve comprehensive coverage include storms, floods, fires, trees, vandalism, theft, riots, and hitting animals while driving. The premiums for comprehensive coverage vary with the value of the car and the amount of the deductible, in a very similar way as seen with collision coverage.

Quite often an accident involves more than cars and people. If the cars ran into each other and then ran off the road into a house, there would be damage to the house. The "property damage" section of your auto policy covers you for this damage. The level needed may be defined by the state you live in, but you want to carry at least $25,000 or you could be looking at making payments on a new addition to someone's house as a result of your accident.

Rental Cars and Your Auto Insurance

Remember that your auto insurance policy covers your car, not you. If you rent a car, your auto policy does not automatically cover the rental car you are driving. For this reason, many people get "car rental" coverage. Some credit cards provide this coverage automatically if you charge the car rental on their card, and the rental dealership is glad to charge $15 per day, or more, for this coverage. I recommend that you pay for it as part of your normal automobile insurance policy. It also quickly pays for itself when compared with the daily charge for rental car company insurance. This coverage, attached to your standard policy, is inexpensive and provides that little extra coverage you might need if you have an accident in another city while driving a rental car.

Dealing with Teenage Drivers

Be prepared. When you add your teenage driver to your auto insurance policy, you might need to take the night off to recover from the sticker shock. Your premiums increase substantially. Why? Simply stated, teenagers are learning how to drive and just aren't very good at it yet. They are teenagers with all the personality complexities that go with being that age. As a result, teens have a higher accident risk, and the insurance company is going to cover its financial position by charging a higher premium.

The following are a few things that you can do to minimize the impact, and every little bit helps:

➤ Shop around for the best rate possible from a reputable insurance carrier.

➤ Have your son or daughter drive a four-door car that is not listed as a sports car or at least a two-door car with a back seat.

➤ Make sure that your kids successfully finish driver's education and that your insurance carrier is aware of this fact.

➤ It is not unusual for insurance carriers to offer a discount for good grades, so this provides a little incentive on the academic front.

➤ Try to keep them from being the primary driver on the car because that also shoots their rates through the moon roof. Listing yourself as the primary driver and your son or daughter as a secondary driver can save enough to lessen the sticker shock.

No matter how you look at it, you should expect to pay a lot of money for teenager insurance. Do everything you can to minimize the expense and put them into the safest car you can that gets them through their teen years.

Voice Of Experience

I have some friends who took a lot of harassment for putting their teenager into a luxury car with an excellent safety record. Their feeling was that this car would protect him through his most accident-prone years and would be worth the expense.

I have some other friends who put their teenage boy into an older pickup truck with a very small engine. Their rationale was that if he had an accident, the truck would probably win the crunching of steel contest and the small engine would keep the truck from becoming a play toy.

In either case, the safety of the teenager was the primary concern with the approach strictly a matter of finances and personal choice.

Getting Discounts on Car Insurance

Don't feel the need to give the insurance company as much money as they ask for without looking for legitimate ways to discount your payments. The following are a few things that may qualify your policy for a discount of up to 15%:

➤ Add a recognized alarm system to your car. Just because your car beeps when you push the little button on the remote doesn't mean that there is an installed alarm.

➤ Don't drive to work if you can car pool. This decreases the number of miles driven per year and decreases your chance of having an accident.

➤ Get a car with antilock brakes, which makes the car stop more consistently.

➤ Successfully complete a defensive driving course.

➤ Keep your driving record clean without moving violations that could indicate that you are a potentially dangerous driver.

➤ Buy cars that have useable rear seats, which should keep it out of the sports car category.

➤ Get a car that has air bags and automatic seat belts that move into place after you are in the car.

➤ Stop smoking, because smoking while driving distracts you and increases the chance of an accident. Cellular phones should also fall into this category.

➤ Stick around long enough to fall into an older, safer age category.

Shopping around for your insurance is a good thing, but don't ever let your insurance lapse. Transferring insurance is pretty easy, as long as you do it at the end of the coverage period. Getting new insurance after your insurance has lapsed can be a little like meeting the Spanish Inquisition.

Using Your Car for Business

There is a temptation to try to use your personal car for business and take the deductions. This is a double-edged sword in that you get reimbursed from your company to the tune of 32 cents per business mile driven and may even get a monthly payment stipend, but your insurance probably goes up because you are driving more miles. And, you put more wear on your car, which means that you might have to trade it in sooner than expected.

I suggest that you take the total number of business miles that you plan to drive each year and multiply that by 32 cents per mile. Does this amount even come close to covering your expenses for the year? If the answer is yes and you may be able to drive the car for both personal and business, and pay for it out of the business portion, you might give this serious consideration. If you are still basically paying for the car out of your own pocket, I suggest that you treat the car as personal with an occasional business trip.

This section covered insurance for your vehicle. The following section covers insurance requirements for your other major personal investment—your home.

Property/Casualty Insurance for Your Home

Imagine the sinking feeling you would have if you came home to your house to find that the refrigerator had caught fire and burned the place to the ground. Now, sink even lower by thinking that you did not have insurance on the house and that the whole place is a complete loss.

Enough depression! You are savvy enough to know that homeowners insurance is a must for anyone who owns property and is trying to manage his finances wisely. The questions usually come up when considering the various options associated with homeowners insurance. This section outlines your major consideration points.

How Much Insurance Do You Really Need?

How much insurance is enough? Your agent, who gets paid on commission, probably believes that you can never have too much. You probably want to make sure that you are covered but don't want to pay more than you need to. Where is the proper middle ground? First, consider the situations covered by homeowners insurance:

➤ The home and associated grounds, or the "dwelling," should be covered for at least 80% of the replacement cost, with 100% replacement cost recommended. Twenty percent of $200,000 is $40,000. This is a lot of money in any book, so go for 100% replacement cost. One hundred percent replacement might be difficult to find for an older home, but it is worth a try. Your mortgage lender requires that you carry a minimum level of dwelling insurance to protect the collateral for the loan that they made to you for the home purchase.

Talkin' Money

Replacement-cost insurance coverage specifies that your lost home and/or contents are covered for the amount required to replace it at current market rates, as opposed to simply covering the original item cost. This can make a huge difference with home insurance because the cost of rebuilding your home has definitely gone up over the years, whereas the initial purchase price of your home has remained the same or even decreased if depreciation is applied.

➤ Insurance for additional structures related to the home such as a garage, shed, sunroom, or other structures that are part of the property but not necessarily attached to the house.

➤ The "contents" of the structure such as your furnishings, tools, appliances, and other items that are not part of the structure itself. Most people underestimate the value of these items, so take a comprehensive look here before deciding on a contents coverage number. You probably want to make this number at least $20,000 and move higher if you have nicer furnishings, electronic toys, personal computer, and other items. Your insurance company may require that certain items such as jewelry, firearms, and electronic equipment be itemized on your policy. Always check with your agent for a clear definition of your policy's coverage requirements. By the way, photos of special items and even a videotape of the house are a really good idea as long as they are kept in a safe place, such as a safe deposit box. Filing a successful claim is a lot easier with more documentation.

➤ If something happens to your home and you must live somewhere else, you need loss of use coverage to cover your living expenses while your home gets back into livable shape. The recommended amount for loss of use coverage is 20% of the dwelling coverage as a minimum or actual expenses, whichever is more economical.

➤ Personal liability is a good idea because it covers you and your family members for injury of damage their actions may cause to someone else. I recently sliced a golf ball through a sliding glass door's window and had it replaced using my homeowners insurance liability. If someone slips and hurts himself on your icy sidewalk, he can sue you for negligence because he might believe the walk should have been cleared. You can always be sued, so $100,000 minimum liability coverage is a must, with as much as $300,000 recommended if you are an easy financial target.

➤ Medical bills coverage of at least $1,000 is also recommended to cover the medical expenses of someone injured on your property. Five thousand dollars is the recommended next level if you want additional protection. Assume a child falls from your apple tree and breaks an arm. This coverage handles the medical portion of the incident with the liability coverage required if the child's family decides to sue for negligence regarding the tree.

QuickTip

Quicken's Home Inventory is a simple tool that quickly enables you to determine your contents coverage requirements by recording information about your existing home inventory items. For additional information on its use, see "Using Quicken Home Inventory to Get It Right" later in this chapter.

Make sure that your dwelling coverage is enough to replace the structure, which is probably a higher number than your initial purchase price for the house. Most policies can be set up for an automatic inflation adjustment so that the coverage automatically increases annually based on a preset level of appreciation.

You might hear your agent talk about HO1, HO2 ,and upward to HO8 coverage. These are blanket policy types that provide standard coverage.

➤ HO1 is the basic policy that covers your loss due to windstorm, hail, riot, aircraft accident, vehicle accident, smoke, fire, lightning, explosion, theft, vandalism, glass breakage on your structure, volcano (for you folks in Hawaii), and civil disturbance.

➤ HO2 adds to HO1 with coverage for freezing of water pipes or water-related appliances, heating and air conditioning system-related damage, fire protection sprinkler systems, household appliances, falling objects, damage from snow, sleet or ice weight, water or steam discharge, and most other accidental items that can occur around your house from appliances, water systems, electrical systems, or standard acts of nature.

➤ HO3 increases coverage to include most other lifelong perils except earthquakes, floods, war, or nuclear accidents. You can get special coverage for these, which is not a silly thought if you live in an earthquake area such as California or a flood prone area. Better to have this coverage before the natural emergency occurs instead of wishing that you had it after the damage is done.

➤ HO5 extends the HO3 level of coverage to include your contents, surrounding structures, and loss of use due to these acts of nature.

➤ HO4 and HO6 are specially set up for folks who rent or live in condominiums, where the contents are covered but the structure is not because the structure is part of the rest of the complex and probably covered by its own insurance policy. This can be tricky insurance to define, so make sure that you understand the coverage. For example, if your neighbor upstairs has a water leak that damages your walls, whose insurance should cover it? Make sure before the fact, not after.

➤ HO8 is basically HO1 coverage applied to an older home.

QuickTip

Don't forget that the higher your deductible, the lower your insurance premiums. A policy with a $250 deductible costs more than a policy with a $1,000 deductible. In addition, always weigh the cost of the insurance with the cost of not having it should the worst happen. I know people in California who did not have earthquake insurance before 1989, who absolutely would not go without it today. Get the hint?

What to Expect if Something Really Does Happen

The insurance company generally covers any claims made as a result of an unexpected or unforeseeable incident that caused the loss. Gradual deterioration of your roof that causes interior water damage is not usually covered. Water damage that results from a serious hailstorm that tears the roof off of your house should qualify for reimbursement.

Assume that you come home one evening and find your house flooded due to a broken toilet tank. The following is the procedure for filing your claim and getting your house repaired:

1. First, make sure that everyone is safe and that you have done what is reasonably possible to minimize additional damage, such as turning off the water in the case of the example. Never put yourself in personal danger trying to minimize an insurance loss. You can always replace a house. You are much more difficult to replace.

2. Call the police or fire department if applicable to instances such as a theft or fire, respectively. Safety is always most important, and getting the proper authorities involved right from the start is the right thing to do.

3. Call your insurance agent or their claims hotline, if after hours. Look in the phone book if your policy is unavailable.

4. Take pictures of the damage. It may take weeks and several groups of people to get things back to normal. You want a solid record of what happened should people start to forget the degree of damage.

5. Save all expense receipts related to living in temporary housing as a result of the incident. This includes car rentals, replacement clothing, food, and any other incremental costs you incur directly because of the incident.

6. Get with the insurance adjuster who evaluates the level of damage and get an estimate of the replacement costs. The estimates are based on the insurance company's industry averages for performing your required work and may not reflect reality. Feel free to verify the numbers with your own contractor.

7. The insurance company issues its assessment of the damage and issues a check to cover the repairs. You can either accept the check and the insurance company's assessment or reject the assessment. Cashing the check may signify acceptance unless you specifically deny its assessment in writing and get its confirmation that cashing the check does not in any way compromise your ability to further negotiate a settlement.

8. You are responsible for getting your house back into livable shape and can spend the money as desired as long as it goes into the house. This means that you can change the house if you want to as long as you understand that the insurance company only pays enough to replace what was there before and does not help you build your dream house from the prior mess.

9. Submit your temporary living expenses to the company for reimbursement on a periodic basis, if you are displaced over a long period of time.

10. If you are not happy with the claim resolution, work your way up through the claims department of the insurance company until you get satisfaction. Ultimately, hire a lawyer and file your claim through the judicial system.

If the amount of reimbursement received from your insurance company does not equal the amount of your loss, you should be able to use the difference as a tax deduction claiming it as a loss on Form 4684, Casualties and Thefts.

Using Quicken Home Inventory to Get It Right

Quicken makes tracking your household contents and estimating their value a simple task by providing the **Home Inventory** feature. **Home Inventory** is accessed by resting your cursor over the **Home and Car** icon and clicking the **Record my home inventory** option. The application starts and is self explanatory.

1. Select the room location from the **View By Location** list box.

2. Type the **Item Description** in the space provided, or double-click one of the items from the **Suggested Items** listing on the right side of the screen. Notice that the listed items change with the **Category** selected. Additional information can be added by clicking the **small page** icon at the right of the **Item Description** field. This **Detail View** enables you to add most standard information related to the item being entered, such as its cost, value, and model number, among others.

3. Select the Quicken category into which this item is to be entered by clicking the down arrow at the right of the **Item Category** field. The default category is furnishings. Multiple categories can be created within Quicken. The category is used for totaling and reporting the information.

4. Enter the **Replacement Cost** and **Resale Cost** as applicable, if not already entered in the **Detail View** screen.

5. Repeat this procedure for each location and each item at that location.

Additional **Locations** and **Categories** are created by clicking the appropriate icon on the Iconbar. Insurance policy information is entered by clicking the **Policies** icon and typing the appropriate information. Claims can also be tracked by clicking the **Claims** icon and entering the required information.

QuickTip

Remember that Quicken helps you shop for insurance using its online research capabilities. Simply rest your cursor over the **Home & Car** icon and select the **Research Insurance Rates** option. You must have an Internet connection and browser for this feature to work properly.

Using the Quicken Home Inventory feature not only enables you to obtain the proper level of contents coverage, but also provides you with a detailed record to back up any claims you may have against the insurance company.

Make sure that you make a backup of your data in both paper and electronic form, and keep that backup in a safe place, such as a safe deposit box. A backup that is caught in a house fire doesn't do you much good, does it?

QuickCaution

If you look around, you should be able to find fireproof boxes that you can keep in your home. They may keep the fire out, but it doesn't mean that the contents won't get super hot in the event of a fire. They also won't necessarily prevent water from getting into the box as the fire department puts out the fire. I recommend that you don't use this means as your only protection for important legal documents or computer data backups. If you choose this route, at least put your items in paper bags that are then placed in plastic bags to protect against water damage. The paper bag protects your contents against melting of the plastic bag.

The Least You Need to Know

➤ Auto insurance is a must, so get adequate coverage from the right company.

➤ Make sure that your auto insurance covers you for your lifestyle by including the proper additional coverage and deductible levels.

➤ Homeowners insurance is required by the lenders to protect the dwelling but not to protect you. All insurance companies are not equal. Get the right policy from the right company.

➤ Your homeowners insurance can cover you for more than your home. Check with your agent if you suffer a loss away from home. It may just be insured.

➤ Quicken Home Inventory is useful for tracking your home contents items and ensuring that you retain adequate coverage and records.

YOUR POLICY'S LAPSED.

Chapter 17

An Apple a Day Won't Keep the Doctor Away

In This Chapter

➤ Get the right medical coverage for your situation

➤ Determine the proper Medicare supplemental coverage

➤ Plan ahead for extended nursing home care

➤ Use Quicken to track and report on emergency medical information

➤ Offset deductible costs with an MSA

Your need for medical coverage changes as you get older, with all things changing when you reach 65 and qualify for Medicare. Read through this chapter and learn the best ways to cover yourself and your family against that unwanted, untimely, and hopefully never to occur, medical emergency.

Medical Costs

If you haven't been sick lately, congratulations, and I sincerely hope that you stay healthy. But if you have been sick or hospitalized lately, or know someone who has been, you know the incredible fees that can run up in just a few days.

A typical stay in the hospital can cost in excess of $1,200, and a day in intensive care can cost as much as $5,000. This is big bucks no matter what language you speak.

Think about saving for years to have a $30,000 nest egg. Now imagine getting into a car accident and winding up in intensive care for a week or so at $5,000 per day. You leave with a hospital bill of $35,000. There goes your savings plus $5,000 more. You have to spend the money or you would probably die. But you sure can get sick when you get home from the hospital to find these bills. Insurance protects you from having to make a medical care versus finances decision.

Medical costs continue to increase annually and are fully expected to increase into the foreseeable future. The cost of uninsured medical care can easily become one of your largest expenses next to your home. The following are reasons for these increases:

➤ More specialists are used to provide the best, most specialized care possible.

➤ The equipment is more sophisticated and simply costs more to purchase and maintain.

➤ Today, medicine has the ability to keep people alive who would have died just a few years ago. These people stay in the hospital longer and at a higher daily expense rate.

➤ The skyrocketing cost of medical malpractice insurance keeps driving up the cost of providing medical services. This is the doctor's claim, but there is debate on this point.

➤ The changing financial shape of the medical industry with the HMO, PPO, and other medical business entities is causing increased costs, which are being passed to consumers.

➤ The costs associated with the federal government's intervention, not only on a regulatory side but also in dealing with Medicare, continue to rise. These costs must be passed on to the consumer.

You may not agree with this list, and you may have a few more that you want to add yourself. The point on which we can all agree is that receiving medical care is an expensive, and often financially serious, situation. If you do not plan properly for your medical insurance needs, you might end up getting substandard care, no care, or paying for care out of your own pocket, if you still have a pocket left when you get out of the hospital.

Medical insurance comes in various forms and is available through many sources. The two basic coverage categories are fee for service plans, which allow you to see any doctor, and managed health care plans (you know these as HMOs), which have an approved listing of doctors where care can be obtained for a standardized fee. The specific term and conditions associated with the various plans differ widely, but the major coverage items generally fall into one of the following categories.

➤ Major medical insurance (also called catastrophic coverage) provides coverage for major medical incidents, such as a car accident or cancer. It is not designed to cover a trip to the doctor for a flu shot. This type of coverage is typically inexpensive compared to full medical coverage but not very economical if you are someone who gets sick on a regular basis. This is usually provided on a fee-for-service basis where you pay a certain amount and the insurance company pays the rest. The amounts vary with the type of coverage, insurance company, and total dollars involved.

➤ Health Maintenance Organization (HMO) insurance is a managed care plan that covers services provided by the sponsoring health organization, which is the HMO. They have their own "in-network" doctors who charge a nominal fee for their services, as long as you are also part of the HMO network. The doctors sign up to be a part of the HMO network. Getting medical treatment from a non-HMO network doctor or hospital can cost you big bucks because it is probably not covered. Some HMO programs are better than others. Although some people are very happy with their HMO, it's always best to check into which physicians are part of the HMO plan. It's also wise to check to see whether you are covered if you must see a doctor who is not part of your HMO. It's possible that you are not covered or can only receive a percentage of the coverage if you visit a doctor outside your HMO network.

➤ Preferred-Provider Organizations (PPO) insurance is a managed care plan that allows you to select your own preferred doctor. This coverage typically has higher premiums because there is more risk on the part of the insurance provider, and they have less control over the doctors involved. Visits to PPO doctors who are in the network are relatively inexpensive. Visits to non-PPO doctors are covered, but only 50% or so of the non-PPO doctor amount is reimbursed. You can go see a non-PPO doctor, but it costs you. You may find plans with differing reimbursement percentages, so look for the one that provides the best care for the least money out of your pocket.

When you go to see the doctor, he or she either charges you for the visit, after which you submit the bill to the insurance company for reimbursement, or the doctor bills your insurance company directly. In either case, you are generally responsible for a copayment, which is either a certain percentage of the visit fee for a fee-for-service plan or a flat fee such as with PPOs or HMOs. You are also responsible for a deductible amount that is paid out of your pocket before the insurance company pays anything at all.

This chapter provides the basic understanding you need to choose the best medical insurance coverage for you and your family. Of course, you should always consult a professional if you have questions about what coverage is right for you.

Employer Versus Private Insurance

One of the benefits that most American workers expect is medical coverage. The company usually has some type of group medical insurance coverage that you become a part of when you join the company. The premiums are either paid in full by the company as a standard benefit, or the premiums are divided between the company and the employee. Often the company simply acts as an umbrella under which employees can get their own insurance. The various insurance programs and the way in which the premiums are paid vary over a wide spectrum, and the only way to know about your company is to talk to its insurance coordinator.

You also have the ability to get your own individual medical insurance policy and circumvent the company policy completely. The benefits of using the company policy are that it is often less expensive and may even offer better coverage than you can get as an individual. On the other hand, I have had individual policies in the past that had better coverage than that offered by my wife's company policy and for less money, so don't take anything at face value.

QuickTip

Most companies provide medical insurance that allows the employee to add family members for a nominal fee. This is often a less expensive way to get coverage than paying for an individual policy. If a married couple both work and have medical insurance coverage, you might want to compare the two plans and decide which provides the better coverage and consolidate under that plan.

One problem with having company-sponsored insurance is that the insurance may have to stay with the company. This means that if you leave and go to another company, you are starting all over again from an insurance standpoint. This is not a big deal when you are 25 and healthy, but it can be a very big deal when you are 55 and have had a stroke but can still function at work.

The stroke is usually treated as a pre-existing condition and subject to a waiting period before another recurrence of the stroke would be covered by insurance. Nobody plans to have a stroke, and if it happens during the waiting period associated with the pre-existing condition, you could have insurance for everything but the stroke. For this reason, many people with some type of serious illness are married to their current company for life because they cannot get alternate medical insurance due to their expensive medical history.

Having your own policy means that you are covered even if you change places of employment. You are relatively immune from the pre-existing condition restrictions because you keep the same policy.

Be advised that you want to keep a record of all medical expenses, including insurance premiums paid, because the money spent is tax deductible. All expenses that exceed 7.5% of your adjusted gross income are tax deductible. If, for example, you had an adjusted gross income of $45,000 and spent $4,500 on medical payments and premiums, you would qualify for a deduction of $4,500 − (.075 × $45,000) = $1,125. By the way, prescription drug expenses can be included in your medical expenses, so keep a record of them also.

You should also keep a record of medical expenses even if your insurance is company provided. Your copayment, deductible, medicine, and any premiums paid can add up. You generally do not get over the 7.5% threshold if your employer pays for the policy, but it is not a big deal to track and may pay off in the form of reduced taxes.

People with High Medical Risk Backgrounds

What if you are someone who falls into a high medical risk category? Getting insurance can be difficult or even impossible. Try looking into Blue Cross and Blue Shield during one of their open enrollment periods when acceptance requirements are relaxed. You can also look into your particular state's health insurance risk pool, which is designed to insure people within the state who are otherwise uninsurable. But think about this. The only people in this pool are those too risky to insure with a normal policy, which means that the premiums for this insurance will be high but cheaper than paying for a heart attack out of your pocket.

Medicare and Old Age Coverage

QuickTip

Congress recognized that health insurance was a problem when people changed companies. It enacted the Congressional Omnibus Budget Reconciliation Act (COBRA), which allows you to carry your company provided insurance benefits with you for up to 18 months from the time you leave the company. You can become either self-employed or unemployed and still qualify. A widow or widower can carry the insurance for up to 3 years. The good news is that you pay the group rate premiums that the company pays. The bad news is that you still have to have an alternate insurance policy after 18 months. You must apply for the COBRA insurance within 60 days of leaving the company to qualify. You are not eligible for COBRA coverage if you are fired for cause or misconduct, so stay out of trouble.

If you are lucky enough to make it to age 65, you qualify for Medicare insurance coverage, which provides a wide variety of insurance benefits. You are eligible the day of your 65th birthday. To ensure that your benefits start on time, contact the Social Security Administration office in your area around three months before your 65th birthday.

By the way, don't overlook the fact that you might retire at age 63 or earlier but not be eligible for Medicare until age 65. These years must be covered by some medical insurance plan other than Medicare, and it usually falls onto your shoulders to get coverage either from your employer or by private insurance.

Medicare falls into two parts: Part A, which covers inpatient hospital treatments, and Part B, which covers doctor's services, medical supplies, and various other medical expenses. Part A is provided for free. You pay a monthly premium of around $36 for Part B coverage.

QuickCaution

Medicare is only designed to cover you in the event of an illness that lasts a short period of time and is of an acute nature. If your illness requires that you stay in the hospital more than 60 days, you better have backup insurance. Otherwise a portion or all the medical fee payments come out of your pocket.

The following is a listing of the coverage provided with Part A and Part B of Medicare:

➤ A $760 deductible is available on your first hospital stay in a benefit period. After that, all costs are covered up to your 60th day in the hospital.

➤ From days 61 to 90, you must pay a $190 per day coinsurance fee.

➤ You are allowed 90 "lifetime reserve days" that can be used at any time during your life. You only have a total of 90 lifetime reserve days for your whole life and each of these days, when used, cost you a $380 coinsurance payment. It is recommended that you treat these days like gold and save them for times when you might need expensive treatment such as intensive care, and your other insurance days are tapped out.

Talkin' Money

Lifetime reserve days are special days that Medicare provides, which can be used to cover any medical expenses. Instead of being related to a specific medical incident or claim, they can be used at any point in your Medicare-covered life. But each day can only be used once, so the reserve of days (90 lifetime reserve days) depletes with each day used. Most people save these days for expensive times, such as those needed to cover intensive care.

➤ The first three pints of blood are not covered by Medicare, but the pints from that point forward are paid 100% by Medicare.

➤ If you have stayed in a hospital for at least three days and are then transferred to a skilled nursing facility, (the step between a nursing home and a hospital) Medicare pays 100% of charges for the first 20 days. Days 21–100 are covered 100% by Medicare as long as you meet the coinsurance deductible amount.

➤ Home health care is covered at 100% for Medicare-approved home health care services and 80% for Medicare-approved home health care equipment.

➤ Hospice care is covered at 100% with some limits set regarding respite (short inpatient stays at a hospice) and outpatient drugs, which are worth confirming with your particular hospice.

➤ Eighty percent of all charges for Medicare-approved outpatient procedures that are performed in a hospital.

➤ Private rooms, private nurses, televisions, telephone, nonemergency hospital care, or medically unnecessary treatments (such as plastic surgery) are not covered.

➤ Don't get sick outside of the United States either because treatment you receive in another country is not covered by Medicare. You might get special consideration if you are in Canada or Mexico when receiving treatment, but don't bet the farm on it.

Part B covers 80% of approved charges for doctor bills, outpatient surgery, some drugs, x-rays, and other medical items. It is important to know that after a healthcare provider agrees to be part of the Medicare system, they cannot go after the patient for more money than is agreed to by Medicare. The Medicare statement clearly states the charges that are your responsibility. So, if you have a major Medicare claim and the doctors or hospital try to get money from you that is over and above that paid by Medicare, don't pay it and turn them in to Medicare to save someone else from getting ripped off. For more information on Medicare coverage, call the Social Security Administration service line at 1-800-772-1213 or stop by any Social Security office for a Medicare handbook.

Covering Yourself Beyond Medicare

Do you notice a pattern forming here with the Medicare coverage? Medicare covers a lot of medical expenses for a limited period of time, but it also misses a lot. For this reason, people take out a Medigap policy that is designed to pick up where Medicare leaves off. These policies are also called MedSup plans.

QuickCaution

Enroll in Medicare Part B within six months of enrolling in Part A or you will be ineligible for the Medigap insurance coverage plans. Bottom line: enroll in both Part A and Part B at the same time.

Medigap insurance was created under federal law as a standardized way for Americans to cover themselves beyond Medicare. Medigap comes in 10 policy types identified by the letters A through J, with A being the most basic plan and J being the most comprehensive. Each plan level has different qualification criteria. Medigap insurance is available through a number of different insurance providers, so shopping around for the best price is a good idea.

Depending on the Medigap insurance you choose, you get a combination of coverage in the following areas:

➤ The basic benefits covered in Plan A cover the coinsurance portions required from Part A coverage to the tune of $174/day for hospital days 61 to 90, $384 per day up to 150 days, and adds 365 extra days where coverage is at 100%. The first three pints of blood and the 20% coinsurance is also covered by Medigap.

➤ The hospital deductible and deductible associated with Part B coverage can also be covered with specific plans.

➤ Beefed-up skilled nursing home coverage is provided with plans C to J.

➤ Foreign travel emergency coverage is provided with plans C to J.

➤ Excess doctor charges coverage is provided with certain plans.

➤ Up to $120 in doctor-recommended preventive screening and testing coverage is provided with Plan E.

➤ Outpatient prescription drugs coverage is expanded with plans H to J.

Medigap coverage is far more complete than that provided by simple Medicare, and you are strongly encouraged to get the additional coverage if you can afford it. After all, can you afford not to have the coverage?

Don't forget that the government defines the coverage, but the insurance comes from private companies and varies as to the price and specific terms. Following are a few things to know about or keep your eyes open for when selecting a carrier:

➤ Make sure that the policy is guaranteed renewable so that a single year of high medical claims on your part doesn't terminate your Medigap insurance coverage.

➤ Know up front whether the policy premiums are going to rise over the life of the policy and by how much.

➤ Get a clear definition regarding the minimum number of days that you must have a condition before you qualify for benefits. It would be a shame to get well sooner than expected and find out that your insurance required a longer illness to provide coverage.

➤ Verify any pre-existing condition clauses that would keep you from getting your medical bills paid on a condition you had years ago.

➤ Test a few real-world scenarios with the insurance provider to see exactly how coverage would work under these circumstances. Write the scenarios down and get them to write their estimated coverage amounts on the same sheet of paper. In this way you minimize the chance of being disappointed later when you present the bills for payment.

➤ Verify the claims procedure and who is responsible for what actions. Does the company have a toll-free number (800 or 888) that you can call for service? Who can you go to if you have a problem? These are all questions you want verified before a medical emergency occurs.

Now, if you are really worried about things and want to prepare for the worst, I suggest you have additional medical coverage over and above that provided by Medicare Part A and Part B and the supplemental provided by your chosen Medigap insurance.

Take a look at the various health insurance policies that do not fall into the Medigap category but still provide supplemental coverage. You might be able to extend your benefits beyond those provided by Medigap and keep your premiums to a reasonable level, possibly negating the need to Medigap at all.

Voice of Experience

Dozens of unfamiliar things happen to you when a loved one has a medical emergency. Many of these things cost money, such as hotel rooms, rental cars, airline tickets, apartment rentals, and hospital meals (ugh). You might even want to have additional services such as a 24-hour sitter service if your loved one is incapable of speaking for herself/himself or in a life compromising condition. These things are usually not provided by a hospital or nursing home and are not covered by Medicare. They also need to be paid for to best ensure your loved one's safety. Start planning today to ensure that lack of money does not compromise the health and safety of your loved one.

It is recommended that you start saving a special medical emergency fund of several thousand dollars. This fund is there for you to dip into without consideration if the situation requires. Hospitals and nursing homes never defend your loved one's interests as much as you or another family member. Having the emergency funds available allows you to do what needs to be done without having your care options limited exclusively to the hospital or Medicare.

No matter what, don't forget that when a serious medical incident happens, the last thing you want to worry about is your insurance coverage. Handle that in advance with the best coverage you can afford so that you can focus on the medical health of the person in crisis.

Paying for Nursing Home or Other Long-Term Care

It appears that you should be insured up to your eyeballs by this time. But, believe it or not, there is another situation that you should seriously consider as an insurance prospect. Medicare and Medigap do not pay for extended stays in a nursing home or other longer-term care facility. This can be a very big deal if your loved one is in a home for many years, because these homes can cost you more than $30,000 per year. Multiply that by 10 years and you are talking a lot of money!

Long-term care (LTC) policies are designed to cover this type of situation. You find that LTC divides covered services into skilled nursing care, intermediate nursing care, custodial care, and home care. Skilled nursing care is the highest level of care, and the most expensive, with trained nursing staff and physicians around 24 hours per day. Intermediate nursing care provides a less intensive level of treatment than skilled nursing but still does not occur at home. The custodial care and home care levels are often performed at the patient's home and rarely involve skilled nursing or medical personnel.

QuickCaution

Your kids are typically covered under your medical policy when they are under 18 year old. From 18 to 23 years old, they must be a full-time student to be covered. If they are over 23, they are on their own unless special circumstances leave them under your policy's umbrella of coverage. Beware that universities provide medical insurance only as long as your child is enrolled as a full-time student. If they drop out or have a serious enough illness that they can't return to school, their school-provided medical coverage could lapse and you might inherit the medical bills. Now that would be a real education!

The LTC policy can be configured to provide the level of care that you desire. The problem with getting too precise with the LTC coverage is that the services needed are heavily dependent upon the patient's recovery, which is often a complete unknown. I suggest that you get the most comprehensive coverage you can afford and make sure that the coverage does not overlap with Medicare's coverage. Another approach is to create enough of an investment portfolio that performs at a high enough return level to pay the required LTC costs indefinitely. This is once again a long-term approach that requires that you think about it far enough in advance to be prepared when the time comes.

Medical Savings Accounts

If you are insured with a small company of 50 or fewer employees and have a medical coverage policy with a high deductible, you can put money into a medical savings account (MSA). The MSA funds are used to offset your medical expenses that are not covered by your insurance. You must be less than 65 to qualify and must not be covered by another medical insurance policy that provides higher levels of coverage. Any financial institution that is qualified to administer IRA accounts can set up an MSA for you.

Tracking Medical Expenses with Quicken

As usual, Quicken can best serve your financial needs if you set up the accounts and categories properly. The following are the recommended procedures for tracking medically related items with Quicken:

➤ Set up liability account called **Medical**. Also set up a separate category for each person in the household who incurs medical expenses. You might consider creating a main expense category called **Medical Exp** and then create subcategories for each person who incurs medical fees. Medical bills are entered as increases to the liability account with disbursements to the proper person's category, such as **Medical Exp:Linda:Doctor**. Reimbursements are entered as decreases to the liability account. Track medical items by account number and healthcare provider payee name.

➤ Repeat the prior procedure for tracking of prescriptions. Create a liability account named **Prescriptions**. Create a main category called **Prescript Exp**, and then create subcategories for each person who uses prescription drugs. Billed prescriptions are entered as increases to the liability account with disbursements to the proper person's category, such as **Prescript Exp:Linda:Drugs**. Reimbursements are entered as decreases to the liability account. Track items by account number and pharmacy or hospital.

➤ Create a special **MSA** asset account to track your MSA contributions. This may require changing deductions from your paycheck. In addition, many of these MSA accounts require that you spend the deposited money within a specified period of time or it is lost. Making deductions from this account when medical expenses are incurred is important, or some of your deposited money could be unused by the end of the qualified period and lost.

239

➤ If you plan to self fund your LTC coverage, you should define an asset account for that purpose. Start making deposits into this account be creating an automatic transaction that transfers funds from your checking/savings account into this **LTC** asset account. The same approach can be applied to tracking an MSA.

➤ Create another account to cover your emergency medical expenses. Call the account **Emergency Med** and define a targeted asset account balance level, such as $3,000, and make deposits into this account until that level is achieved. I suggest that you make this a money market fund that is tracked through your brokerage.

➤ Enter pertinent information into the **Quicken Emergency Records** application. It is activated by resting your cursor over the **Planning** icon and selecting the **Organize Emergency Records** option. This feature allows you to enter medical information about family members, designate doctor and hospital information, and print out a summary report for quick access at a later date, if needed. (In some versions of Quicken, you need to use the **Home & Car** icon to access the **Organize Emergency Records** option.)

Tracking medical expense items is similar to any other expense item with the exception that you are tracking expenses and reimbursements through a medical liability account. And if you think about it, this makes sense. Until the insurance company reimburses you, you must carry a liability debt to the health care provider. If your reimbursements equal your medical bills, this liability account should generally be at zero balance.

The Least You Need to Know

➤ Major medical is highly recommended minimum medical insurance coverage.

➤ Insurance premiums vary with the level of coverage required, your health, your age, and the deductible chosen.

➤ You can get insurance from your employer or get private insurance that is independent of your place of employment.

➤ Medicare coverage applies when you reach age 65 but still requires Medigap coverage and possibly supplemental coverage.

➤ Ignoring long-term care (LTC) coverage can cost a lifetime of savings in a short period of time. Make sure you are prepared for this possibility.

Chapter 18

Taking Risks Doesn't Mean Betting the Farm

In This Chapter

➤ Blend high- and low-risk investments for the optimal investment portfolio

➤ Evaluate your risk tolerance

➤ Use Quicken to track your investments

➤ Update your portfolio for timely performance feedback

➤ Use compounded interest to build your wealth

We have all heard the success stories of people who bought Yahoo!, Dell, or Microsoft when they were just starting out. Those people are often millionaires from the success of their stock. But there are others who have lost money on high-risk stocks and don't talk about it as much.

It is good to take risks, because along with the risk comes the reward of a big success. It isn't necessarily a good idea to take such a huge risk that could seriously hurt or bankrupt you if it doesn't work out.

This chapter takes a look at the relationship between risk and reward, and outlines the steps you can take to get the best rewards of high-risk and conservative investment.

What Kind of Risk Taker Are You?

Ever been to Las Vegas, Nevada? A lot of things can be said about Las Vegas, but one thing most people agree on is that it's an interesting place.

Everyone who goes to Las Vegas to gamble must weigh his or her risk tolerance with the temptations provided. You can play the higher stakes games, such as private card room poker with a minimum $1,000 ante, or the lower stakes games, such as the nickel slot machines. I heard a rumor on my last visit that some casinos now have penny slot machines. It just doesn't get more low-risk than that.

What about these state lotteries where the jackpots get into the hundreds-of-millions of dollars? Each ticket costs only a dollar, but some people take out second mortgages on their homes to buy thousands of the tickets. Each ticket by itself is a low-risk venture, but the overall amount of money risked is substantial.

Risk, as defined in the dictionary, is "exposure to the chance of injury of loss." The injury in financial terms may be a loss of lifestyle caused by a financial loss. The more you are willing to expose yourself to loss, the higher your tolerance for risk and the higher your expected return is for taking that risk. Conversely, the lower your willingness to expose yourself to potential loss, the lower your tolerance for risk and the lower your expected return.

Take a look at yourself and determine where your risk tolerance threshold lies. Risking more money than you can tolerate is a poor approach because you not only lose sleep but also probably make poor money management decisions along the way. If you risk less than you can tolerate, you might be giving up opportunity cost income by leaving your investments in lower-risk accounts.

Risk is also in the eye of the beholder. I know wealthy people who don't gamble because they would never forgive themselves if they lost even as little as $100 on something that self-indulgent. I also know people with no money who don't give a second thought to going to Las Vegas, taking out an advance on their credit card, and gambling the night away.

If you are taking a risk simply for personal enjoyment, I suggest that you set a dollar amount that you are willing to lose. Congratulate yourself if you walk away making money, and console yourself with the fact that you had a good time if you lose it all.

Otherwise, you want to treat your investments as financial decisions, weighing the amount of risk against the possibility for income return on your investment.

Think about assessing your investment risks in the following three areas:

➤ Will the interest return you make off of your investment be greater than the amount of decrease in value due to inflation?

➤ Could you make more money if you invested your money elsewhere, leaving you with an opportunity cost?

➤ Will the place where you made the investment default on their payments, leaving you with a partial or complete loss of your investment?

Notice that the first item on the list is tied to inflation, which in recent years has run around 2%. This is a very low inflation rate, and most people expect this inflation rate to remain relatively constant into the year 2000. So, concern about inflation eating away at your investment is minimal if the projections are accurate.

The opportunity cost risk should be clearly understood before the investment is made. Leaving your money in a savings account because you think the stock market will crash is a great strategy if it really crashes and a poor strategy if it increases 40% over the next 12 months. You weighed the risks at the beginning of the investment period and took your chances appropriately. (See Chapter 3, "Keeping Score with Accounting," for additional details on assessing the opportunity cost.)

The risk of default (that the borrower will not pay you back) is the most likely risk area in today's investment environment. The more you look at various investment opportunities, the more you see a strong correlation between the amount of risk associated with an investment and the interest rate offered.

Think of risk and interest rate in the context of the following example. Assume that you have two people who are asking you for a loan. You have enough money to lend to both, so don't worry about selecting one or the other. You plan to lend to both, but you need to determine the interest rate to charge each of them.

Borrower A has a solid credit record and is already prequalified for a loan from his local bank for 8%. You want to lend to him so you can make money off of his loan instead of the bank.

> **QuickCaution**
>
> Trying to undo the past only costs you anguish and probably money because today's investment environment doesn't look anything like the one that existed a year ago. Make your investment decisions based on what you know today and hope you are right.

Borrower B has a spotty credit record and has been turned down by the standard financial institutions. You want to lend the money, but you want to be compensated for taking the risk.

Notice that the risk associated with borrower B is higher than with borrower A because A has historically shown that he pays back his loans, whereas there is a question about repayment with borrower B.

Making a loan to both A and B at the same 8% rate doesn't make sense under these circumstances. So, you apply some type of "risk premium" to the borrower B loan to compensate you for taking the increased risk. The amount of that risk premium is up to you and driven by market conditions, but you might charge him a 10% interest rate (8% plus a 2% risk premium) to provide you with some incentive for making the higher-risk loan. In some cases, you want some type of collateral, such as a car, as security for the loan so that if borrower B defaulted on the loan, you could use the proceeds from the sale of the car to pay off the outstanding loan balance at the time of default.

The reverse situation is true when you are investing in stocks, bonds, mutual funds, or U.S. government treasury bills. The treasury bills pay the lowest interest rate because they are the lowest risk of the bunch, requiring the default of the U.S. government for lack of repayment. From there you get a wild mix of various investments that provide a wide range of interest return rates, which are all higher than the treasury bill based on their higher risk.

Think about the following things when assessing your risk tendencies:

Low-Risk Takers (Risk Averse)

➤ Tend to worry excessively about things not working out as planned.

➤ Never comfortable risking money needed to ensure lifestyle security.

➤ Think others take unnecessary risks.

High-Risk Takers

➤ Like the excitement of letting it all ride again on the same number.

➤ Willing to take a change on a compromised lifestyle for the chance to win big.

➤ Think that low-risk takers are way too conservative.

Medium-risk takers are somewhere in between these two.

I have found that few people fit cleanly into one category or another, and that risk tendencies change with age, family responsibilities, and life shocks. For example, a parent of two young children is less likely to "bet the farm" than a 23-year-old professional making $65,000 and no family. A death in the family can change a person's view from one extreme to the other in either direction. As people get older, they realize that they have less time to recover from risky ventures that don't pay off, and often turn to less risky investments as a way of not compromising a secure retirement.

Everyone must make the investment decisions that are right for them, and these decisions should be made with eyes wide open to the risk and rewards.

I personally favor a mixed approach where you allocate a certain amount of money for your risky side and put the rest of your investment money into an account that takes advantage of the long run through compounded interest.

Long Term Is Generally Better in the Long Run

Have you ever noticed that doing a little of a large project every day eventually leads to getting it done completely? This is absolutely true when it comes to building a nest egg. You are always better served by putting a little away every month as opposed to trying to make a lot of money that you invest all at once.

Any weight loss professional will tell you that long-term weight loss is accomplished by consistently losing a certain amount of weight every week or two.

Trying to lose a large amount of weight on a crash diet over a short period of time has minimal likelihood of success. For example, losing a pound every two weeks doesn't sound like much until you do this over a 6-month period and lose 12 pounds. Do this over a year and you lose 24 pounds. And so forth.

The same applies to investment in that a little bit of interest earned on an account every month adds up to big money over time. Money actually multiplies over time so that the interest that your account earns today actually earns more interest for you in the future. This in effect is called "compounded interest."

Compounding Interest to Real Wealth

Compounded interest means that the money you place into an account today earns interest, and that total money earns interest next year. The net result is that you earn interest on the interest or your earnings are compounded over time. This is the secret to building wealth over time.

Assume that you put $5,000 into an account today that earns 10% annual interest and do not add any more money to this account for 25 years, and then check your balance. You would find your account balance at $54,000! Not bad for having done nothing but put that $5,000 into an account and wait.

Now get ready for something mind blowing. Assume that you monthly put $100 into this 10% account. At the end of the same 25 years, this monthly $100 ritual would earn you $132,683 dollars. Now, that is big bucks! Notice that you actually only deposited $100 × 12 × 25 = $35,000, yet wind up with over $132,000 due to the effects of compounded interest.

The moral of this story is to always make a deposit to yourself every month into the highest interest-paying account your risk tolerance level lets you stand. As you might have heard from other financial advisors, "Pay yourself before you pay anyone else." Allocate at least 5% per month of what you make toward this deposit, allocating more if you possibly can. If you think about it, $100 a month is not that much money, but it can really add to your financial independence if performed as a ritual monthly act.

Try to shift your investment horizon from the near term of less than 12 months to the longer term of 10 years, or more. This applies for all your investments. The longer your investment horizon, the more you can use the power of compounded interest to your benefit.

Trying to Make a Killing Can Leave You Broke

Do you know anyone who is always trying to work that "one deal" that will set them up for life? Most of us have either experienced this desire ourselves or know someone who has. You should now see the problem with using this approach as your long-term investment strategy. There is no long term in this approach. It is exciting, invigorating, nerve-wracking, and makes for good stories at cocktail parties, but it usually doesn't pay the bills when you retire.

This strategy does not put the power of compounded interest to work for you. Your investments aren't given enough time to compound before they are removed and used for your latest "get rich quick" scheme. If that scheme fails to pay off as you optimistically planned, you are left starting all over again.

Voice of Experience

I spent my late 20s and early 30s with a number of start-up companies in the Silicon Valley area. I took all my energy, time, and money and put them into making these companies succeed. After all, I had founder's stock that would make me a ton of money when it sold for big bucks. Well, I now own some of the coolest looking, yet worthless, stock certificates around.

It is true that I would have made a lot of money if the companies had done well, but they didn't. I should have realized at the time that the high payoff opportunity is possible because there was an associated high risk that it wouldn't work. I really never let myself absorb the high-risk portion of the equation, and I paid for my oversight when the companies folded. High risk means high reward, and high reward means high risk. This is a two-way street.

It is okay to buy a lottery ticket, but don't make it your only ticket to building your nest egg. I suggest a two-pronged approach where you take higher risks with a certain amount of your money, and lower risks with the rest. Always pay yourself with a lower-risk investment deposit before putting the money into the higher-risk investments.

Following this approach allows you to speculate on the higher-risk ventures without risking a financially insecure retirement.

What Is a Lower–Risk Investment?

Lower-risk investments provide a lower return on the money invested, but provide a high likelihood that you not only get your initial investment money back but also get the agreed-upon interest on that invested money.

Typical low-risk investments include, but are not limited to, the following:

➤ Real estate in a stable neighborhood that you use for your primary residence.

➤ U.S. Treasury bonds.

➤ Corporate bonds with high ratings such as AAA or Aaa. See the later section in this chapter for details about the various bond ratings.

➤ Certificates of deposit provided by your lending institution.

➤ Your standard savings account that is insured for up to $100,000 by the Federal Deposit Insurance Corporation.

➤ Money market funds.

Notice that all these investments pay lower interest rates when compared with medium- and higher-risk investments. For example, a standard savings account at the time of this writing pays around 3%. A CD may pay as high as 5% if you leave it for a few years, whereas real estate on average appreciates at 2–5% per year (and you can live in it—try doing that with a savings bond.)

Also notice that no individual stocks were included in this list. You can minimize your stock investment risks by investing in mutual funds instead of individual stocks, thus avoiding placing all your eggs into one corporate stock basket. (See Chapter 19, "Protecting Your Dough with Investments That Aren't So Risky," for additional information about mutual funds.)

You can count on these types of investments to pay off as expected unless the entire economy falls into a tailspin, which can and does happen, but very rarely.

You might be surprised at my inclusion of real estate, especially if you have lived through Texas, New England, or other U.S. real estate difficulties that existed in the late 1980s up until the mid-1990s. Investing in a home is still the best investment decision you can make as long as you plan to hold it for a few years. You have to live somewhere, and you are almost always financially better served by owning your home instead of renting it. (See Chapter 12, "There's No Place Like Home," for additional information.)

Looking at Medium-Risk Investments

Keeping all your money in a savings account may guarantee the safety of your money and provide you with a solid 3% annual interest income, but you may feel a little too conservative when you see people making 2 to 5 times that amount of interest per year and not losing any of their initial investment. At some point you start to wonder whether you are being too conservative. Once again, this depends on your risk tolerance and how you handle your money.

Talkin' Money

Volatility is a measure of the stability of the returns that are received from an investment. If the return can vary significantly over the term of the investment, this is considered a more volatile investment than one with a guaranteed return.

Instead of jumping into the high-risk stock game, you might choose to take a portion of your money out of savings and put it into a medium- or moderate-risk investment. These are investments that have a higher volatility because the amount of return is not fixed and can vary over the term of the investment, which makes the overall investment less predictable.

The following is a partial listing of moderate-risk investments:

➤ Blue-chip stocks that pay a high dividend

➤ Other stocks that show a high stock price growth and pay high dividends

➤ Mutual funds that track the various indexes

➤ Mutual funds comprised of government-backed securities such as Ginnie Mae mortgages, which are bundled mortgage loans that are guaranteed by the federal government

Talkin' Money

The blue-chip stock listing is a listing of companies based on the size of the company, its profitability, and its stock's overall performance.

Notice that stocks appear on this list, but only those stocks that have been around for a long time and have a consistent performance history, such as IBM, AT&T, and the other blue-chip stocks. The blue-chip stock list changes because stocks that qualify for inclusion at one point may not qualify at another due to performance irregularities.

Remember that your risk of losing money on an investment goes higher as your investment return increases.

Living on the Financial Edge

Assume that you drive a fast car, fly on all your vacations, and eat dinner standing up. Waiting a long time to see results just isn't for you. You want to be where the action is. Well, the higher-risk investments fit right in with your personality type and investment desires.

Higher-risk investments provide the possibility of higher investment returns at the very real risk that you lose either part or all your initial investment. If you have money, there is always someone out there willing to use it for you. The question is whether giving it to them is worth the risk on your part.

The following is a partial listing of higher-risk investments from which you can choose:

➤ New companies with new technologies in emerging marketplaces. Getting in at the investment ground floor with these companies can really pay off big if this company hits pay dirt. These companies are often not publicly traded, so you may have to look to find them.

➤ Small, publicly traded companies whose securities are traded on the secondary exchanges, such as the NASDAQ or the Over The Counter exchanges. Many small companies first introduce themselves on the Canadian Stock Exchange and trade for a few cents per share.

➤ Investment real estate in transitional areas of cities presents interesting, yet higher-risk opportunities. Buying a run down building on the fringes of an up-and-coming neighborhood allows you to buy the building for a reasonable price, fix it up, and hopefully sell it in a few years as part of the trendy section that migrated into your neighborhood.

➤ Purchasing stock in a company that recently fell on hard times and whose stock is trading at all-time low levels. If you believe that the stock will rebound, buying now pays off well for you when it does rebound. If the slide continues, you might just lose everything as the company goes out of business.

➤ International investing can provide great returns but not without exposing your investment to the tides of that particular country.

There are too many high-risk investment opportunities in the marketplace to list them all here. My primary interest (no pun intended) is to give you a feeling for what constitutes a low-, medium-, and high-risk investment. Notice that the higher-risk investments give you the excitement of knowing that your entire investment could be at risk, whereas the lower-risk investments give you the comfort of knowing that your money is there next year even if you make less money from it.

Being Realistic with Yourself Is Less Disappointing

It is written somewhere that you should always try to be true to yourself, and the same applies to managing personal investments. If you extend your risk level too far, you won't sleep well at night, and any rewards gained might be overshadowed by the nervousness associated with taking the risk.

For those of you at the other end of the risk spectrum, you might beat yourself up for not having taken a bigger chance when you see others "making a killing" while you slug along at your measly 8% annual return.

A solution is available for both of you. Why not create a blended portfolio that combines some low risk with some moderate risk and high risk. This way you create a scenario where you do not risk everything but still can take advantage of the opportunities provided by the higher-risk/higher-return investments. Look at Table 18.1 to see the various ways that your investment risk can be distributed over low-, medium-, and high-risk investments. Also notice how they blend together to provide an overall risk rate.

Table 18.1   Varying Investment Risk Mix at Different Ages

Age Group	Low-Risk	Medium-Risk	High-Risk	Blended-Risk
Under 35	20%/6%	30%/10%	50%/20%	14.2%
Age 35–55	25%/6%	40%/10%	35%/20%	12.5%
Over 55	40%/6%	40%/10%	20%/20%	10.4%
Retirement: As needed to accommodate required cash flows.				

The examples shown in the table show the blended interest rate you would see if you put a specific percentage of your money into low-, medium-, and high-risk investments paying 6%, 10%, and 20%, respectively. The upper percentage number indicates the percentage of your money you have invested in that bracket, and the lower percentage number indicates the expected return from that investment category. The blended rate of return is calculated by multiplying the percentage of money in each category by the return in that category and adding those three numbers together. For example, the under-35 blended return rate is calculated as: $.20 \times .06 + .30 \times .10 + .50 \times .20 = .142$ or 14.2%. Perform the blended calculations for the other age brackets to prove to yourself that the blended rates are accurate.

The table shows that keeping some of your money in low- and medium-risk investments drops the under-35 bracket's possible investment return. If all money was put into a high risk (that could also all be lost), the return would be 20%, whereas the return is 14.6% if blended over the three investment categories. You might think of this as giving up 5.8% in possible income, but take a look at the return if all your money is in a high-risk investment, and you lost all the money—0%. Ouch! Losing all your high-risk money in a blended investment still provides you with an 8% return on what was not in the high-risk investment. Don't forget that you also lost 50% of your money, but you are not broke thanks to your lower-risk investments.

Take some time to build up your risk money and try it again. You can afford to take a few risks when you are under 35 and still have 20+ years of earning power ahead of you.

The risk factor changes when you are over 55 and looking at retirement. You really cannot afford to lose it all at this point because you just don't have the number of earning power years ahead of you to make up for losing it all on a risky venture. For this reason, the investment percentages shift more toward the conservative with a little left for the higher risk. If the lower-risk investments provide you with the needed income, you might consider shifting it all to lower risk. After all, as a retired person you first want to ensure that your financial security is intact, and then secondly worry about maximizing the amount of money you make off of your investments.

Notice that this blended risk approach keeps you from putting all your investment eggs in one basket, while still allowing you to take advantage of higher-risk opportunities.

QuickCaution

Don't risk more than you are willing to lose. Putting money into high-risk investments puts it at risk for being lost completely. If you can't afford to lose it, protect it with lower-risk, lower-return investments. Wasn't there a story, once upon a time, about a turtle and a rabbit? I think the turtle won.

This approach also allows you to easily adjust your investments to your particular risk tolerance level. You simply vary the percentage of your investment fund that is earmarked for each investment risk category based on your personal propensity for risk. The blended risk level adjusts accordingly.

Quicken's Investment Features and Tools

Quicken has a set of investment-tracking features that truly makes portfolio management easier. The following are some of the things you can do with these handy tools:

➤ Track mutual funds as a single fund or as a group of funds.

➤ Track the purchase and sale of individual stock securities.

➤ Group investments by personal goal description, such as college savings, high-risk, low-risk, or custom descriptions that mean something specifically to you.

➤ Group investments by type, such as CD, stock, bond, and mutual fund.

➤ You can also perform most stock-transfer-related activities, such as tracking of splits, reinvesting dividends, and options.

➤ Provide an overall report of your portfolio performance based on its cost basis and current market value.

➤ Use the Internet to update the current status of the stocks and funds included in your portfolio.

(See Chapter 19, "Protecting Your Dough with Investments That Aren't So Risky," and Chapter 20, "Rake in More Dough with Riskier Investments," for specific information regarding investment tracking with Quicken.)

The Least You Need to Know

➤ Taking too much risk can not only cost you sleep, but it can also cost you your retirement nest egg.

➤ Taking too little risk can cost you money in terms of lost investment opportunities and can erode your nest egg if the rate of inflation becomes higher than the return on your investments.

➤ The best portfolio contains a mixture of high-, medium-, and low-risk investments that shift in relative percentages to each other as needed.

➤ Quicken has some great investment tracking and management tools that make stock, bond, and mutual fund tracking an easy process.

➤ Information is king when it comes to investing, and the online update features easily keep you updated on the market in general and your investments in particular.

Chapter 19

Protecting Your Dough with Investments That Aren't So Risky

In This Chapter

➤ Determine the low-risk investments that are right for you

➤ Understand bond ratings and their impact on returns

➤ Learn how mutual funds diversify your portfolio

➤ Demystify bond jargon and understand its place in your investment portfolio

➤ Use Quicken to find the mutual funds that are right for you

---

Making money is hard enough. Making the money just to lose it on a poor investment decision is even harder. As outlined in Chapter 18, "Taking Risks Doesn't Mean Betting the Farm," a well recognized investment approach is to invest in low-, medium-, and high-risk investments. This chapter reviews several of the more common lower-risk investment alternatives that lay the solid foundation for additional higher-risk investments.

Money Market Funds

Money market accounts fall into two large categories: money market deposit accounts and money market mutual funds.

A money market deposit account is available through a standard financial institution such as a bank and pays an interest rate just slightly higher than a savings account. They usually have a minimum balance level that keeps you from having to pay a maintenance fee. You can write checks against these accounts, but the checks often have a minimum amount and there is a limit to the number of checks you can write against the account in a given time period. The good news is that the money market deposit account is federally insured, so the risk with this investment is very low.

QuickTip

Your standard financial institution's savings accounts (passbook), checking accounts, certificates of deposit (CD), and money market deposit accounts are usually federally insured by the Federal Deposit Insurance Corporation (FDIC) for up to $100,000 per account if your bank is a member.

This insurance is great as long as your balance is less than $100,000. What happens when your account balance is more than $100,000 (which I certainly hope it is)?

If the financial institution goes into default, the amount more than $100,000 might be placed in jeopardy. Ask your financial institution for detailed information about the federal insurance coverage on your account, and take out multiple accounts such as a savings account, CD, and money market account to make sure that the federal insurance covers your deposits.

A money market fund is a lot like a money market deposit account, except the fund actually invests your deposit in other financial instruments such as short-term corporate debt (called commercial paper), treasury bills, and short-term municipal debt. You should be able to write checks against the account, but there is usually a minimum check amount and maximum number of checks allowed during a given calendar period.

Money market funds come in two flavors: tax free and taxable.

At the time of this writing, a taxable money market fund paid interest in the range of 5.3% to 5.85% depending on the minimum allowed investment and who offered the fund. The government-only money market funds paid around 4.99%. The interest income obtained from investing in these funds is taxable income, which means that the after-tax return is actually lower than the numbers shown. If you are in a 36% federal tax bracket and pay 3% in state income tax, you must decrease the interest income by 39% to get an idea of the after tax income you actually receive. For example, the 5.3% interest rate really gets you 5.3% × (1 − .39) = 3.2%. The tax-free funds make a lot more sense after this discussion.

A federal tax-free fund is one that provides interest income that is not subject to taxes because the underlying money funds are derived from debt associated with municipalities. At the time of this writing, these funds pay an average of 3.30% interest rate, with some funds paying as high as 3.66%. Notice that a taxable fund has to yield a higher return than the 3.66% to provide an equal return after taxes. In fact, if you are the 39% tax bracket person discussed in the preceding paragraph, the taxable fund must pay 3.66% / (1 − .39) = 6% to provide an equal after tax return. For this person, the tax-free fund would be a better option because none of the taxable funds pay more than 5.85% interest. Funds may be tax free at the federal level, but taxable at the state level, so check both federal and state tax status before investing.

For someone in a lower tax bracket of 15% federal plus 3% state (18% total tax), the taxable funds would be a better investment. Prove this to yourself by multiplying 5.5% × (1 − .18) = 4.51%, which is the after-tax return on a taxable fund and is higher than the 3.66% by the tax-free funds.

No matter how you slice these funds, their rate of interest return is low compared with other higher-risk investments. They are very secure and pay a higher return than your savings account, which at the time of this writing showed a taxable yield of around 2.26%, which really puts the after-tax yield at something lower than that. All of a sudden, a very secure tax-free yield of 3.66% looks better to you low-risk investors, doesn't it?

Certificates of Deposit

A certificate of deposit (CD) is an investment typically offered by a financial institution that pays a little higher interest rate than a money market deposit account. Why? Because money invested in a CD is tied up for a specific period of time, which can range from a few months to several years. And there are penalties associated with removing your money before the end of the agreed-upon period.

The penalties are levied because of the way banks manage money. Remember that banks make money when it is loaned out, which is exactly what is done with your CD money. It is offered as loans to borrowers, and the period of the loans corresponds to the period of your CD. If you want your money earlier than expected, the bank must come up with the money from elsewhere, because the money you deposited is out on loan and not due back until a later date. The bank did not make the planned amount on your CD and charges you a penalty for changing your mind.

These accounts are federally insured by the FDIC, making them a very safe place to put your money, but know that you may not be able to get at it for an extended

Talkin' Money

Liquidity is determined by the speed with which something of value can be turned into cash. Your checking and savings accounts are treated as cash, so they have a high liquidity. Your house may have value, but if you have to sell it in a slow real estate market to turn that value into cash, it has very low liquidity.

period of time, which makes them less liquid than a money market deposit account or a savings account.

You can hedge against this time frame dilemma by getting your CD through a brokerage house instead of your financial institution, such as a bank or credit union. A brokerage house can help you sell your CD should you unexpectedly need the money before its termination date, and they may have access to CDs from other parts of the country with more attractive terms that may get you a higher interest rate. Verify that a brokered CD is also federally insured, or make sure that you are compensated with a higher interest rate for absorbing that additional risk.

A typical CD may pay an interest rate that is a few percentage points higher than a standard savings account. At the time of this writing, taxable CD rates varied from around 5.41% for a one-month CD to 7.21% for a five-year CD. By the way, the one-month CD requires a $100,000 deposit.

Only you can decide if this slight increase in interest rate is worth tying up your money for an extended period of time. If you think that you might need the money that you plan to put into the CD at some point during the CD term, don't invest it. Only invest the money that you are sure you won't need or the penalties can offset any interest gain that you see. Naturally, if an emergency comes up, you do what it takes to get through it. Don't forget, cash today is almost always worth more than the promise of cash tomorrow.

Bonding as a Secure Investment

A loan is paid back over a period of time, in little increments as outlined in the amortization schedule. What if you could borrow money from someone, agree to pay it back at the end of a few years, and only make interest payments between now and then? Notice that this approach enables you to get the money you need today and minimizes the periodic payments you must make over the period of the loan. This is the approach used when a company, government, or government agency issues bonds.

A bond is an IOU from the issuer of the bond to the person who buys the bond. The IOU outlines the par value of the bond (or the amount of money loaned usually in increments of $1,000), the interest rate paid over the life of the bond, and the bond's maturity date, which is the date when it must be paid back. This bond differs from stock in that a bond is a legal loan agreement that must be repaid whereas stock represents a speculative investment that can be lost entirely. When you hold a bond, you become a creditor to the entity issuing the bond. Therefore, if a company goes bankrupt, the bondholders get their money back before the stockholders.

Talkin' Money

The par value of a bond is the amount that is paid for the bond when it reaches maturity, also called the face value of the bond. Usually issued in increments of $1,000.

A bond's maturity date is when the amount owed by the bond issuer must be paid to the holder of the bond.

Bonds have interest rates, also called coupon rates, associated with them that determine the interest payments that can be expected by the bond holder over the life of the bond.

Yield is the total amount of money made from a bond over its lifetime, which may be different from the interest rate depending on whether the bond was sold during its life and historical interest-rate fluctuations.

Bond ratings classify bonds as to their level of risk. Ratings are issued by Moody's and Standard & Poor's, which are two recognized rating agencies whose information is readily accessible by any brokerage or is listed on the bond issue itself.

Junk bonds are bonds with very poor ratings of Ca/CC or lower that have a high risk of going into default and not being repaid.

Investment-grade bonds are bonds with a rating of Baa/BBB or higher that have a high likelihood of being repaid.

How Does a Bond Rate?

Just as people have credit ratings, so do companies and governmental agencies. Moody's and Standard & Poor's have an industry-accepted bond-rating system that provides an independent assessment of a bond issuer's ability to repay the bond amount. Take a look at Table 19.1 for a listing of the various bond rating levels and their meaning.

QuickTip

The federal government bonds are not rated because it can always come after you and me in the form of increased taxes to pay its debt. If the federal government falls into default, we are all in trouble.

Table 19.1   Rating Bonds and Determining Their Investment Risk

Moody's	Standard & Poor's	Meaning	Comment
Aaa	AAA	Best quality	Investment Grade
Aa	AA	High quality	Investment Grade
A	A	Med High quality	Investment Grade
Baa	BBB	Medium quality	Investment Grade
Ba	BB	Moderate security	
B	B	Solid but shaky	
Caa	CCC	Poor quality	
Ca	CC	High risk	Junk Bond
C	C	Lowest rating	Junk Bond
D	n/a	In default	Junk Bond

See Talkin' Money, earlier in this section, for more on Investment Grade and Junk Bonds.

As you should expect by this point, the lower the rating, the higher the likelihood that the bond issuer defaults on the interest payments, repays the bond upon maturity, or both. The higher the risk, the higher the interest rate must be to attract investors. Junk bonds are issued to fund smaller companies with little track record or a poor track record. They entice investors, who clearly know the risks associated with providing the money, with the promise of much higher interest rates on the bonds. Once again, the higher the risk, the higher the expected reward must be.

Bond investments can be at risk in the following ways:

➤ The initially invested money might be lost if the issuer simply does not pay off the bond when it hits maturity.

➤ If the issuer does not make the interest payments as agreed upon, it diminishes the investment yield of the bond over its lifetime.

➤ If inflation and interest rates rise during the bond's term, the value of your bond investment as compared to other investments decreases. If you hold the bond to maturity, you receive the agreed upon amount of money that yields your expected return, but your investment might have an opportunity cost associated with it due to the effects of inflation and interest rates.

The first and second bulleted items are pretty obvious at this point. The third bullet point may need a little explanation.

Bond Values Change Over Time

A thorough understanding of bond sale prices and yields is a pretty complicated topic, and somewhat counter-intuitive. There is really no way to discuss the topic without performing financial calculations similar to those presented in this section. If you are not interested in bond value calculations, or if you find a lot of math confusing, I suggest that you skip this section. But, for those of you who want to test your financial understanding, take a few moments to work through this example. If you get to the point that you understand bond valuation discussions, you are well on your way to understanding the time value of money and the importance of bonds in financial markets.

Assume that you purchase a tax-free bond that has a par value of $10,000, an interest rate of 5.5% and a maturity date 10 years in the future. This bond pays $550 per year in after taxes and preinflation adjusted interest income.

Also assume that inflation is 3%. Notice that your after inflation interest rate is 5.5% – 3% = 2.5%, which is still a positive number. You are making .025 × $10,000 = $250 per year on the bond investment, after accounting for inflation.

Assume that you are now beginning the fourth year of the 10-year term, and the inflation rate has jumped to 6%. Your bond is still paying 5.5%, but now notice that inflation is eating away at your interest rate to the point that you are now losing money to the tune of 5.5% – 6% = –0.5% per year, or $50 per year after adjusting for inflation. Ouch!

This is no longer a great investment, and you decide to sell the bond. A problem exists. Other investments on the market are paying higher interest rates, such as 8% or higher. For someone to purchase your 5.5% bond, you must give them incentive, so you wind up dropping the sale price on the bond to some negotiated level less than $10,000 to entice another investor. Notice that over the three years that you held the bond, you made $750 (3 years × $250 per year = $750). You might consider dropping the sale price on the bond to $9,250 so that you can get out with your skin and not have to lose money in the upcoming years.

Your prospective buyer might now be interested because the bond still pays $550 per year in tax-free interest, and their investment is only $9,250. Notice that he owns a bond that pays $10,000 at the maturity date. Notice also that $550 / $9,250 = 5.95%, which means that he is just breaking even today when inflation is considered. If the buyer believes that inflation will drop next year, he can expect to make money over the rest of the bond's life and still collect his $9,250 investment plus $750 when the bond pays off $10,000 at its maturity date.

Complicated formulas are involved with calculating the total percentage return that this buyer sees over the life of the bond, called the "yield." The simplest way to determine the yield is to check with your broker for current yield information on your specific bond issues.

Understanding Bond Information in the Newspaper

I have dropped a huge amount of jargon on you over the last few sections. Now, I put it all together by looking at typical bond-reporting information.

Table 19.2 Evaluating Financial Status of Two Bond Issues

Bond	CurYld	Vol	Close	NetChg
JackSt 11-3/4 02	10.8	33	109-7/8	+1/8
NickTr 8-1/4 99	7.9	20	104	–1/8

The preceding two table lines contain a lot of information about the bond offerings shown. (Note: These are fictitious offerings from fictitious companies, so don't try to look them up for comparison purposes.)

QuickTip

The "eighths" section of a bond price refers to the number of "eighths" of a $10 increment and represents the number that sits in the "ones" and "cents" section of the price. For example, 1/8 = $1.25 ($10/8), 1/4 = $2.50, 3/8 = $3.75, 1/2 = %$5.00, 5/8 = $6.25, 3/4 = $7.50 and 7/8 = $8.75. A bond selling at 96-1/2, is really selling for $965, calculated as $960 + $5.00 = $965. Are you thoroughly confused yet? It takes time, so hang in there.

Two separate bond offerings are shown: one from Jackson Strip Mining (JackSt) and another from Nickerson Trailers (NickTr). The abbreviation, also called a "ticker symbol," may not be obvious, so your broker may be able to help you find the company issuing the bond.

Working from left to right for the JackSt offering, you see that the interest rate on the bond is 11-3/4%. Next to the interest rate is 02 indicating that the bond matures in the year 2002, with the 20 assumed. Notice that the 19 portion of 1999 maturity date is assumed for the NickTr offering. Next to the maturation date is the current yield (10.8%) for the bond if purchased at the close price listed. The Vol column indicates the dollar volume of this bond that traded yesterday, which is shown in thousands of dollars. The 33 indicates that $33,000 worth of this bond traded hands yesterday. The Close column indicates the market price that this bond closed at on the previous day's trading (109-7/8). This means that the current market value for this bond is $1,098.75. The NetChg column indicates the net change between yesterday's market price and today's.

In this case, the bond increased by +1/8, which means that the bond increased in market value by $1.25.

Notice that the current yield of 10.8% is under the 11-3/4% interest rate offered on the bond. Also notice that the bond is selling at a premium of $98.75 (sale price of $1,098.75) over its $1,000 par value. Because the current buyer pays $98.75 more to own the bond, its yield to that owner must be lower because the interest paid remains the same as does the redemption value of $1,000, but the amount paid for the bond is higher than the originally issued $1,000 par value rate.

It is natural to question, at this point, why someone would pay more than face value for a bond? Assume that the interest rates offered for other investment vehicles had dropped to a lower level that that available when the bond was first issued. The bond pays an interest rate of 11-3/4%, and assume that the current interest rate on other investment vehicles is 8%. This makes the bond a more valuable investment vehicle when compared to the other, available investments. As a result, it is worth more to the buyer, which is why the investor is willing to pay more than the face value for the loan.

Two ways exist for you to buy bonds: you can purchase them through a broker or some banks, or you can buy new treasury bonds issued directly from the Federal Reserve Bank as long as you have first set up a Treasury Direct account. Interest payments and the final payoff distribution are made directly into your bank account from the Treasury Direct account. If you want to sell your treasury bond before they mature, you must first transfer them into a brokerage account from which they can be traded.

Bonds are traded on the New York Stock Exchange, the American Stock Exchange, and privately within brokerages. Be aware that most bonds require a large upfront minimum investment of at least $5,000. There is some talk going around that this minimum may drop to $1,000 for most bonds. Check with your broker for additional details regarding bond trading.

QuickTip

Following is a rule of thumb that is worth keeping in mind. If you think that interest rates (and usually inflation) are going to drop, it is safe to assume that bond prices will go up, which is good news if you already own bonds because this increases the value of your investment as compared to other investments. If you think that interest rates are going to increase, it is safe to assume that bond prices will decrease as other investments pay higher interest rates, which is a bad thing if you already own bonds because the value of your investment probably drops as compared to other investments.

261

What about Savings Bonds?

Did your parents buy savings bonds for you when you were a kid? I was always told that the savings bond was an investment in America, and I bought them for years. They are still around and readily available from most banks. Stop by almost any bank to find the current value of your savings bonds or to cash them in. Although they are not really a great investment, savings bonds are offered in smaller denominations that make it easier for investors to get started. The savings bond purchase/redemption process is as follows:

➤ At the time of this writing, you pay 50% of the face value at the time of purchase. So, a savings bond with a $100 redemption value costs you $50 to purchase today. This is around a 4% annual interest rate.

➤ Hold the bond for 18 years and cash it in for the full redemption value—in this case, $100. You can hold the bond longer if you choose and still collect interest, up to 40 years in some cases.

➤ Any gain realized when you redeem the bond is then taxable at the federal level but exempt from state and local taxes.

➤ Savings bonds are not transferable, which means that they are issued to you alone, and only you or your heir can cash it in. If you lose your savings bond, write to The Bureau of Public Debt, Parkersburg, West Virginia 26106-1328 to get another issued.

Annuities

Annuities have been around for a long time and represent an agreement between you and your insurance company. You make payments into an account that is managed by the insurance company, which invests the money for you and, in exchange, agrees to return a fixed number of payments of a certain amount or to make payments of a fixed amount for the duration of your life, which I certainly hope is a very long time. You can also arrange to receive a single lump sum payment if desired.

Annuities come in two basic types: immediate and deferred. Immediate annuities require that you deposit immediately into the account usually as a lump sum deposit and the insurance company starts paying you immediately. Deferred annuities require that you start depositing today and the insurance company does not need to start paying you until a later date, usually when you are 59 1/2 to avoid paying a 10% early withdrawal penalty.

Talkin' Money

An immediate annuity starts paying you during the same year that the annuity is started with any earned interest left in the annuity fund remaining tax deferred. Applicable to those over 59 1/2.

A deferred annuity starts making payments to you at least one year in the future, and usually after you are 59 1/2 years old to avoid early withdrawal penalties.

Annuities provide you with a payment on a regular basis for either a fixed number of years, or for the rest of your life, depending on the type selected.

A fixed annuity provides you with a fixed investment vehicle with an interest rate that might vary annually over the life of the annuity.

A variable annuity allows you to move your funds around into different investment vehicles but makes no guarantees about the future annuity level or total value of the annuity account.

The annuitant is the person who receives the funds distributed from the annuity contracted account.

An annuity is annuitized when it starts to make annuity payments to the annuitant. This usually happens after the annuitant reaches age 59 1/2.

The immediate annuity is most applicable to a person older than 59 1/2. Assume that you have $50,000 that you want to invest at 12% annually, which equates to $6,000 interest income per year or around $500 per month. Also assume that you only need $250 of that money as monthly supplemental income. The extra $250 would be taxable interest income if not part of a tax-deferred annuity. Because you set up an immediate annuity, you can immediately deposit your $50,000 and start taking out $250 per month with the balance retained in the annuity fund as tax-free interest income.

The tax-deferred annuity is the most popular because it defers tax payments on the interest earned until the interest is drawn out of the account after you reach the age of 59 1/2. This is often beneficial because you usually draw the money out after age 59 1/2, or in retirement, when your income is lower along with your tax bracket, compared to today when your earning power is typically much higher.

Deferred annuities also come in the fixed and variable flavors. The fixed is similar to a CD with a deferred tax clause attached because you do not pay tax on the accrued interest until withdrawn, but you also cannot move the money from one account to another. The interest rate paid by the insurance company can vary periodically, usually annually, over the life of the agreement.

Variable annuities allow you to move money between asset types or even split your invested money over multiple asset types such as mutual funds. In a lot of ways, the variable annuity is similar to a mutual fund with the added attraction of deferring paying tax on any gain until age 59 1/2. In fact, you can set up annuity accounts so that they invest in mutual funds, obtaining mutual fund performance levels, but are tax deferred because the funds are part of an annuity account. This is an attractive benefit for you higher tax bracket folks.

Talk to your insurance agent or brokerage firm for additional information regarding the annuity programs offered by the company.

Mutual Funds with Lower Returns

Putting all your eggs in one basket can be dangerous if you have slippery fingers. At best you might end up with scrambled eggs. At worst, you might end up with no breakfast.

The same is true for investments. Placing all your money into a single investment might be fine if that investment is performing well, but can be disastrous should that investment have problems.

Financial people use "diversification" as a hedge against any single security taking a nose dive and possibly taking the entire investment portfolio with it. Diversification spreads the investment risk over a number of different investment vehicles so that a rapid decrease in one is tempered by the performance of the other investments.

Talkin' Money

An investment vehicle can be any asset type that provides some type of return on investment, from treasury bonds to stocks and junk bonds.

When brokers talk about various securities, they are referring to stocks as opposed to other investment vehicles.

Spreading investment risk over a number of different investment vehicles is called diversification. The more diversified your investment portfolio, the more insulated you are from a single security's performance in either a positive or negative direction.

Shrewd investors have practiced diversification for a long time, but it takes a full-time commitment to ensure that the investment vehicle blend is right. Most investors don't have the time to study the markets and ensure that their money is distributed over the optimal securities or the large amount of money needed to purchase the wide array of investments needed to achieve the maximum benefits of diversification. This is where the mutual fund comes in.

Mutual funds have a portfolio fund manager whose only purpose in life is to make sure that the fund's overall performance is as high as possible and that the fund is protected from radical downswings.

Mutual funds typically invest in hundreds of investment vehicles that can range from secure investments such as government securities all the way to high-risk investments such as junk bonds. You choose the fund that targets your investment area of interest, place your money into that fund, and let the fund manager do the rest. The diversified fund portfolio is an excellent hedge against any single stock taking a nosedive and taking your nest egg with it.

The least risky of the various mutual funds include the following:

➤ Bond funds that invest in municipal, government, or corporate bonds. These typically have low risk associated with them and also have a lower interest rate.

➤ Money market funds that invest in the higher-quality bonds, commercial notes (paper), and bank notes. These investment vehicles are very secure, but they also pay a lower interest rate.

Both of these fund types are susceptible to interest rate fluctuations and inflation, just as any bond would be. These funds typically provide a secure income stream but do not show high investment return rates.

You find out in Chapter 20, "Rake in More Dough with Riskier Investments," that the recommended approach for the casual investor who is willing to absorb some level of risk is to invest in various mutual funds. Selecting funds with a lower risk and some with higher risk allows you to take advantage of high growth investment opportunities without losing everything on a single bad investment.

Using Quicken's Mutual Fund Finder

Finding the information you really need from the mounds of financial data that exist is truly a daunting task. Quicken helps substantially in this area by providing a **Mutual Fund Finder** tool that sorts through the more than 4,400 mutual funds that are out there and finds the ones that match your investment criteria. From this information, you can investigate the ones that are right for you. Don't be afraid to click **Help** to find details regarding Quicken's definitions for its various fund categories. Be informed that these are not the only fund categories out there, but you have to start somewhere. (See Chapter 20 for additional information regarding selecting the right mutual fund for your investment needs.)

Activate the Mutual Fund Finder by following this procedure:

1. Click the **Features** menu.
2. Select **Investments** (or **Investing**, depending on the version of Quicken you use) from the list.
3. Select the **Mutual Fund Finder** from the displayed list.
4. Follow the wizard's instructions to define the search criteria that **Mutual Fund Finder** is to apply to its mutual fund information database.

5. After you're finished with the wizard, you should have a listing of the mutual funds that match your criteria.

6. Select any of the funds, and then click the **Fund Details** button to see detailed information about this fund's performance and management.

7. Click **Criteria** to change the sorting criteria and bring up a new listing of funds that match your new criteria.

QuickTip

Some versions of Quicken follow a different set of steps. If the set of steps presented don't work for you, try the following:

1. Choose **Features**, **Investing**, **Investment Research**. The Quicken Investment Research window appears.

2. Scroll down until you see the Mutual Funds area. Click the **Fund Finder Link**, which launches your Internet connection (provided that you have one).

3. In the **Mutual Fund Finder**, choose your criteria for performance, expenses, and so on.

4. Click the **Show Results** button. You (eventually) get a list of mutual funds with some performance data you can review.

My version of Quicken had historical fund data that was more than a year old, which in today's marketplace is ancient. You can update this information for $4.95 per calendar quarter by clicking the **Online** menu selection and clicking the **Mutual Fund Update** option. This invokes a wizard that leads you to the quicken.com Web site, where you then select the link to update the mutual fund data. (This may or may not apply to you, depending on which version of Quicken you have.)

I think that $4.95 to have this information readily at your fingertips from within Quicken is a reasonable expense and one that you should make if you are interested in mutual funds.

The Least You Need to Know

➤ Savings accounts are secure but provide very low interest rates.

➤ CDs provide slightly higher interest rates but tie up your money for a longer period of time.

➤ Any time you give up flexibility, or increase the amount of risk in an investment, you should expect to get a higher interest rate.

➤ Mutual funds are a great way to pay someone else to manage the diversification of your investment portfolio.

➤ Quicken's **Mutual Fund Finder** is a great tool for sifting through the market data to obtain the fund information that is right for you.

Chapter 20

Rake in More Dough with Riskier Investments

In This Chapter

➤ Learn how to read the financial section of the newspaper

➤ Understand the meaning behind the various stock market performance indexes such as the Dow Jones Industrial Average

➤ Work with either full-service or discount brokers as required for your personal financial needs

➤ Find the mutual funds that match your higher risk investment needs

➤ Use Quicken to instantly determine the performance level of your investment portfolio

You can't listen to the radio or television without getting some type of financial data shoved at you. The robust economy combined with the incredible performance of the stock markets in this decade has moved many people into the securities markets and for good reason overall.

It is one thing to own securities, and it is another to know what you own and determine whether the securities you own are the right ones for you. This chapter introduces the most important fundamental concepts associated with stocks and other forms of securities. The goal of this chapter is to get you to the point that you can read the financial section of the newspaper and understand what you are reading. You will be much better prepared to understand the various securities included in a mutual fund so that you can determine whether the level of risk provided by the included securities meets your investment goals.

Private and Public Stocks

Every corporation is actually owned by whoever owns its shares of stock. This applies from the smallest family-owned corporation to the largest corporations in the world.

People buy stock because it represents a good financial investment, which is determined by the amount a shareholder makes off of the stock each year in the form of dividends and the amount that the stock increases in value over time.

Talkin' Money

A share of stock represents a portion of corporation ownership. The owner of the stock is called the stockholder, or shareholder.

Some corporations pay their shareholders periodically—usually annually—by issuing dividends to them. Dividends are paid out of after-tax, retained earnings.

Stocks increase in value as the perceived value of the corporation increases and the number of issued shares remains constant. For example, assume that a corporation is worth $100,000 and 10,000 shares have been issued. Dividing $100,000 / 10,000 = $10/share of stock.

Assume some time later that the company is valued at $200,000 and the number of issued shares is still 10,000. Notice that $200,000 / 10,000 = $20/share and the stock value has doubled. Assuming that the marketplace recognizes this increase in value, a shareholder who bought at $10 per share can make $10 per share by now selling that share at $20 per share. If that shareholder also received dividends of $2 over the time of ownership, the total profit seen by that shareholder is $10 + $2 = $12.00, which can represent a nice profit if the time frame for holding the shares was only a year or two.

Stocks can be traded either between individuals or through the various stock exchanges. Stocks traded between individuals are restricted only by the bylaws of the corporation, and small company stocks are traded between people and companies as a regular part of business. Stocks traded over the exchanges must be registered with the Securities and Exchange Commission (SEC) and comply with very specific information disclosure guidelines.

Privately traded stock does not pass through one of the exchanges. It is transferred through privately negotiated sale agreements. Publicly traded stocks pass through the exchanges and must comply with SEC regulations.

The beauty of publicly traded stock ownership is that you can make money from the purchase and sale of stock and never meet the people who run the companies or the other parties in the stock transaction. Simply contact a stock broker, inform him or her about the shares you want to buy or sell, and let the broker do the rest—for a fee, of course.

Voice of Experience

You always want to make sure that the stock you buy can be resold. I know people who bought privately held stock only to find out that the stock could only be sold back to the company and was not transferable to another individual without company approval. These shareholders owned a piece of the company but had no means for converting that ownership into cash or other securities except through the company that had created a monopoly market for itself.

This is an uncomfortable position for an investor and one that you should avoid or at least be aware of before you buy the shares.

Buying privately held shares of stock may be a solid investment, but you should categorize these investments as high risk and expect higher returns that compensate for that risk. That stock being sold by one of your friends or family members as a great opportunity may not be such a great deal if you can never sell it and recover your investment.

The Various Stock Markets

Movies such as *Wall Street* portray the stock market as a place of high stakes poker and backstabbing. The reality of stock trading is actually pretty mundane. The excitement comes from seeing your stock purchases increase in value or decrease in value from your purchase price. When the stock price increases, you make money when you sell. When the stock price decreases, you lose money when you sell. For this reason, you always want to buy stock when it is at its low point (assuming you think that it is going to later increase in price) and sell it at its high point.

This "buy low, sell high" strategy makes great sense in theory but recognizing a stock's low and high points is an art form that most people refine over their entire lives.

The stock markets provide you with a central clearinghouse for your stock trades.

The following is a listing of the various exchanges, some of their attributes, and the types of securities that they handle:

➤ The primary stock exchange is the New York Stock Exchange (NYSE), which was founded in 1817 and is located on Wall Street in New York City. NYSE stocks are typically the largest, best-known companies in the country, such as IBM, AT&T, and General Motors. There are more than 2,500 listed companies that trade their stocks on the NYSE.

➤ In 1842, an alternate stock exchange named the American Stock Exchange (AMEX) was started as alternative to the NYSE. Smaller companies are listed on the AMEX, so it tends to cater to mid-size companies. Around 850 companies trade their stock on the AMEX.

➤ The National Association of Securities Dealers manages the Nasdaq Stock Market that exchanges the stocks of smaller companies all the way up to Microsoft and Intel. The minimum requirements are less for the Nasdaq than for either the NYSE or AMEX, and more than 4,700 companies trade their stocks on the Nasdaq. Nasdaq also handles Small-Cap Issues, which are new companies with very small capitalization that may not even have been profitable for a long enough period of time to provide any credible historical financial information.

➤ The Over The Counter Stock Exchange was created to handle trading of new and smaller companies, many of which are offering their first publicly traded stocks. The minimum requirements to be traded OTC are so low that most companies ready to be publicly traded can qualify. More than 28,000 companies trade their stocks OTC.

➤ There are regional exchanges located in Los Angeles (Pacific), Chicago, Cincinnati, Boston, and Philadelphia. Some stocks are only listed on the regional exchanges, but their results are posted on the NYSE Composite Trading columns.

The various stock exchanges have minimum financial requirements that companies have to meet to list their stocks. When a company's stock becomes unlisted it means that the company no longer meets those requirements and is no longer listed on that exchange.

When looking at the financial pages of the newspaper, you come across certain stock-specific jargon. This information may look similar to that covered in Chapter 19, "Protecting Your Dough with Investments That Aren't So Risky," which discusses the symbols used in regard to tracking bonds. Just keep in mind that we are talking about stocks here.

The following is a list of some stock-specific jargon:

➤ 52 Weeks Hi and Lo represent the highest and lowest trading price for this stock in the last 52 weeks.

➤ The Stock name is not necessarily the same as the ticker symbol by which the stock is traded. For example, Computer Sciences Corporation has a NYSE listed Stock name as CompSci, whereas its trading symbol is CSC.

➤ The Yld (yield) for particular stock is the dividend rate divided by the current close price for this stock, expressed as a percent. For example, a stock paying a 40-cent dividend that had a closing price of $26.67 shows a 1.5% yield.

➤ The Div (dividend) amount for a stock is the estimated annual dividend for this stock on a per share basis, as expressed in dollars or cents. If a stock pays a dividend, it tends to be less volatile because the investors aren't relying completely on the stock value increase for a return on their investment.

➤ The P/E (price to earnings) ratio indicates the number of times that the stock is valued compared to the company's earnings over the last four quarters. For example, a stock selling at $43-1/4 that had earnings of $9.25 per share shows a price-to-earnings ratio of $43.25/$9.25 = 4.7, rounded up to 5. The higher the P/E ratio, the more the marketplace is basing the value of the stock on its future earning potential as opposed to historical performance. New stock issues typically have high P/E ratios because their earnings are typically low, whereas established stocks typically have lower P/E ratios. A stock with a lower P/E ratio that pays dividends is usually a less risk stock than one that pays no dividends and has a high P/E ratio.

➤ The volume of shares traded on the prior day are listed under the Vol column. The number shown should be multiplied by 100 to get the actual number of shares traded unless the number is preceded by a Z, which indicates that the number shown is the actual number. When a stock shows a high trade volume, it generally indicates that the market knows something about that stock and is either buying or selling because of this new information. For example, a number of 112 under the Vol column indicates that 11,200 shares traded on the prior day.

➤ The Hi, Lo, and Close columns show the highest traded price, lowest traded price, and the price the stock finally closed at from the prior day's trading.

QuickTip

Share prices are listed in fractions of a dollar from 1/8 to 7/8. 1/8 = 12.5 cents. 1/4 = 25 cents. 3/8 = 37.5 cents. 1/2 = 50 cents. 5/8 = 62.5 cents. 3/4 = 75 cents. 7/8 = 87.5 cents. For example, a share price of 55–7/8 really means a price of $55.875 cents.

➤ The Net Chg column shows the net change in the share close price between the listed day's trading and the trading prior. A change of +1/4 with a close price of 22-1/2 means that the stock closed at 22-1/4 on the trading day prior to that listed. Shares that change by 5% or more are listed in boldface so that they are easily recognized.

A comment is due here regarding the difference between dividend and earnings. A company that makes money after all its taxes are paid has "retained earnings" or income that remained with the company after all expenses and taxes were paid. Dividends are then issued out of these retained earnings at the discretion of the board of directors. Notice that dividends are paid out of after-tax corporate earnings. The P/E (price to earnings) ratio is based on the earnings, not the dividends paid. The last four quarter's dividends are used to calculate the yield based on the closing price.

If you got all that, you have a pretty good foundation for understanding the stock pages and the implications of the information shown.

P/E ratios have slowly crept up through the 1990s as they typically do during robust economic times. Investors are more willing to bank on the future, which is indicated by a higher P/E ratio. When times are less robust, the P/E ratio drops to reflect the more conservative view of the future.

When the stock market goes through a correction, as it did in mid-1998, it generally means that stocks drop to a more reasonable level based on the reported and expected earnings of the traded companies. This also means that the P/E ratio also drops to a level where investors feel more comfortable.

I heard an analyst report in July 1998 that he felt the market would keep dropping until it showed a market-wide average P/E ratio of 18, lower than the average that existed in early 1998, which was in the high 20s. In August 1998, the market dropped to a low enough level that the P/E ratio more closely matched the analyst's prediction. Now you understand his rationale.

The Dow Jones Average and Other Index Insights

You can't listen to the radio or watch television without somebody telling you the percentage change in the Dow Jones Industrial Average (DJIA), or the Dow as it is called. The following are some of the averages related to the Dow:

➤ **Dow Jones Industrial Average**   A weighted index of 30 major industrial companies. These companies represent around 25% of the total stock value listed on the NYSE. This is a dynamic list with companies being added and removed from the list.

➤ **Dow Jones Transportation Average**   Monitors 20 airline, railroad, and trucking companies.

➤ **Dow Jones Utility Average**   Monitors 15 electric, gas, and power companies.

➤ **Dow Jones 65 Composite Average**   Monitors all 65 of the stocks contained in the other Dow Jones averages.

By watching these averages, you get a feeling for the market's movement across a number of different major markets. Notice that industry, energy, and transportation are all monitored in one of the Dow Jones averages. Due to its limited number of tracked companies on the Dow indexes, some people think a broader index would more accurately represents market trends. This gives rise to the various other indexes that are surely worth watching:

➤ **Standard & Poor's 500 Index (S&P 500)**   Monitors 500 stocks, of which 400 are industrial, 20 are transportation, 40 utilities, and 40 financial. The broader company base and more diverse mix make this a more attractive index for many investors.

➤ **The NYSE Composite Index**   Tracks all stocks listed on the NYSE.

➤ **The AMEX Market Value Index**   Tracks more than 800 stocks listed on the American Stock Exchange.

➤ **The Nasdaq Composite Index**   Monitors changes in stocks traded on the Nasdaq. Notice that these stocks are typically smaller than those listed on the NYSE or AMEX, which means that this index often shows wider fluctuations than the NYSE and AMEX indices.

➤ **The Value-Line Index**   Reports trends with 1,700 common stocks.

➤ **The Wilshire 5000 Index**   Represents information for all stocks traded on the exchanges and also OTC.

➤ **The Russell 2000 Index**   Shows the performance of the smaller 2/3 of the largest 3,000 companies. In other words, the largest 1,000 companies of the 3,000 largest companies are excluded from the index.

A natural question at this point is, "Which of these indexes do I believe?" And the right answer is, "It depends on what you are looking for and what you want to find."

The DJIA reflects the activity of the largest valued stocks on the exchanges. If this number drops, then that indicates that the most valuable companies on the exchanges are perceived by investors as having troubles, and you should take a hard look at your future projections.

If the DJIA increases by 10% over a few months, but the S&P 500 drops by 5%, this might indicate that the rally seen by the DJIA is related to a few large stocks, and does not reflect a market-wide positive trend.

Assume that the Wilshire 5000 drops by 10% while everything else is stable or increasing. Remember that the Wilshire 5000 tracks the OTC stocks and smaller companies are more susceptible to market economy downturns than the bigger companies. This might be an early warning indicator of hard times ahead for all stocks.

If there was a hard and fast rule for all investment decisions, there would be no risk associated with these investments. You are the ultimate decision maker for your investments. Take your time. Learn the various indexes and listen to the financial reports. They make more sense to you after reading this chapter.

Nobody can read the future, but you can certainly use the indexes as possible barometers of the financial weather to come.

Stock Option and Purchase Plans

You might be one of those lucky employees who work for a company that is publicly traded and that offers its employees a stock purchase plan. These are usually great investments and you are highly encouraged to look into it.

These plans allow you to purchase your company's stock at a percentage under the prevailing market price. Assume, for example, that your company's stock is trading at $20 per share, and that your stock purchase plan allows you to purchase shares for 20% under market price, or $16. If you exercise this right, you just made $4 per share on the day that you bought the stock.

If the company is doing well and you expect the share price to increase, you are just that much further ahead of the rest of the investment community due to the reduced purchase price. More than one person I know created a substantial nest egg simply from buying company stock at a reduced rate and holding it for an extended period of time.

Stock option plans provide employees with an incentive to stay with the company for an extended period of time. Stock option plans provide the employee with an option to purchase a specified number of shares for a specified price, but the employee becomes eligible to purchase a certain number of the optioned shares after specified periods of employment.

Assume, for example, that your company has offered you an option on 5,000 company shares of common stock at a price of 50 cents per share, that you have become eligible for stock purchase, and that you vest these shares over a five-year period. This would mean that you vest 1,000 shares at the end of year one, 1,000 shares at the end of year two, and so forth until year five. At the end of year five you could exercise your option to purchase the shares at 50 cents each by spending $2,500. Depending upon the corporation bylaws and the restrictions on the stock option plan, you might be able to sell the shares on the public market for more than 50 cents each meaning that you would show a gain on the stock option purchase.

Talkin' Money

A vesting period is the time frame over which an item gradually becomes yours. For example, a stock purchase plan that allows for vesting over a four-year period usually allows you to acquire 25% of your stock each year, for four years, until all 100% is vested.

Stock option plans are usually used in dynamic company situations where the option price is low and the shares are redeemed by the employee after the company does a public offering. If you owned these 5,000 shares at 50 cents each and the company sold its shares to another company for $10 per share, you just made $9.50 per share or $47,500. Not bad.

The down side of stock options is that the company might not financially perform as well as needed, and the stock value may drop to less than the option price. In this case, you would not exercise the option to purchase your shares if it costs you 50 cents to buy a share that has a market value of only 25 cents. I have been through this a few times, and it really breaks my heart.

Also, you may exercise your option and find that you cannot sell the shares to anyone but the company. In this case, you are on hold until the company buys the shares, sells its shares and yours to someone else, or folds its tent, taking your shares with it. Your particular stock option agreement outlines methods for transferring shares covered by the option plan.

The Mechanics of Securities Trading

Securities trading is a pretty routine activity that happens thousands of time per day. Your investments are such a small part of a daily trading volume that you should try to work within the systems already in place.

Buying or selling a security is a three-part transaction:

1. You, as the customer, place an order to either buy or sell a specific security.
2. You contact your broker who then initiates the trade request.
3. The actual transaction is handled by the stock exchange. Your broker is notified of the transaction's completion, who then notifies you.

There are various ways that you can work with a broker, and the wide availability of the Internet is continually spawning even more. You can work directly with your broker, or you can work through the brokerage house using an online connection. The fees generally drop when less human involvement is required.

Independent of the specific transaction procedure you choose, you generally must set up a money market fund with your selected brokerage house. This fund acts as a central holding pool for funding your investment transactions.

When you execute a purchase, the buy money is taken out of the money market fund. When you execute a sale, the proceeds from the sale are placed in the money market fund, which is then ready for your next purchase. The money market account bears an interest rate that is higher than a savings account and you can generally write checks against the account.

Buying and Selling Securities Through a Broker

Brokers come in different flavors from full-service brokers, to discount to deep discount. The full-service broker charges a higher fee, or commission, on the transaction but is supposed to provide advice and other research services in exchange for the higher commission. The discount broker charges a much lower fee, as much as 70% less than a full-service broker, but provides fewer services. The deep discount brokers are the least expensive, and might even charge a flat fee for each transaction up to maximum number of shares.

Use a discount broker if you track your investments carefully and do your own securities research and make your own purchase/sale decisions. If you feel uncomfortable with your knowledge you might be better served by paying the higher fees associated with a full-service broker.

QuickCaution

Know that some brokerage houses have their own "pet" securities on which the brokers may receive higher commissions. If you completely rely on the broker for advice, and that broker gets paid a higher commission on one security over another, then there is a possible conflict of interest situation. Does she recommend the best security for your personal situation or recommend the one on which her commission is the highest? You would like to think that ethics would prevail and the right security for you would be recommended. This is probably what happens in most cases, but it is up to you to ensure that your interests are taken care of before the brokers commission interests are served.

The more comfortable you get with trading securities, the more you want to control the process. I suggest you look to a full-service broker such as A.G. Edwards when you first start out, and then move to a discount broker such as Charles Schwab when you find that you are making your own choices and the broker is really just implementing your wishes. There is no reason to pay full-service fees if you don't need them.

Online (Internet-based) Trading

Many of the brokerage houses have set up online trading that allows you to execute your security buy/sell requests from your home computer. You must have Internet access, which costs you anywhere from $10 to $25 per month along with the associated modem and other software that must reside on your home or office computer to take advantage of these online trading. In addition, you must be affiliated with a brokerage house because a broker must still execute your trade. The brokerage fees associated with online trading are so low that you should absolutely start laying the groundwork to take advantage of it when you are ready.

QuickCaution

Remember that some mutual funds charge a fee, called a load, when you either join or leave the fund. These fees are over and above those charged by the broker. Each of these fees takes a little more out of your pocket and puts it into someone else's.

More of our world is moving toward computerized automation, and trading is no exception. I read an article the other day that predicted that the standard person-to-person trading that happens on the floor of the NYSE will eventually be replaced with computerized transactions.

We all know that automation is here to stay and you should prepare yourself for completely automated transactions using your home computer.

Online Investment Tracking

One great feature of online investing is the ability to track your overall portfolio performance right from your living room. You simply connect over the Internet to your broker's Web site then make a secure connection into that site using your personal ID and password. The site now knows who you are and displays your personal portfolio with updated current market values. Check with your broker to determine the level of online investment tracking capability provided by their Web site.

In a matter of moments you can update your portfolio and know exactly where your investments stand. No more calling into your brokerage, asking for current prices, entering that data into a sheet, and manually determining your overall performance. Let the computers do it for you automatically—a great use for computers.

Using the Quicken Portfolio and Security Detail Views

Quicken includes a great tool for tracking the performance of your overall portfolio. These tools are all included on the menu displayed if you rest your cursor over the Investments icon.

➤ The **Track My 401(k)** option is used to create a 401(k) account and track the distribution of investments within the account.

➤ The **Enter a new investment** option enables you to create a new investment that is tied to an existing account, such as My Broker account, or to create a completely new account such as My Broker 2 account. This might apply if you trade securities through multiple brokers.

➤ The **View my portfolio** option provides you with a summary view of all investments that you added to the Quicken portfolio under the **New** Investments option. You can get updated market values for your securities by clicking the **Update Prices** button, and then selecting the **Get Online Quotes Only**, **Get Online Quotes & News**, or **Edit Price History** options. The online options requires the **Symbol** (entered on the specific security's properties screen) so that the proper security information is obtained. **Edit Price History** is a manual way for you to enter historical data if you don't have an Internet connection. The historical data is obtained from the newspaper and manually entered using the provided screens.

➤ The **View Security Detail & News** option provides detailed information regarding the various securities that you select from within the view itself. You can chart the **Market Value** or **Price History** for this security along with any buy/sell activity entered into the Quicken portfolio view. Click **Easy Actions** to see options for buying/selling and others that are pertinent to a specific security. You are not actually making the trade by clicking **Buy**, but you are telling Quicken about what you are going to do through your broker. Make sure to check the options under the **Advanced** option to reassure yourself that the things you want to do are covered.

➤ **View Market Indexes** is used to get updated market index information. You can either use the information already stored on your computer or quickly get it updated by clicking the **Update** button. (This might work differently in some versions of Quicken.)

➤ **Use My Investment Register** enables you to access your investment account's register and make entries directly into it. You can do the same thing by selecting the **Accounts** view, **Investments** tab.

Following are a few things to remember when setting up your Quicken investment accounts:

➤ Quicken treats your 401(k) account as a separate unique account, even though it is an investment account.

➤ You must first create an investment account, which typically is tied to a broker. You then transfer funds in or out of this investment account as you buy/sell securities such as stocks, bonds, or mutual funds.

➤ You can create an account that is tied to a specific security such as when you do buy some of Uncle Bill's small company stock.

➤ Try to group your investments according to your personal investment goals. Remember that you can add goals as needed to meet your needs. You should try to keep your low-, medium-, and high-risk investments spread so that your personal risk requirements are met. You have to calculate the percentage breakdowns yourself based on the information contained in the portfolio views.

The investment information provided by Quicken is only as accurate as the information entered into the program. You must have current information or your investment decisions may be inappropriate for the current market conditions. Quicken quickly updates your portfolio securities information using the online update features, but you must first make sure that your securities are listed as part of the portfolio. Working with Quicken, you can make informed investment decisions that work best for you.

Mutual Funds with Higher Returns

Every investor is looking for an investment that shows above average returns but involves minimal risk. Mutual funds are an excellent place to look for this blend of return and risk.

This may be the most important section of this chapter, so sit up and take notice. Chapter 19 introduced mutual funds in the context of lower risk investments.

Mutual funds have very specific investment goals that are spelled out, in detail, in the fund's prospectus. There are thousands of mutual funds available today, and it is hard to believe that there isn't one right for you.

Remember that a mutual fund invests in hundreds of securities to diversify the fund's portfolio. Diversification minimizes the likelihood that a single security can dominate the fund's performance in either a positive or negative way. You could perform this diversification yourself by purchasing individual stocks until you have several hundred included in your portfolio, but then you have to monitor it daily to ensure that the fund's overall performance is maximized.

Mutual funds are managed by people whose only job in life is to ensure that the fund makes the most possible money for its members within the published investment objectives.

Funds come in high-risk categories, such as those that only invest in very small companies with a high risk of failure and also a high risk of explosive stock performance. They come in low risk such as those that only invest in government securities or blue chip stocks. And they come in medium risk flavors that include a balance, or blending, of stocks and bonds.

QuickCaution

Unfortunately, all mutual funds are not created equal in how they charge for membership. Some have a front end load, which charges you at the point that you buy into the fund. Some have a back end load, which is charged if you leave the fund. This back end load usually decreases over time, usually five years, until there is no fee for leaving the fund. My favorite funds are no-load funds that charge no front end or back end loads when moving money into or out of the fund. Loads can be in the range of 0.5% to 5%, depending on the fund and how you get into it. Always ask about how people get paid when working with mutual funds, and you avoid potentially expensive surprises later.

Heck, they even come in colors, such as green, that only invest in environmentally conscious companies or those involved with environmental clean up.

Finding the right fund for you is the difficult part, and Quicken helps in this regard with its **Mutual Fund Finder** feature, which is located on the **Features** menu, **Investments** option. (Depending on the version of Quicken you use, this feature might operate differently. See Chapter 19 for information on how to use the Mutual Fund Finder.)

The Least You Need to Know

➤ You must go through a broker to buy/sell publicly traded stocks.

➤ The financial section of your newspaper gives you a ton of information about the publicly traded securities.

➤ The stock market averages provide quick insight into the overall condition of the stock markets.

➤ Quicken provides portfolio management features that give you current security value information and let you know the performance status of your securities at any time.

➤ Mutual funds come in all kinds of shapes, sizes, and risk levels. The Quicken Mutual Fund Finder helps sift through the thousands of funds to find the ones that are right for you.

Part 5

The Future Starts Today

The time to plan your estate is before you have passed away. Sounds pretty basic, doesn't it? Yet, many people pass away without leaving behind a will that instructs their heirs. This situation can cause internal family friction and can hand tax money to Uncle Sam on a silver platter.

You can't start saving for retirement after you retire, and it makes no sense to start saving for your kid's college expenses when they go off to school. Taking a last-minute approach to these predictable personal financial phases puts you and your family at a disadvantage because you cannot use the time value of money to your benefit.

Work your way through this part to ensure that you have the funding necessary for a secure retirement, have enough put away to pay for college, and make sure that your wishes are implemented after your life's journey comes to an end.

The rest of the book has really led up to this part, so don't stop here. Take the final steps to financial freedom.

Chapter 21

Mom, Dad, Can I Borrow $250,000 for College?

In This Chapter

➤ Calculate the total cost of education for various university and college types

➤ Determine the future cost of college 18 years in the future

➤ Use Quicken to determine a budget today and provide a future education for your child

➤ Investigate scholarships, grants, and loans as a way of paying for college

➤ Determine whether an expensive school is really worth the extra money

Education is critical to your child's professional future. A degree says that your child has a minimum level of understanding and perseverance. Perhaps the best gift you can ever give your child is the opportunity to get a solid education. Planning today for that education is the best way to ensure that the gift gets delivered.

How Much Will College Cost?

One thing is certain about future college costs. College will cost more tomorrow than it does today. How much more is a matter of personal conjecture, and different people give you different answers.

College costs are divided into several basic categories, each of which varies with the school, study program, geographic location, and personal living standard.

➤ Tuition and fees, which include the expenses related to having a seat in a classroom for a full-time course of study and all associated fees such as athletic facilities, library usage, and so on. These costs vary widely with the type of college and the study program selected. See Table 21.1 for representative costs.

➤ Books needed for the classes taken. This can run into hundreds of dollars per semester or quarter. For this example, books are assumed to cost $450 per year.

➤ Living expenses, which includes things such as a room in a house or dormitory and food. This probably also includes a computer and telephone. For this example, living expenses are assumed to cost $3,500 per year, though it could be higher.

➤ Travel expenses between college and home. This includes gas and car expenses if the student commutes and might include airfare if the college is in another state. You are going to have to estimate these yourself, but assume at least two trips home per year to be on the safe side. This amount is assumed, for this example, to be $400 and is more if airfare is required.

➤ Also be aware that some students just don't finish in four years, and that fifth year can be an expensive indulgence that you provide your child. There are some schools that guarantee that your child graduates in four years if all classes are passed and the mandated course loads are taken.

Take a look at Table 21.1 to see some recent Illinois educational institution costs for tuition and fees. Assume that these costs are typical and your state has a similar cost and category breakdown for its colleges.

Table 21.1   Typical College and University Tuition and Fees Costs

	In-State		Out-of-State
Type	**1996-97**	**1997-98**	**1997-98**
State University	$4,186	$4,340	$10,956
Well-Known Private	21,300	22,476	22,476
Local Private	13,100	13,780	13,780
Community College	1,198	1,258	6,718

The dollar amounts used in this table are from colleges in Illinois for 1997 and 1998. You should consider these dollar amounts estimations, and you should obtain actual tuition pricing from the colleges and universities of your choice.

From my own observations, the actual costs for the various colleges vary by state, but the comparative costs for the various schools remain constant. A few obvious conclusions are to be taken from the tuition prices shown in the table.

➤ The community college is by far the least expensive college route but only takes the student through the first two years of study. Students can receive an associates degree but cannot receive a full four-year degree such as a Bachelor of Arts.

➤ The well-known private school is by far the most expensive option. The cost for a student commuting from home to this private school is almost 18 times higher than commuting to a community college. By the way, this school has an excellent academic reputation and a nonexistent sports reputation, so students certainly don't go here for the sports legends that it has created. On the other hand, several Nobel Laureates still teach here.

➤ The local private school is well-respected in the local area, provides at least a four-year degree program, costs about 60% of the well-known private school, and still is three times the cost of the state university.

➤ The state university chosen has a solid academic reputation and a marginal sports reputation. Its sports reputation is slowly spreading, but it is years before it ever has the reputation of a Northwestern.

➤ The private tuition prices increased by 5% whereas the public school tuition increased by between 3% and 5%.

➤ Out-of-state tuition is much more expensive for public schools than in-state tuition, whereas the in-state and out-of-state tuition for the private schools is a nonissue.

➤ None of these costs include living expenses or books, which adds thousands to these numbers. Check with the intended college for annual living estimates for on-campus and off-campus housing arrangements.

Talkin' Money

Residents of the state where the academic institution is located, pay the in-state tuition and fees rates.

Residents of one state who choose to go to school in another state generally pay the out-of-state tuition in the destination state. They come from out-of-state to go to school.

Most experts agree that tuition costs will continue to increase annually at between 5% and 6% per year, which is approximately what you found in the table of costs for Illinois. Assuming Illinois is reflective of the rest of the country, you can estimate the tuition and fees costs for a year of college at some point in the future. It is done using the following formula:

1. Assume an annual cost increase of 5%, or .05.

2. Add the .05 to 1 = 1.05.

3. Multiply 1.05 times itself once for each of the years you have between today and the year your child starts school. For example, a child starting school 18 years from now would require that 1.05 be multiplied by 1.05 18 times. If you are familiar with exponentiation, you can take (1.05) to the 18th power and get the same result (x^y, where x=1.05 and y=18). Performing this calculation returns a result of 2.4.

4. Multiply the factor calculated in step 3 by the current costs for the school of your choice to estimate the costs 18 years in the future if they continue to increase at 5% per year. Assume the example of a state university with a current annual cost of $4,340. The estimated cost in 18 years is 2.4 × $4,340 = $10,416.

The Quicken Investment Savings Planner can be used to calculate the same result. The Planner is provided with the Quicken Deluxe version but not with all others, so you must verify its inclusion with your particular version. It is designed to show the increase in your savings account over the years based on annual contributions and a percentage interest rate yield. The same calculations can be applied to estimating a future value of something, which is why this tool can be used.

1. Open the **Quicken Investment Savings Planner** by clicking **Feature**, **Planning**, **Financial Planners**, **Savings**.

Use the Quicken Investment Savings Planner to estimate future tuition costs.

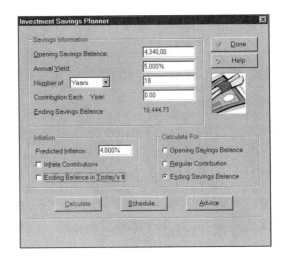

2. Set the **Opening Savings Balance:** value to the current costs, which for this example is **$4,340**.

3. Set the **Annual Yield:** to your expected percentage annual increase in costs, which this example assumes to be **5%**.

4. Set the **Number of Years:** value to the number of years between today and the future date for which you want the estimated costs calculation, which in this example is **18** years.

5. Make sure that the **Contribution Each Year:** value is set to **0.00**.

6. Make sure that neither of the options contained in the **Inflation** section of the dialog box are checked.

7. Check the **Ending Savings Balance** option contained in the **Calculate For** section of the dialog box.

8. Click **Calculate** and notice that the **Ending Savings Balance:** field updates to **$10,444.73**, which is approximately what we found with the Windows calculator example.

9. Vary the starting tuition costs, the number of years, and the expected annual increases, and notice the effect that each assumption has on the future tuition estimates.

I want to emphasize that the Quicken Investment Savings Planner is really designed to estimate the future value of a regimented savings plan. It works in this specific case, and I recommend using it merely as a convenience. Make sure that steps 6 and 7 are always executed, and this tool can be used to calculate the future value of any present valued item.

Your college expenses don't stop with tuition and fees. You have the other expenses associated with college such as books ($450/yr), living expenses ($3,500 if away at school or $1,800 [$200 × 9 months] if commuting from home), and travel expenses to/from school ($400 if away at school). Take a look at Table 21.2 to see the various costs associated with two different college scenarios.

➤ Scenario 1 is a student that completes his or her first two years at a community college (tuition and fees = $1,258 per year, commuting = $1,800 per year, and miscellaneous travel = $0 per year). This scenario also assumes that this student completes his or her last two years away at a state university (tuition and fees = $4,340 per year, living expenses = $3,500 per year, and miscellaneous travel = $400 per year).

➤ Scenario 2 is a student that spends all four years away at a nationally recognized private school (tuition and fees = $22,476 per year, living expenses = $3,500 per year, and miscellaneous travel = $400 per year).

Books for both scenarios are assumed to cost $450 per academic year.

Table 21.2 Comparing Costs For Two Different School Scenarios

Item	Years 1 & 2	Years 3 & 4	Total
Scenario 1			
Tuition/Fees	$ 2,516	$ 8,680	$11,196
Books	$ 900	$ 900	$ 1,800
Living Exps	$ 3,600	$ 7,000	$10,600
Misc Travel	$ 0	$ 800	$ 800
Total Scenario 1:			$24,396
Scenario 2			
Tuition/Fees	$44,952	$44,952	$89,904
Books	$ 900	$ 900	$ 1,800
Living Exps	$ 7,000	$ 7,000	$14,000
Misc Travel	$ 800	$ 800	$ 1,600
Total Scenario 2:			$107,304

QuickCaution

Your children typically do not all start college at the same time, which affects your analysis. This might work in your favor. Can you imagine two kids simultaneously attending a scenario 2 college! If you don't plan ahead to have enough money socked away for college tuition, you are never able to do it unless you are already wealthy enough to foot the bill.

Using the earlier presented procedures for calculating the future cost of these two college scenarios based on their current costs, 5% annual increase and 18 years into the future, you find that scenario 1 estimates a future cost of $58,712 and scenario 2 estimates a future cost of $258,240! Neither of these numbers is trivial, and scenario 2 is roughly $200,000 larger than scenario 1.

If you have three children and expect all of them to go to a four-year college, you must multiply your estimated costs by three to get the estimated college education costs. If you have two, multiply the estimated costs by two, and so forth.

A question to ask yourself is whether the added expense of the nationally recognized private school is worth it—especially for an undergraduate degree.

I have always contended that my education at state universities was excellent and have never felt that I lacked in any educational way from having a state school education.

The environment in the private school is different. The fellow students at the recognized private schools create a network of friends and associates who can greatly aid a person in career activities, simply because many of these students come from families with highly successful parents.

No matter where you go to school, you still have to prove yourself after you leave school. A Harvard degree wouldn't save someone who doesn't do her job, and graduating from a local college wouldn't hold her back if she is a true performer.

I encourage you to look at this decision from both a personal and financial standpoint:

➤ From a personal standpoint, you might want your kids to go to Harvard because you did, and your father did before you. It is just the way things are done in your family. The cost is irrelevant.

➤ From a financial standpoint, you spend an extra $200,000 sending your child to a nationally recognized private school. Assume that your child's income upon graduation is $20,000 higher than that of a student with the same degree but from a state university. Your child must work for 10 years to break even on the additional expense. Is it worth the money?

➤ Financial aid was not factored into this discussion, and most schools have financial aid programs that can help substantially with tuition costs and fees. Make sure that you include these financial aid benefits in your analysis.

Using Quicken's College Planner

Once again, the folks at Intuit anticipated your need to calculate your children's future education expenses. More importantly, they anticipated your need to start saving today in such a way as to have enough money around when college time comes around. This tool is the Quicken College Planner, which is included in the Quicken Deluxe versions and not included with others. Verify its inclusion with your particular version.

1. From the **Features** menu, select the **Planning**, **Financial Planners**, **College**. The College Planner dialog box appears, as shown in the figure.

2. Type the estimated total cost for a single year of college at today's prices into the **Annual College Costs:** field. For the example, I used the scenario 1 four-year total divided by four, or $24,396/4 = **$6,099**.

3. Type the number of years between today and when your child starts college (which for the example is **18)** into the **Years Until Enrollment:** field.

4. Type the expected number of years that your child will be in school into the **Number Of Years Enrolled:** field. For the example, and for most children, type **4**.

5. Enter the amount you currently have saved for college into the **Current College Savings:** field. For the example, leave this number at **$0**.

291

Use the Quicken College Financial Planner to calculate the deposits needed for future college expenses.

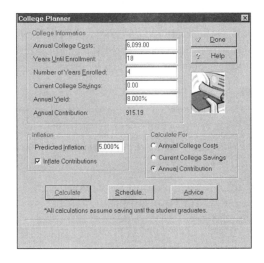

6. Set the **Annual Yield:** field to a reasonable expected annual return on your investments. For the example, set this value to **8%**.

7. In the **Inflation** section, set the **Predicted Inflation:** number to **5%**, and check the **Inflate Contributions:** field. These settings indicate that you expect inflation to increase prices at 5% per year (which is what is estimated for college fees), and you increase your annual contributions by 5% per year to keep up with inflation.

8. In the **Calculate For** section, select the **Annual Contribution** option to provide you with the amount you must deposit annually to have enough money for the future college expenses entered in step 2.

9. Click **Calculate** to display the required annual deposit amount (**915.19** for the example) in the **Annual Contribution:** field. This amount is only $76.27 per month, which is really not very much money to ensure your child's future education.

10. Select **Annual College Costs:** to shift the calculation to one that determines the maximum amount of money you can spend annually, in today's dollars, for education expenses for a specified annual deposit amount. Leave everything else as it was for the earlier part of this exercise, and set the **Annual Contribution:** amount to **$1,200**, or $100 per month. The **Annual College Costs:** amount jumps to **$7,997.03**.

11. Select the **Current College Savings:** option, set the **Annual College Costs:** to **$10,000**, and click **Calculate**. You must have a current savings balance of **$4,627.82** and deposit $1,200 per year at an 8% interest rate yield for 18 years to pay the expected future costs of a college that today costs $10,000, assuming a 5% increase in college costs annually and that you increase your payments annually by 5%.

12. Click the **Schedule** button to display a schedule of deposits, amounts adjusted for inflation, and withdrawals that start at year 18 and continue for four years. Click the **Print** button to print out this schedule.

You now know the minimum amount that you must budget to meet your projected education expense goals. And, by the way, the sooner you start the more likely you are to make your financial goals a reality. I also suggest that you initially put this money into a higher interest bearing account, with a little higher associated risk, to build up some equity early in the fund's life. This way, the later years have more account balance to work with when compounding interest. Set this budget amount in Quicken as an automatic transaction so that you don't forget to pay the college fund, or you could be facing a nasty bill later.

The Quicken College Planner is a great tool for providing you with a solid starting point with regard to college expense planning. There are a few problems with the tools. One major problem is that taxes are not included in the analysis, and all interest income is taxed at your personal tax rate unless you take precautions to shield the income.

One such tactic is to put the education savings account in your child's name. In this way, you gain some minor tax advantages because any interest gained on the account is taxed at your child's income tax rate, which is a little different from yours. If the child is under age 14, the first $1,300 is subject to around a $100 tax (As a humanitarian gesture, I skip the calculations on the $100 tax) and everything more than $1,300 is taxed at your rate. This might save you up to $450 in taxes on the first $1,300, and you gain little after that. But $450 invested over a 14-year period at 8% turns into almost $11,000 in money savings that would have otherwise gone to Uncle Sam.

After your child turns 14, he or she is taxed at his or her own rate, which is typically 15%. This rate should be lower than your rate, which could be 28% or higher. This can really add up to savings over the remaining years until he gets out of college. Your contributions to the account are always tax free to the child because you can give up to $10,000 annually to someone as a gift without that person paying tax on the money. You already paid tax on it when you earned it, so you are really not getting away with much on this one.

QuickCaution

Here is the big downside. After you transfer that account to your child, he owns it. You have no say on how it is spent. Should he or she get to age 21, see $50,000 in the account, and decide that scuba diving on the Great Barrier Reef looks better than trigonometry, you have no legal way to stop him or her from taking all your hard-earned money and spending it on a wet-and-wild vacation. Only you know your child, but this should be considered if you try to outwit the IRS.

As a final thought on transferring funds to your child, know that the financial aid funding formula used by colleges requires that any money that your child owns be spent completely before any financial aid can be provided. This is not the case with parents because they are assumed to need those funds for other familial obligations.

QuickTip

Education IRAs have been set up to allow up to $500 per year to be contributed to a specified account for a specific beneficiary. As with any IRA, there are a number of exclusions, exemptions, time frames, and penalties associated with an Education IRA. For example, these IRA's have some income exclusions when adjusted gross incomes for singles get more than $95,000 and $150,000 for couples filing jointly. Verify the tax benefits for your situation with your tax professional before investing here.

Other potentially beneficial tax actions you might consider are the Crummey Trust, Minor Trusts, U.S. Series EE Bonds, Lifetime Learning Credit, and the Hope Scholarship tax credit. Finally, interest paid on loans that were specifically used to fund education are tax deductible. Once again, there are limits and exclusions associated with this interest deduction, so check all this out with your tax professional.

Student Loans and Financial Aid

Funding education has become big business. There are people out there who, for a fee, walk you through the financial aid maze. Some even guarantee you a grant or loan. Watch these folks and talk to your chosen education institution's financial aid office before you go anywhere else. Even better, talk to them today, 18 years before your child even starts school to get your budgetary estimates as accurate as possible.

Funding falls into three categories: grants, scholarships, and loans.

Grants are free money given to you as a way of assisting with education expenses. There are federal, state, local, and school-specific grants out there, and your child might qualify for one of them. Don't let all the paperwork put you off, and it can really look like a mountain sometimes. Take the time to fill it out and submit it. You will be glad you did if you get thousands of dollars back for your efforts. The most common type of grant is the Pell grant, which usually provides up to $3,000 to low income families, dependent upon need. You start here, because you won't be considered for other financial aid unless Pell has first evaluated your need. Try 800-4FED-AID for more information.

Every school has its own scholarship programs that are provided from all types of sources, from alumni to businesses to rich benefactors. If your child has good grades and/or has some special talent, he might be eligible for one of these scholarships. You should absolutely talk to the financial aid office and department of your child's study interest for scholarship eligibility requirements.

Loans come in all shapes and sizes, from home equity loans to pay tuition to federal loan programs such as Student Loan Marketing Association (Sallie Mae). Talk to your financial aid office about Stafford Loans, Parent Loans to Undergraduate Students (PLUS), Perkins Loans (for those with under $30,000 family income), and specific state loan programs. By the way, you will find that state loans are usually only available for in-state students.

Finally, talk to your bank about education assistance loans that they offer. They know you and your family and might be able to point you in the direction of a loan that is best for you.

QuickTip

Some states have full tuition payment incentive programs for students who maintain a high enough grade point average or who study particular career paths. I have a friend whose daughter maintains a B average and attends a state school with all tuition and fees paid. Another state pays tuition for those studying to be school teachers as long as the student works a certain number of years in that profession after graduating. How is that for incentive?

The Least You Need to Know

➤ College is already expensive and increases in cost at around 5% per year.

➤ The Quicken College Planner is a simple, yet effective tool for calculating required deposits to meet future college goals.

➤ The future cost of college is estimated by multiplying today's costs by a special factor that is related to education cost inflation rates and the number of years between today and the first day of college.

➤ Scholarships, grants, and loans are great aids when paying education expenses.

➤ Planning today for future education expenses is the best way to protect your child's professional future.

Chapter 22

Retirement: Getting There in Style

In This Chapter

➤ Determine your retirement income and expenses

➤ Plan for extra money during retirement

➤ Provide for your heirs after you pass away

➤ Use Quicken to easily estimate future savings needs

➤ Choose the deferred tax account type that is right for you

We all wonder about retirement and how we are going to pay for it. Part of the anguish that accompanies retirement is the financial uncertainty of living on a fixed income. Fixed income doesn't necessarily need to mean poor. It simply means that your retirement pension and Social Security are predictable but usually not very large. Tapping your retirement nest egg to pay for your retirement may sound a little strange, but living off of the interest from your portfolio without actually using some of your portfolio equity may not be feasible for many people. Take a look through this chapter and discover several ways that you can plan for and use your nest egg for a productive and comfortable retirement.

This chapter has some overlap with Chapter 2, "Planning Ahead in Your Middle Years," which covered the general aspects of retirement. In this chapter, we build on the foundation created previously to define the details that financially prepare you for a financially solid retirement.

Planning for Retirement

There should be no doubt in your mind by this point that planning is the best way to ensure a financially secure retirement. The sooner you create a plan and begin its implementation, the earlier you can retire and with greater peace of mind.

Retirement planning is done in a few stages:

1. Determine your current financial position.

2. Determine your expected financial needs when you retire.

3. Determine the number of years that you have between today and when you plan to retire.

4. Plan to start implementing your plan today and really do it, or it won't get done.

QuickTip

Assuming that you've read Part 2, "Getting It into the Computer," you should know where you stand today. If you haven't read Part 2 yet, I suggest doing so before actually sitting down to work out your retirement plan. The Quicken skills you learn there help make the planning process much easier.

By simply running a Cash Flow report you get comprehensive information about your income, expenses, and net income. It basically tells you the amount of money left over for retirement planning purposes. The Net Worth report tells you the value of your assets such as your house, car, bank, and investment accounts. The net worth amount displayed on the report is computed by Quicken by subtracting what you owe from what you own. In accounting language, subtracting the liabilities from the assets provides you with your net worth.

Increasing this net worth amount is your ultimate goal when planning retirement. Your salary income goes away when you retire, and your net worth is then used to fund those retirement expenses that are not covered by your pension and Social Security income.

Liquidity—Keeping an Even Flow

Your net worth is comprised of several components with each component having a different level of liquidity, which is the speed with which an asset can be turned into cash without sacrificing asset value. As you can see in Table 22.1, some items can be liquidated more quickly than others.

Table 22.1   Typical Mixture of Assets That Make Up Your Net Worth

Item	Description	Liquidity
Bank Accounts	Checking, savings, and so on	High—all cash
Money markets	Investment	High—usually
Real Estate	Market value—loans	Low to medium
Car Equity	Market value—loans	Low to medium
401(k) Acct	Tax deferred until 59 1/2	Low until 59 1/2
IRA Accounts	Tax deferred until 59 1/2	Low until 59 1/2
Other Tax Deferrals	Tax deferred until 59 1/2	Low until 59 1/2
Stocks	Investment	Medium—usually
CDs	Dependent on term	Low to High
Mutual Funds	Investment	Low to medium
Bonds	Investments	Low to medium
Furnishings	Market value—usually low	Low to medium
Cash Value Insurance	Useful for loans	Low

Many other investment vehicles exist in today's financial climate, but they should all fall into a low-, medium-, or high-liquidity category based on how quickly you can turn the asset into cash without sacrificing the value of the asset, such as by offering the asset at a highly reduced price to sell it quickly.

A highly liquid asset is one that can be converted to cash within a few days, such as a money market or bank account. These are essentially cash holding accounts. It is recommended that you maintain at least six months of living expenses in highly liquid investment vehicles to cover you in case of emergency. The theory being that this gives you time to sell the other, less liquid assets, such as real estate, without being in an emergency situation causing you to sell below market price.

An investment vehicle with medium liquidity is one that can be converted into cash within six months without sacrificing the value of the asset. Many investment vehicles waver between low and medium liquidity, based on the current market for the asset involved. Your home may sell in 30 days or in several years, depending on the real estate market in your area at the time you choose to sell. The same is true for your other assets. Stocks can quickly be converted to cash, but you might have to take a loss depending on the current stock price compared to your initial purchase price.

A low-liquidity investment vehicle is one that requires more than a year to convert to cash. A certificate of deposit with a five-year term is a low-liquidity investment because you cannot easily convert it to cash. Your 401(k) and other tax-deferred accounts are low-liquidity investments unless you are over 59 1/2, which is the minimum age for withdrawal without paying a penalty.

Voice of Experience

It is common for people to put the majority of their retirement planning money into a tax-deferred account such as their company's 401(k) plan. On the surface, this looks like a sound strategy and really is one as long as you work until you are 59 1/2 and never need extra money until that time.

But what if you retire early or have some type of emergency cash need come up long before you reach 59 1/2? Now you have a problem because you cannot touch the 401(k) money to solve your immediate need for cash if you retire early and can only access the money through a loan if still working. Spreading your investments over low- to high-liquidity investment vehicles provides you with breathing room while still taking advantage of the tax benefits associated with retirement accounts.

It is interesting to note that the return provided on an investment vehicle is often related to that vehicle's liquidity. For example, a bank account is highly liquid but provides very low return rates. Stocks that fluctuate a great deal have high return rates but may provide either high or low liquidity depending on the performance of that particular stock at that particular time. Bonds that tie up your money for a longer period of time, which are less liquid, pay higher interest rates. In general you find that the lower the liquidity of an investment vehicle, the higher the interest rate of return provided by that vehicle.

Looking back to Chapters 1, 2, and 18, I made a few recommendations on the percentage of your portfolio to put into low-, medium-, and high-risk investments. You can now extend those discussions to managing your liquidity as well.

➤ Always maintain at least six months of living expenses in highly liquid accounts. Should something happen, you are thankful for this breathing room.

➤ When younger, invest in higher risk, less liquid investments because your salary covers you if you need to convert these less liquid vehicles into cash. (See Chapter 1, "It's Never Too Early to Start Planning," for additional early years investment information.)

➤ As you get closer to retirement, start moving your investments into more liquid vehicles that provide lower returns but more ready access to cash as your salary income turns into retirement pensions and Social Security. (See Chapter 2 for additional information on preparing for retirement as you approach it.)

➤ Real estate is almost always a good investment unless you get yourself "house poor." This means that all your income goes to paying for the house, leaving over no liquid assets for daily living. This is a stressful, risky tightrope act that is best reserved for those with many years until retirement. (See Chapters 12, "There's No Place Like Home," and 13, "Make It a Dream Home," for additional information about housing ownership benefits.)

➤ As you approach retirement, make sure that less of your net worth is tied up in your house and more is with income producing, more liquid investment vehicles.

➤ Retirement often means that the mortgage on your house is paid off, and you have substantial equity in your house. This might be a good time to take your $250,000/$500,000 exemption and move into a smaller house. By doing this, you can trade in the equity on your home for cash that can be placed into more liquid assets. Also know that you probably qualify for a home equity loan if you need to draw cash out of your paid off house. (See Chapter 12 for additional information about your primary residence as an investment.)

Managing your investments is always a juggling act, and it remains a juggling act as you approach retirement. Just remember that your emphasis probably shifts from high capital increases, such as seen with high-risk stocks, to a dependable income stream required to pay your bills.

QuickTip

This tip might sound a little morbid, but please bear with me. If one of you is sick and close to dying and you have more than $250,000 equity in your primary residence, you might consider selling it while that spouse is still alive so that you qualify for the $500,000 tax exemption level instead of the $250,000. You must be married filing jointly to qualify for the higher exemption level and you can only file joint returns during the year that your spouse passed away. That extra $250,000 ($500,000 – $250,000) is a lot of money and can go a long way toward helping you financially after your spouse is gone.

I know that this is a lot to consider if a loved one is seriously ill, but I thought you should know about the option before it passes away with your spouse. Check with your tax professional to verify the details regarding timing and the actual benefit you can expect.

An overall strategy of decreasing your expenses while increasing your income is a solid way to move into retirement.

How Much Will You Need?

Much of this section was already answered in Chapter 15, "Cover Your Personal Assets." You performed an analysis in that chapter that determined the amount of life insurance you should have to protect your family. As part of that discussion, you determined your family's living expenses after you had passed away. The same type of analysis applies here except that you are now planning your investment portfolio so that it can provide the income stream needed to cover the "expense gap" that exists between your expected retirement income and expected retirement expenses (see Table 22.2).

Table 22.2   Estimating Income and Expenses After You Retire

Monthly Income When Retired	
Your Social Security income	$_____
Your Spouse's Social Security income	$_____
Your Pension income	$_____
Your Spouse's Pension income	$_____
Any other retirement-related income	$_____
1. Total Pension And Social Security Income:	**$_____**
Monthly Continuing Expenses	
Utilities	$_____
Food	$_____
Car payments	$_____
Mortgage payments	$_____
Property taxes	$_____
Insurance	$_____
Household maintenance	$_____
Second home expenses	$_____
Family member support, as required	$_____
Clothing	$_____
Federal, state, and local taxes	$_____
Recreation (Don't skimp here)	$_____
Education	$_____
Other living expenses	$_____
2. Monthly Expense Total:	**$_____**
3. Monthly Income Surplus (Gap):	**$_____**
(Subtract line 2 from line 1)	
4. Annual Income Surplus (Gap):	**$_____**
(Multiply line 3 by 12)	

If line 4 in this table is a positive number, you have an income surplus, which means that you have more retirement income than is needed to pay your expenses. If line 4 is a negative number, then you have an income gap. This means that you have less retirement income than is needed to pay your expenses. The after-tax income from your investment portfolio must be used to cover this gap or you must decrease your expenses to match your expected income. It is that simple.

QuickCaution

A word of caution is probably due here regarding the future viability of Social Security. Some people believe that Social Security may not even be available in another 20 years, due to the large number of baby boomers who will reach retirement and the smaller number of workers who will be supporting the Social Security system. Talk exists today in Congress about methods to save Social Security, which implies that our congressional leaders also have concerns. This means that planning is even more important. The bottom line is that you want to consider the possibility of having to make your way through retirement without Social Security. That way, you're prepared.

QuickCaution

It is also a good idea to repeat the exercise outlined in Table 22.2 for the possibility of either spouse's passing away. Social Security income typically drops to that of the spouse with the higher level of income, and the pension income is typically cut in half, or goes away completely. This is another "surprise" that you want to avoid if possible.

Calculating the portfolio needed to cover your retirement income gap is a straightforward process once you have gotten this far. You can calculate the amount based on two scenarios:

➤ You leave the investment intact and live only off of the interest.

➤ You deplete the portfolio by treating it as an annuity.

Use the following procedure for calculating the scenario 1 portfolio target amount:

1. Enter the annual income gap required: $_____

(For example, using the information you gathered in the previous table, $650 × 12 = $7,800)

2. Estimate your annual portfolio return: _____%

(for example, 8%)

3. Portfolio Value: (Divide line 1 by line 2) $_____

(For example, $7,800 / .08 = $97,500)

This example indicates that a $97,500 investment portfolio generating an after-tax 8% return covers the expected annual income gap. If you expect to be in a 15% tax bracket, your portfolio must generate 8% / .85 = 9.4% overall pretax return rate.

Notice that as the income gap increases, so does the required portfolio value and/or the required portfolio return. Looked at another way, the larger your portfolio at retirement, the lower the required return that allows you to select lower risk investments. How do you make sure that your portfolio value is as large as possible? By starting early and paying yourself first. Have you heard that before in this book? Now you know, by the numbers, why this is the best strategy to take.

The first scenario assumes that you only live off of interest gained from your portfolio. When you pass away, your entire portfolio is left behind. The second scenario assumes that you plan to deplete your portfolio over your retirement years and leave nothing behind. You live off of both the principal and interest related to your portfolio. (See Chapter 19, "Protecting Your Dough with Investments That Aren't So Risky," for additional information about annuities.)

How Much Do You Plan to Leave?

Another important part of retirement planning is to determine the amount of money you want to leave behind as part of your estate. This is a tough question to answer in any standard way, because it is heavily dependent upon your particular family situation.

➤ You might be the type of person who wants the last dime that you own dropped in the coffin before you are buried.

➤ You might have a sick child that needs extended care after you are gone, and you want to ensure that your estate covers his needs. (See Chapter 15 for assistance in this regard.)

➤ You might want to leave as much as possible to your heirs to provide them with a financial boost.

➤ You might want to leave a substantial amount of money to a charity or medical research group.

If you plan to leave a lot behind, your portfolio must be large enough to support your income gap without depleting the portfolio amount.

If you plan to leave little to no money behind, you can use the annuity approach and deplete the portfolio value as you pay for your retirement.

Like most people, you are somewhere in the middle and will probably leave some money behind, because it just doesn't make personal sense to optimize this game too much.

How Long Do You Plan to Stick Around?

Don't forget that your investment portfolio is more than just a means for generating interest income. It also has an intrinsic value of its own that can be used as needed to pay expenses. This way, the portfolio can be treated as an annuity because you can receive payments from your portfolio that are part interest income and part asset from the portfolio. In fact, some people put their investments into a tax-deferred immediate annuity when they retire so that the income generated by the investment account is tax-free, but they still have access to their money.

The good news with this annuity approach is that your nest egg value does not need to be as large to provide the income gap required. The bad news is that you must estimate accurately the number of years that you plan to deplete the account value because the annuity payment is designed to remove a little of the account value with each payment until the account value drops to zero.

Voice of Experience

Whatever your personal desires, I suggest that you first worry about your own financial and personal well-being, and then worry about what you leave to your heirs. After you are personally covered, then get fancy about your financial planning.

QuickCaution

It is important that you review the specific insurance needs that apply to you when retired. Take a look at Chapters 15, "Cover Your Personal Assets," and 17, "An Apple a Day Won't Keep the Doctor Away," for information regarding life and medical insurance coverage.

If you have enough control over your life to pass away with your last annuity payment, there are Hindu masters that would like to make your acquaintance. If you are like the rest of us, you hang around until it is time for you to leave, which is not heavily dependent on your investment account balance. So, if you plan the annuity for a 15-year period and live for 25 years, the last 10 years are without annuity income, which could be a problem. If you plan for 25 and only live 15, you leave some money behind in the account. There is just no way to know until your passing away is a historical note, so I suggest that you plan to live more years instead of less, because aging without money is an undesirable condition.

The 401(k) Plans, IRA Plans, and KEOGH Plans

You know that you have to invest somewhere. The next question is where? The first place to look is at your tax-deferred plans that are either offered by your employer or set up on your own. This section looks at 401(k), 403(b), individual retirement account (IRA), Roth IRA, Keogh, and other plans. Selecting the right one for your situation may be simple or complicated, depending on your circumstances.

Saving Through Your Employer with 401(k) and 403(b) Plans

I think that the 401(k) plan is one of the greatest savings vehicles around. You enroll in the plan through your employer. After enrolled, you have an account that you can take with you if you leave the company. Any money deposited into your 401(k) account is tax deferred until you draw it out after you reach the magic age of 59 1/2. After retirement, you must pay tax on the withdrawn funds at an assumed lower tax rate because you are retired and have a much smaller income.

The nice thing about 401(k) plans is that the employer can match your contributions in a number of ways. This means that money you contribute to the plan is essentially multiplied by a percentage related to the company's contribution. Free money from the company that you use for your retirement is always a good thing. But there is often a catch. For example, you may have to stay with the company for a period of time, such as five years, before you can take the matching funds with you to another company. This is the company's way of holding you for a longer period of time. By the way, these company benefits can make a big difference in your overall compensation package. For example, a company that provides four-year vesting is better than one that provides five-year vesting.

The 401(k) plan also allows you to invest your money into different investment vehicles such as mutual funds, money market funds, or even your company stock. You can also put a percentage of your money into a combination of low-, medium-, and high-risk investment vehicles, which is my recommendation. This plan can grow into a lot of money over time, and you should not ignore the benefits of enrolling in a 401(k) plan. The following are some other significant 401(k) plan features:

➤ Withdrawing money before age 59 1/2 incurs a 10% penalty plus income tax payments on the funds withdrawn unless you meet very specific exceptions.

➤ You can borrow money against your 401(k) plan and repay the loan to yourself, interest and all! This is a pretty sweet deal because the interest you pay actually goes to fund your retirement.

➤ You are generally allowed to contribute between 2% and 10% of your salary into the account, up to the IRS limits that change every year due to inflation.

➤ Account deposits are usually taken directly from your paycheck before taxes are taken out because they are tax deferred. Automatic deduction means that you pay yourself first and regularly.

➤ You can roll over the plan to another qualified tax deferred investment plan if you leave this company. Check with your plan coordinators for specific instructions regarding the roll over and expect the process to take weeks. You can also choose to leave the money in your last employer's plan. If you don't roll over your 401(k) money and deposit in your standard savings account, you are charged income tax on the money plus penalties. Ouch!

The 403(b) plan is established for religious, public education, and charitable organizations and works almost identically to a 401(k). Both are great plans, but remember that your money is locked up until you reach 59 1/2 or you pay stiff penalties.

Saving for Yourself with IRAs and Roth IRAs

An IRA is a tax-deferred plan that allows you to deposit up to $2,000 for a single person and up to $4,000 for a married couple, if only one spouse works. The amount deposited into the plan is deductible in the year that the money is added to the IRA account. IRA money is also unavailable until 59 1/2, and you incur a 10% penalty for early withdrawal unless you meet certain exceptions. One important exception is that up to $10,000 can be withdrawn to pay for the down payment on your first house, or an unlimited amount can be withdrawn to pay for higher education. As your income increases, the IRA tax exempt portion disappears depending upon whether you are a participant in another qualified plan, single or married.

The Roth IRA is a special account type that also allows you to deposit up to $2,000 per year, subject to various income limitations. The deposits into the Roth IRA account are not tax deductible in the year of the deposit, but can be withdrawn along with their interest earnings on a tax-free basis after you reach any one of the following criteria:

➤ You reach age 59 1/2.

➤ You become disabled.

➤ You are applying the withdrawn money to the down payment on your first house (up to $10,000).

➤ Your account is passed to your beneficiaries after you die.

QuickTip

If your current tax rate is low, invest in the Roth IRA to avoid the taxes. If your current tax rate is high, you might be better served by depositing into a standard IRA today and bearing the tax consequences later when your tax rate might be lower.

The basic difference between the two IRA plans is that withdrawals from the standard IRA are taxed when you retire and the interest income is taxed. The Roth IRA charges you taxes today and allows you to withdraw tax-free when you retire, and the interest income is also tax-free.

A Retirement Plan for You Self-Employed Folks

If you are the owner of an unincorporated business, you have a way to defer tax on some of your income by putting it into a Keogh plan. This plan comes in various types that allow you to contribute today and draw out after you reach age 59 1/2. You can choose a "money-purchase Keogh" that requires you to deposit an annually fixed amount between 2% and 20% of your earnings up to $30,000 or a "profit-sharing Keogh," which allows you to annually decide whether you want to contribute up to 13.04% of your earnings up to a $30,000 maximum. There is also a "combined Keogh" plan that allows you to select aspects of both plans.

Employees can also be covered under a Keogh plan in similar percentages to the plan you establish for yourself. This is a potentially big decision, so talk with your tax professional before getting yourself into something that you later might regret.

The Keogh must be set up by December 31 of the tax year in question, and you cannot withdraw from your Keogh account without incurring stiff penalties. You don't manage the Keogh plan. Instead, you find a brokerage house to administer it for you. Keoghs can be complicated to set up, but they offer a higher level of potential tax shelter than the simplified employee pension (SEP) plan.

Making Life Simpler with the SEP

The simplified employee pension (SEP) plan is set up to allow employees to have their own, separate retirement account. This account can be transferred from one qualified retirement plan to another if the employee changes companies. If you are self-employed, you can contribute up to 15% and $30,000 into the account. There is a 10% penalty for early withdrawal before age 59 1/2. Other deferral opportunities and complexities are associated with an SEP, so talk with your tax professional for the details.

Using Quicken's Retirement Planner

Once again, Quicken comes to your calculator's rescue by providing Retirement Planning, which is accessed from the **Features** menu, **Planning**, **Financial**

Planners, **Retirement** option. This handy tool enables you to estimate your annual future income based on current financial parameters, estimate what you must contribute annually to reach a specific future investment goal, or determine your current savings requirements to reach specific future retirement income goals. The exercises that you performed earlier in this chapter, and the estimated percentage return calculations you performed elsewhere in this book, all feed into using this particular tool. This tool is not available in Quicken versions other than the Deluxe. Please verify its availability for your personal version.

Operating the tool is the easy part. Knowing the proper amounts to enter is the hard part.

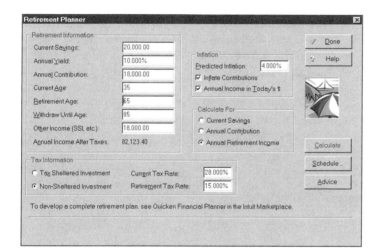

Planning today's savings actions to reach tomorrow's goals.

Enter the Retirement Information to include the following:

➤ **Current Savings**, which is the amount you currently have in your total portfolio including all assets. Assume **$20,000** for this example.

➤ Enter the **Annual Yield:** that you can reasonably expect from your investments between today and when you die. For this example, assume **10%**, which equates to a lower after-tax rate.

➤ Enter the amount you plan to add to your retirement fund into the **Annual Contribution:** field. Assume that this amount is **$18,000**.

➤ Enter your **Current Age:**, which is assumed to be 35 for this example.

➤ Enter the age at which you plan to retire into the **Retirement Age:** field, which is assumed at **65** for this example.

➤ Enter the age at which you expect to die in the **Withdraw Until Age:** field. Assume this number at **85** for this example.

➤ Type your estimated total annual retirement income in the **Other Income (SSI, etc.):** field. Assume this amount at **$18,000** or $1,500 a month for this example.

➤ In the **Inflation** section, set the **Predicted Inflation:** amount to **4%** for this example, but use your own estimate for the future inflation rates.

➤ Check **Inflate Contributions** if you plan to increase your **Annual Contributions:** by the inflation rate every year. Check **Annual Income In Today's $** to see your answers in today's dollars as opposed to the inflated dollars of your retirement future. For this example, check both options.

➤ In the **Tax Information** section, select whether your investments are tax deferred (**Tax Sheltered Investment**) or taxable (**Non-Sheltered Investment** should be checked for this example). In addition, define your **Current Tax Rate:** (assumed **28%**) and your **Retirement Tax Rate:** (assumed **15%**).

➤ Finally, set the options in the **Calculate For** section to designate whether you are looking to determine the expected **Annual Retirement Income** (checked for this example), or determine the **Annual Contribution** to achieve a specific future savings goal or the **Current Savings** required to achieve a future savings goal.

This example shows that, given the savings procedures outlined, you can expect to have the retirement dollars equivalent or $82,123 of today's dollars. Not too bad considering that your mortgage is probably paid off.

The Least You Need to Know

➤ The amount of money you need in retirement from your investments is dependent upon the income gap between your retirement income and expected expenses.

➤ The Quicken Retirement Planner helps you define a current savings plan that creates your future required portfolio value.

➤ Various retirement plans can be used to create your tax-deferred nest egg, from the 401(k) plan to the SEP.

➤ Estimates of future inflation and expected return on your investment portfolio make a huge difference in your ultimate portfolio value.

➤ The more you know about your expected retirement style of living and the amount you want to leave behind, the better you can plan a comfortable retirement.

Chapter 23

You Can't Take It with You, So Plan Your Estate Now

In This Chapter

➤ Avoid extended court intervention in the processing of your estate

➤ Make sure that the right people get the right stuff after you pass away

➤ Set up different types of wills to cover both your death and becoming incapacitated

➤ Use Quicken to keep track of important legal and financial information that are needed to resolve your estate

➤ Know what to expect from your executor and the probate courts

The one thing you can be sure of is that someday you pass away. Although this certainly is not a happy thought, it's even worse to think about your family struggling to survive emotionally and financially without you.

That's why having a well-thought-out estate plan makes good sense. It not only makes it easier for your relatives who are left behind, but also better ensures that your estate goes to the people you choose and not to the government in the form of estate taxes. A lot of detail is associated with estate planning, but the basic concepts are simple. Work your way through this chapter and start preparing today for that day down the road when your will has to speak on your behalf.

Expressing Your Will

It is ironic that you work your entire life to provide for your family, and that upon your death, they might very well have to struggle to keep what you intended for them to have in the first place. This situation might very well happen if you do not explicitly outline what you want done with your estate before you die, because even Houdini couldn't do it after he passed away. You define these instructions by creating a "will" that contains your instructions. The will is read upon your death, and the instructions are followed.

Talkin' Money

A will is a legal document drawn up while you are still alive that outlines your wishes for your estate, after you pass away. Think of the will as instructions from the grave. You typically include instructions regarding division of your estate assets, guardianship of minor children, funeral wishes, and the designation of an executor or person who manages the distribution of your estate.

It is important that a copy of your will be maintained in a readily accessible place so that it is not sealed off when you die. It is also important that the people around you know that a will exists and where to find it. A safe deposit box is often used, but some states seal these boxes when someone dies. So, if the will is in the box and the box is sealed, your estate might be tied up for a very long time. Leave a copy with your attorney, another in a safe place at home, and another in your safe deposit box. This way, a copy is always readily available when you pass away.

When a person dies without a will, they are said to have died "intestate," which legally means that your estate is divided up according to law, not according to how you want it to be done. If you think about it, the law has no other choice because you did not leave specific instructions.

This really becomes a big deal if both you and your spouse die in an auto accident and you have children under age 18. It is very possible that the state would turn around and appoint a guardian for them that you would never have picked in a million years. Designating a guardian in your will takes care of this issue and protects your children. Telling someone isn't good enough. It needs to be in writing and is best prepared by an attorney.

Everything that passes through your will is treated as part of your estate and subject to the estate tax laws. A number of other legal mechanisms exist that help you keep things out of your will and possibly minimize estate taxes:

➤ **Revocable trust**   A legal instrument that allows you to designate the distribution of your estate but allows you to revoke the designation at any time while you are still alive. It become irrevocable after you pass away and is used by the estate executor to implement your wishes.

➤ **Irrevocable trust**   A legal instrument that you create to pass an asset to one of your heirs that cannot be altered after created. This trust allows you to give someone a gift, but it keeps his or her hands off of it until you pass away. Tax benefits are associated with an irrevocable trust because the assets covered by the trust are not included as part of the estate (for estate tax calculation purposes), which can help a lot if your estate is larger than the applicable Unified Credit, which is $625,000 in 1998.

➤ **Power of appointment trust** Allows the person you entrust with this power to designate when your beneficiaries receive their assets and other property. This power might be used to ensure that the assets are transferred to your heirs at a time when they need them the most, not necessarily when they want them the most.

➤ **Durable powers of attorney** Given to someone you trust to handle your financial affairs if you become incapacitated, but remain alive. This is a big deal because those surviving need to administer your estate to pay for your medical bills if you have a incapacitating medical condition. These powers can be given on a general (handle anything) or special (handle only specific things) basis. A person designated as power of attorney has the right to write checks in your name, liquidate assets, and do everything else that you could legally do, so choose this person carefully.

➤ **Living will** Used to define your wishes if you are medically compromised to the point that you are being kept alive by life-support equipment. This instrument explains your desire to refuse medical treatment and the circumstances under which you would want to be taken off of life support. This is a very special responsibility so you want to ensure that this person is someone you trust.

➤ **Durable health care power of attorney** Allows another person to make medical decisions on your behalf if you are not able to make those decisions on your own.

Talkin' Money

The Unified Credit is the amount of estate value that transfers to your heirs on a tax-free basis. It is actually a tax credit of $192,800 that covers the tax due on what I call the excluded amount. The excluded amount for 1997 was $600,000. It increased to $625,000 in 1998 and continues to increase to $1,000,000 from 2006 onward. Your 1998 estate gets a Unified Credit and so does your spouse's for a total of $1,250,000 that can be transferred to your heirs on a tax-free basis.

QuickTip

There are software packages on the market that lead you through the creation of a will. One of these packages is the Quicken Family Lawyer. I suggest that you start off your will creation process with one of these packages, but have the will inspected by an attorney to make sure that the software generalities are right for your specific situation. See Intuit's Web site at www.intuit.com for more details regarding Quicken Family Lawyer.

It is important that the completed versions of the preceding list of documents be kept current and be applicable to the state (for example, Idaho) that you live in. If you live in two states, you should have these documents drawn up to comply with the laws of each state, which require separate sets of documents.

The last three instruments deal with situations where you are still alive and require others to make decisions on your behalf. Providing these documents is a tremendous service to family members who want to do the best they can, under difficult personal circumstances, to handle things as you would want.

Who Needs It the Most?

All the items that comprise your net worth are passed to someone when you die. It either is your spouse, family, designated heirs, or the government in the form of taxes that can go as high as 55% to 60% for very large estates. Advance planning maximizes the amount given to your heirs and minimize the portion given to the government.

I suggest that you determine the relative percentages that you want to pass onto various people or organizations based on a list that looks something like the following:

➤ First ensure that your spouse or significant other is taken care of in a way sufficient for the rest of his/her life. Of course, this varies depending on your specific situation.

➤ Next ensure that the most needy members of your family are taken care of in a way sufficient for the rest of their lives. This might include children, parents, or other relatives.

➤ Next look at major contributions that you could make to help out others, such as paying tuition or medical expenses.

➤ You might want to donate to a charity of some type, such as a group doing cancer or diabetes research.

Whatever your chosen heirs, it is important that you define your wishes or the government defines them for you and takes a huge share for its efforts. In addition, remember that your family, and particularly your spouse, feels both the personal and financial impact of your loss. I encourage you to provide for her/his welfare before making some grand gesture.

Items typically evaluated when you pass away include the following:

➤ Your cash reserves such as bank accounts, money market funds, and cash value insurance policies.

➤ Major asset items such as real estate and vehicles.

➤ Stock, bonds, and other financial instruments.

➤ Any interest you may have in a privately held company such as a company that you started and left behind when you died.

➤ Any debts that people owe you such as personal loans you might have made to people or organizations that they agreed to pay back.

➤ Life insurance benefits that may come from your personal policies or those provided with your retirement benefits.

➤ Miscellaneous assets such as jewelry, paintings, clothing, tools, furnishings, and intellectual properties such as patents, copyrights, and trademarks that have some type of value associated with them.

➤ Liabilities associated with the various assets. These are naturally deducted from the value of your estate before calculating your estate's worth.

QuickTip

Keeping your Quicken accounting records current makes this process a snap. The net worth report shows you all asset items of value and their worth at the time that you run the report.

Asset items that are not liquid, such as real estate or jewelry, contribute to the value of your estate but do not provide any cash with which to pay estate taxes. This is a potentially precarious position for your heirs because they may need to come up with cash to pay the estate taxes on items of high personal and/or market value but no cash value. Planning ahead can minimize the tax impact on your heirs and allow you to sleep better before your death.

Dodging the Tax Man

When someone, such as Uncle Sam, is looking to take up to 60% of every nickel you ever made, you should be looking for ways to keep his hand out of the cash box. In short, advance planning can keep your estate from paying more taxes than are needed. If you play things right, your estate might pay no taxes at all. Table 23.1 shows you the maximum nontaxable estate values for 1998–2006 and later. Basically, if your estate is worth more than the amounts shown in this table, any higher amount is subject to taxation.

Table 23.1 The Unified Tax Credits Applicable to Estates of Persons Dying in Various Years

For persons dying in:	Estate value amount excluded:
1998	$625,000
1999	$650,000
2000–2001	$675,000
2002–2003	$700,000
2004	$850,000
2005	$950,000
2006 and later	$1,000,000

The Basics of Estate Taxes

The following are a few points that are fundamental to estate tax planning:

➤ A unified estate and gift tax credit provided by the IRS basically pays the tax on your estate's first $625,000 in 1998 and progressively more each year up to $1 million from 2006 into the future. This means that estates with a value of less than the threshold ($625,000 in 1998) owe no estate tax.

➤ Any assets passed through your will are considered part of your estate and summed to determine its value.

➤ Both you and your spouse qualify for the unified estate and tax credit, which means that up to $1,250,000 ($625,000 × 2) could be tax exempt from estates calculated in 1998. More can be exempt in subsequent years because the credit increases annually until the year 2006.

➤ Funeral and estate administration expenses are deducted from the estate value before determining estate taxes. This includes most funeral expenses along with estate administration costs such as executor fees (usually 2% to 5% and usually well-earned), appraisal fees, court fees, attorney fees, accounting costs, and other related fees. These fees can really add up if the estate is at all complicated or must first go through the court system.

➤ Assets can be valued at the time of your death or six months after your death. If the values of your estate assets are expected to decrease, choosing to have your assets valued six months after you pass away may be the right move because the estate taxes would be less.

➤ One-half interest in property owned as "joint tenants with right of survivorship" or "tenants by the entirety" passes to the surviving partner, who is typically a spouse but does not have to be. If the partner is not a spouse, the tax treatment is more complicated because the property is assumed to be owned completely by the first party to die; the surviving partner must then prove that he or she financially contributed to the estate expenses. Comprehensive record keeping at that time is appreciated, so make Quicken your friend today if you are not married and own property under one of these two legal designations. The person with the most paper wins when working with the IRS.

Talkin' Money

Joint tenants with rights of survivorship and tenants by the entirety are both legal ownership designations that automatically transfer all ownership rights to the asset in question to the surviving partner. If that partner is a spouse, no tax is paid on the transfer because the Estate Tax Marital Deduction umbrella protects the transferred assets from tax.

The estate tax marital deduction allows one spouse to transfer an unlimited amount of estate assets to a surviving spouse without paying any taxes at all. The good news is that no assets are taxed when passed to the spouse. The potentially bad news is that all these assets are subject to tax when the second spouse dies.

➤ If your estate is expected to be under the unified estate tax and gift credit threshold ($625,000 in 1998), no fancy estate planning is needed to avoid paying taxes because none will be due.

Check out this little trick to see how you can save more than $250,000 in estate taxes. Assume that you and your spouse own an estate valued at $2 million and your spouse dies. His or her half of the $2 million is $1 million, which could pass to you directly through the marital deduction. No estate taxes are due, so far.

Now assume that you pass away and want to leave the entire estate to your children. The estate is now valued at $2 million of which only your $625,000 is excluded. This means that your estate pays tax on the remaining $1,375,000 ($2 million minus the maximum credit of $625,000 in 1998). From the following table, you can calculate that this requires taxes of $448,300 (the base tax rate for this estate value is shown on line 13 + $53,750 (($1,375,000 – $1,250,000) × .43) = $502,050.

	Value over	But not over	Base Tax due	Marginal %	Of amount over
1.	$0	$10,000	$0	18%	$0
2.	10,000	20,000	1,800	20%	10,000
3.	20,000	40,000	3,800	22%	20,000
4.	40,000	60,000	8,200	24%	40,000
5.	60,000	80,000	13,000	26%	60,000
6.	80,000	100,000	18,200	28%	80,000
7.	100,000	150,000	23,800	30%	100,000
8.	150,000	250,000	38,800	32%	150,000
9.	250,000	500,000	70,800	34%	250,000
10.	500,000	750,000	155,800	37%	500,000
11.	750,000	1,000,000	248,300	39%	750,000
12.	1,000,000	1,250,000	345,800	41%	1,000,000
13.	1,250,000	1,500,000	448,300	43%	1,250,000
14.	1,500,000	2,000,000	555,800	45%	1,500,000
15.	2,000,000	2,500,000	780,800	49%	2,000,000
16.	2,500,000	3,000,000	1,025,800	53%	2,500,000
17.	3,000,000+		1,290,800	55%	3,000,000

Now assume that you and your spouse agree that you can live on your $1 million half of the total estate and that your spouse's half should pass to the children. Your taxable estate is now calculated at $1,000,000 – $625,000 (his credit) = $365,000. You see from the table that this taxable amount owes taxes of $70,800 (base tax rate for this estate value shown on line 9 of the previous table) + $39,100 (($365,000 – $250,000) × .34) = $109,900.

QuickCaution

The marital deduction is not applicable if the surviving spouse is not a U.S. citizen. This is a critical point for those couples where one is a U.S. citizen and the other is not. See a lawyer and tax professional to set up other ways to transfer assets to the non-U.S. citizen spouse.

If you assume that the same calculations are applied to your $1 million estate when you pass away, which now also qualifies for a $625,000 estate value exemption, your estate also has to pay $109,900 in taxes. Your combined estate taxes are $109,900 (your spouse) + $109,900 (your estate) = $219,800.

You can now calculate the estate tax savings derived from this simple switch in tax handling. It is calculated by $502,050 (prior single-estate scenario) – $219,800 (split estate scenario) = $282,250 less than if you simply relied on the marital deduction as was done in the first scenario. Keeping $282,000 in taxes out of the government's hands would even make Bill Gates smile!

The basic concept is to get your taxable estate down as close as possible to the tax credit amount applicable for the year of death ($625,000 in 1998) so that the majority of your estate is excluded from estate taxes. A number of techniques are available for reducing your estate value and minimizing taxes while still providing benefits to your heirs:

➤ Use joint ownership only on those items that you absolutely want to pass to your spouse, and explicitly define beneficiaries for other assets.

➤ Give gifts annually to your beneficiaries to reduce the size of your estate. Obviously, you don't want to compromise your financial security to beat taxes (especially because you won't be around to pay them), but you can give gifts of up to $10,000 per person, per year to as many people as you want without you or them having to pay tax on it. Every $10,000 you give as a gift means that this person gets $10,000 instead of only $4,500, which would be their net benefit after the 55% estate tax is applied.

➤ Pay someone's college tuition costs and/or medical expenses directly to the college or medical caregiver and not to the person himself. This way, the "gift" is not taxable to either you or him, but you definitely have helped that person out. Make sure that you keep accurate Quicken records of the transactions.

➤ Set up trusts that exempt the amount dedicated to the trust from estate tax and make your intended heir the beneficiary of the trust. Trusts are complicated to set up and cost hundreds to thousands of dollars to create, but they can also provide huge estate tax savings while still providing for your heirs. See your attorney for the tax and legal details on trusts. There are many types in existence today, and more types being created all the time.

➤ Don't try willing the money directly to your grandchildren because it is immediately taxd at the generation-skipping transfer tax rate of 55%! A $10,000 annual gift to a grandchild is not subject to this generation-skipping transfer tax, but everything over that amount is.

QuickTip

Make sure that you check out the bypass–trust, which is also called a nonmarital trust. This legal construct allows you to leave money behind for the use of your surviving partner and even allows him/her to access the principal if needed, but it also allows this amount to not be included in the surviving partner's estate, thus preserving your tax credit. This trust has a maximum limit that is equal to the applicable unified estate credit, which was $625,000 in 1998.

If you are getting the impression that this estate planning is complicated from both a legal and tax standpoint, you are getting my message loud and clear. If your estate is anticipated to be less than the unified estate credit, a will and simple precautions protect you. If you plan to leave a lot behind, and want control over where it goes while minimizing estate taxes, you need to spend the time to do it right. I encourage you to work with a lawyer and tax professional to get it right, because the dollars involved and potential personal impact on your heirs is so large.

After you have completed your first will, don't expect it to last you a lifetime. You should evaluate it at least every five years or when a major life event occurs such as marriage, divorce, the arrival of children, a death in the family, buying/selling a house, changing jobs, and so forth. The more precise you are in your estate planning, the more frequently you need to review things.

The Executor's Role

Coordinating the resolution of someone's estate is not a trivial task, even if everything is in order. There are people and companies to be notified, government paperwork needs to be complete, and other family members to deal with. Unless you want a state-appointed person performing these functions, you must appoint this person, called an executor, yourself. The executor's job is to execute your instructions as outlined in your estate documents. After a court recognizes your will as legal, your will officially designates your executor, who is then put in charge of your estate. The court then backs out of the process except to verify that the executor does his/her job as designated—a sort of quality control check.

This process of verifying the validity of a will is called "probate" and is unavoidable because your will must first be deemed legal before it can be executed. If you die intestate (without a will), probate becomes a difficult process because the court must now guess at your intent and follow the laws instead of your expressed wishes.

The executor is usually paid a fee that ranges from between 2% and 5% of the estate value for performing his/her duties. This may seem like a lot, but just assume that resolving someone's estate may take several months to several years. That person should be compensated for the involvement.

The clearer you make your will, the less involved the probate process because your wishes are legal, clear, and above contention.

Do your family and your executor a favor. Work with a lawyer and accountant to create a solid will that clearly outlines your wishes, and make sure that this will is easily accessible when you pass away.

Using Quicken to Organize Your Estate Paperwork

Finding emergency documents when they're needed is important, because these documents are designed to inform others of critical information. When an emergency happens, the last thing you want to be doing is frantically looking for the very information that was created to deal with the emergency. Having this information in a consistent, clearly marked spot is very important. When a person dies, the first thing that a funeral home asks is whether the deceased person had any special funeral requests. Those documents should already be in hand, and usually on the day that the person dies. Get the picture?

Quicken Deluxe helps in this regard with its **Emergency Records Organizer**, which is accessed under the **Features**, **Planning** menu option. This feature is not available with all Quicken versions, so you need to verify its inclusion with your particular version.

This is a great tool that provides a central storage location for all kinds of important personal information, and it prints reports that can then be stored for easy access. Some of the information stored includes the following:

➤ Medical, dental, personal, and emergency contact information for both adults and children. This includes doctors' names and numbers, Social Security and driver's license numbers, and maiden name information.

Use Quicken's Emergency Records Organizer to save documents related to your estate.

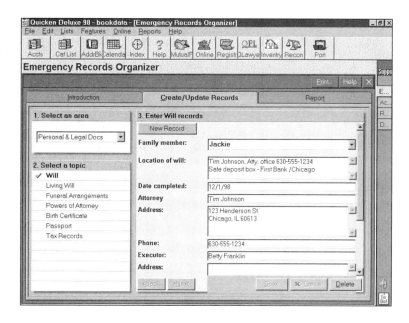

➤ Legal information regarding attorneys' names and numbers, wills and their location, funeral arrangements, and other information related to your family.

➤ Banking and other investment account information including institutions, numbers, and contact information.

➤ Detailed property information including automobile titles, location of ownership deeds, safe deposit box information, safe locations plus combination, and other information that only a few people would know.

➤ Insurance information including life, auto, disability, and health. You can include the policy numbers, agent name and phone numbers, face values, and other pertinent information.

➤ Loan information including the account numbers and contact information for the lender.

Much of this information is linked to the specific account type as designated in the properties section of accounts, such as the investment accounts. Properly defining the accounts Info and Tax information for the account automatically transfers the information to this screen.

This tool is also easy to use by following these simple instructions:

1. Click the **Create/Update Records** tab to access the specific information divided by category.

2. From the **Select an area,** section 1, select an area of interest from the list provided, such as **Personal & Legal Documents**, as shown in the figure.

3. Under **Select a topic**, section 2, select the specific topic areas of interest that are then displayed in the right side of the window, such as **Will**, as shown in the figure.

4. Complete the information requested in the right side of the screen such as the **Enter Will Records**.

5. Click **Save** to save the entered information.

6. Click another topic from section 2 of the screen to get information related to that particular topic area or click **New Record** to add will information for another person. Click **Delete** to remove this information from the stored file.

7. Click the **Report** tab to view various reports that contain the information added. Reports can be printed to contain information pertinent to **Caretakers**, **Survivors** and **Emergency** situations. **Summary** and **Detail** reports are provided that print all information entered. Select the desired report type along with its associated options and click **Print** to get a paper copy of the information. These printed reports should be kept in readily available locations for emergency purposes.

Creating reports that summarize emergency information.

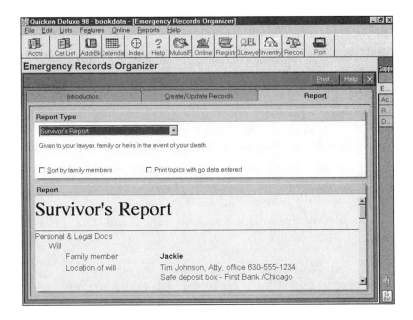

A word of caution is due at this point. Although this feature is a great help to the people who actually own the information, it is also a great help to those who want to fraudulently use your credit information. If you look at the amount of personal information contained in these reports, you realize that they contain information that you wouldn't tell your best friend.

Although you want these reports readily accessible, you also want them in a secure spot. My suggestion is that you put the Emergency Report information into a binder so that anyone can easily get at it. The other information should be stored in a secure place, such as with your attorney and in a safe deposit box. This covers you in case of fire, theft, or death in the family. Once again, make this determination for yourself as applies to your particular situation.

The Least You Need to Know

➤ Without a will, your estate goes into probate where the courts decide the fate of your estate and children.

➤ The marriage deduction is a great thing for couples but does not apply to life partners who are not married or to those who are not U.S. citizens.

➤ Optimizing the use of the unified tax credit can greatly reduce estate taxes.

➤ Your will should be stored in a place that is accessible after your death, such as your attorney's office. A safe deposit box might be sealed and can only be opened by the courts.

➤ Using the Quicken Emergency Records Organizer can greatly simplify tracking of financial and legal information in the event of a death or medical emergency.

Index

C

P

P/E (price to earnings) ratio, stocks, 273-274
paperwork, attorneys, 165
par value, bonds, 257
parents
    caring for, 24-25
    things to consider when having children, 14-16
    see also children
Paycheck Setup Wizard, 48
payee, 102
paying bills electronically, 107-110
paying off loans, 132-133
payment periods, loans, 134-135
payments
    loan amortization table, 138
    loans, acclerating, 139-140
    tracking, 49
Pell grants, financial aid, 295
penalties, CDs (certificates of deposit), 255
people, single
    credit ratings, 9
    financial guidelines, 9-11
    investments, 9
    planning for retirement, 11
    saving, 9
    see also couples
Personal Identification Numbers (PINs), 95
personal injury protection (PIP), automobile insurance, 216
personal liability, homeowners insurance, 223
PITI (principal, interest, taxes, and insurance), 169
planning
    accounts for tax preparation, 117-118
    for retirement, 298, 300-306
        without Social Security,303
    for taxes, 114-117

power of appointment trust, 313
power of attorney, 313
PPOs (Preferred-Provider Organizations), medical insurance, 231
pre-existing conditions, 232
preparing
    to care for aging parents, 24-25
    for retirement at middle age, 18-20
prepayment penalty clause, loans, 137
printing checks, 104-107
private colleges, 287
probate, 320
property damage, automobile insurance, 218
property gain, 180-181
Property Tax Expense Account for New Residence, 183
Property Tax Expense Account for Prior Residence, 183
property taxes, appraised value, 170-171
providers of Medigap, 236-237
purchase plans, 276

Q

Quicken
    accounts, 92-93
        Asset Account for Prior Residence, 182
        Asset Accounts for New Residence, 183
        Depreciation Expense Account for New Residence, 183
        Depreciation Expense Account for Prior Residence, 182

Maintenance Expense Account for New Residence, 183
Maintenance Expense Account for Prior Residence, 182
Property Tax Expense Account for New Residence, 183
Property Tax Expense Account for Prior Residence, 183
and TurboTax, 121-122
bills, entering, 85-87, 89, 91
budgets, setting goals, 81-83
Canadian version, installing, 69
car, tracking costs, 194-196
checkbooks, balancing, 62, 93
CheckFree, 108
checks, writing, 102
creating
    car loans, 141-144
    reports, 79-81
defining categories automatically, 70-71
EasyAnswer Reports, 80
Emergency Records Organizer, 320-323
entering
    deposits, 90-92
    miscellaneous charges, 90-92
features of, 38
Home Inventory, 226
home sale items, tracking, 182-184
installing, 68-70
    Web browsers, 70
insurance research, 211
insurance transactions, tracking, 211-212
InsureMarket, 211
investment accounts, 280-281

333